WOMEN, THE NOVEL, AND THE GERMAN NATION
1771–1871

Domestic Fiction in the Fatherland

Todd Kontje surveys novels by German women over the one-hundred-year period that stretches from the beginnings of a German national literature to the founding of its nation-state. Introducing readers to the lives and works of fourteen women writers of the period, including Sophie von LaRoche, Sophie Mereau, Fanny Lewald, and Eugenie Marlitt, he shows the historical and thematic coherence of a body of fiction by women that has been obscured by traditional literary histories. He explores ways in which novels about traditionally feminine domestic concerns also comment on patriarchal politics in the German fatherland. Finally, he argues that we must view the history of the German novel in the context of both the history of sexuality and the rise of German nationalism, and that novels by German women, often marginalized or trivialized, played a central role in shaping attitudes toward class, gender, and the nation.

Todd Kontje is Professor of German at the University of California, San Diego. He is author of *Constructing Reality: A Rhetorical Analysis of Friedrich Schiller's "Letters on the Aesthetic Education of Mankind"* (1987), *Private Lives in the Public Sphere: The German Bildungsroman as Metafiction* (1992), and *The German Bildungsroman: History of a National Genre* (1993), and he has written many journal articles on German literature from the eighteenth to the twentieth centuries.

CAMBRIDGE STUDIES IN GERMAN

General editors
H. B. Nisbet, University of Cambridge
Martin Swales, University of London
Advisory editor
Theodore J. Ziolkowski, Princeton University

Also in the series

ERNST BEHLER: *German Romantic Literary Theory*
0 521 325854

MICHAEL BUTLER (editor): *The Narrative Fiction of Heinrich Böll:*
Social Conscience and Literary Achievement
0 521 46538 9

J. P. STERN: *The Dear Purchase: A Theme in German Modernism*
0 521 433304

SEÁN ALLAN: *The Plays of Heinrich von Kleist: Ideals and Illusions*
0 521 49511 3

W. E. YATES: *Theatre in Vienna: A Critical History 1776–1995*
0 521 42100 4

MICHAEL MINDEN: *The German "Bildungsroman":*
Incest and Inheritance
0 521 49573 3

WOMEN, THE NOVEL, AND THE GERMAN NATION
1771–1871

Domestic Fiction in the Fatherland

TODD KONTJE

CAMBRIDGE
UNIVERSITY PRESS

PUBLISHED BY THE PRESS SYNDICATE OF THE UNIVERSITY OF CAMBRIDGE
The Pitt Building, Trumpington Street, Cambridge CB2 1RP, United Kingdom

CAMBRIDGE UNIVERSITY PRESS
The Edinburgh Building, Cambridge CB2 2RU, United Kingdom
40 West 20th Street, New York, NY 10011–4211, USA
10 Stamford Road, Oakleigh, Melbourne 3166, Australia

First published 1998

Printed in the United Kingdom at the University Press, Cambridge

Typeset in Baskerville 11/12.5 pt   [CE]

A catalogue record for this book is available from the British Library

Library of Congress cataloguing in publication data

Kontje, Todd Curtis, 1954–
Women, the Novel, and the German Nation 1771–1871: domestic
fiction in the fatherland / Todd Kontje.
p.   cm. – (Cambridge studies in German)
Includes bibliographical references and index.
ISBN 0 521 63110 6
1. German fiction – 18th century – History and criticism.   2. German
fiction – 19th century – History and criticism.   3. Domestic fiction,
German – History and criticism.   4. German fiction – Women authors –
History and criticism.   5. Feminism and literature – Germany.
6. Women and literature – Germany.   I. Title.   II. Series.
PT759.K66   1998
833'.0099287–dc21   97–35264 CIP

ISBN 0 521 63110 6

for Nick and Tim

Contents

Preface   *page* xi

1   Introduction: women, the novel, and the German nation   1

2   The emergence of German domestic fiction   18
    Introduction   18
    Richardson: Clarissa's sacrifice   21
    Rousseau: Julie's compromise   25
    Sophie von LaRoche: Sophie's survival   30

3   German women respond to the French Revolution   41
    Introduction   41
    Caroline von Wolzogen: for a kinder, gentler patriarchy   43
    Friederike Helene Unger: Julchen Grünthal's father fixation   51
    Therese Huber: patriarchy vs. patriotism in *Die Familie Seldorf*   60
    Sophie Mereau: experimental fictions   74

4   Liberation's aftermath: the early Restoration   94
    Introduction   94
    Caroline de la Motte Fouqué: Romantic nationalism
        confronts modernity   98
    Henriette Frölich [Jerta]: a cosmopolitan in Kentucky   107
    Karoline von Woltmann: cosmopolitan conspirators at home   114
    Johanna Schopenhauer: Gabriele's renunciation   122
    Annette von Droste-Hülshoff: Ledwina's lethargy   129

5   Feminists in the *Vormärz*   136
    Introduction   136
    Ida Hahn-Hahn: the curse of the idle rich   140
    Fanny Lewald: republican, feminist, Jew   152
    Louise Aston: "Amazons," aristocrats, and other revolutionaries 170

6   Eugenie Marlitt: the art of liberal compromise   183

Notes   202
Works cited   221
Index   238

Preface

Although I didn't realize it at the time, this book had its beginnings on or around November 9, 1989, in West Berlin. A few days earlier I had completed work on a study of the German *Bildungsroman*, which focused on canonical texts by such authors as Goethe, Tieck, Novalis, and Hoffmann. While completing this project I had become increasingly curious about women writers in the "Age of Goethe." Did they exist? (I had certainly never heard about them in graduate school.) If so, why had they been forgotten? And were novels by German women anything like the canonical *Bildungsromane* by men? With these questions in mind I began to read and reread Sophie von LaRoche's *Geschichte des Fräuleins von Sternheim* [The History of Lady Sophia Sternheim] (1771). LaRoche's work soon sent me back to Richardson and Rousseau, and led me on to German women writers of the next generation, including Therese Huber, Sophie Mereau, Friederike Helene Unger, and Caroline von Wolzogen. The novels were scattered throughout the libraries of the still-divided city, and in January, 1990, I was able to take advantage of a new law that allowed German nationals and other residents of West Berlin to travel without a visa and without the compulsory monetary exchange into what was still the German Democratic Republic. Thus one grey morning found me boarding the S-Bahn to read the copy of *Elisa oder das Weib wie es seyn sollte* [Elisa or Woman As She Should Be] (1795) housed in the *Staatsbibliothek* in the heart of East Berlin. By the time I left Germany in August, 1990, at least two things were clear: that my initial queries about German women writers had opened up a vast area of research, and that German reunification would take place in a matter of weeks.

The fall of the Berlin Wall was only one of the most dramatic (and telegenic) moments in a stunning sequence of events that saw the most significant realignment of national borders since at least 1945.

Separatist movements from Serbia to Chechnya and from Sri Lanka to Quebec seem to support Benedict Anderson's claim that nationalism remains a vital force in late twentieth-century society.[1] At the same time, however, new global networks have emerged that cut across national boundaries, including Hollywood film, multinational corporations, and the World Wide Web, each of which buttresses E. J. Hobsbawm's insistence that "nationalism, however inescapable, is simply no longer the historical force it was."[2] The collapse of former colonial empires has further complicated questions of national identity. Homi Bhabha, for instance, writes of the "hybridity" of the partially assimilated postcolonial subject, who is no longer quite "native," but who will also never quite be accepted as an equal member of the dominant society.[3] Conversely, the increasing percentage of "foreigners" in England, France, and Germany have forced its citizens to confront the ethnic diversity of what once seemed relatively homogenous cultures.[4]

The political climate that has spurred such intense thought about the complexity of national identity in the 1990s has led to an investigation of nationalism's nineteenth-century origins. Benedict Anderson's *Imagined Communities* has been particularly influential in calling attention to print culture's role in creating a sense of common national identity in nineteenth-century readers, while such path-breaking studies as Doris Sommer's *Foundational Fictions* and Peter Uwe Hohendahl's *Building a National Literature* have explored links between romantic fiction, literary history, and nation-building in Latin America and Germany. What was once portrayed as the spontaneous uprising of a unified people now seems the product of a complex cultural strategy based at least as much on the exclusion of the Other – the foreigner, the Jew, the homosexual – as the inclusion of the same.

My own work on the still-nebulous project involving German women novelists was interrupted during the early 1990s by a commission to write a history of *Bildungsroman* criticism for the Camden House series "Literary History in Perspective." In tracing the history of the genre from 1770 to the present, I became increasingly interested in the link between canon-formation and nation-building in the critical discourse about the German novel. Beginning around 1870, German scholars began to view the maturation of the hero in the *Bildungsroman* as a parable for the development of the German nation toward cultural independence and political unification. The link between narratives of male development in the novel and the maturation of the fatherland began to explain why women writers were largely ignored in the building of a national literature. It also began to suggest new questions for my study of German women and the novel: what role did their works play in the construction of a national identity? How do novels about traditionally feminine domestic concerns comment on public politics? In short: how does the fatherland look from the perspective of its mothers and daughters? In exploring these questions I expanded the historical scope of my original project to include women writers of the early Restoration, the *Vormärz*, and the *Gründerzeit*; *Women, the Novel, and the German Nation 1771–1871* is the result.

I have borrowed the term *domestic fiction* from Nancy Armstrong's study of the English novel[5] as a way of avoiding the pejorative connotations of the German *Frauenroman*,[6] and the awkwardness of the "female *Bildungsroman*."[7] Certainly there were novels by women with female protagonists who go through a process of maturation; I will discuss several in this book. Yet two main considerations make me hesitate to designate them as "female *Bildungsromane*." First, the term has sparked endless debate. Everyone seems to know vaguely what the *Bildungsroman* is supposed to be, but no one seems certain that such novels actually exist.[8] I can think of no canonical *Bildungsroman* whose status as an example of the genre has not been challenged at one time or another, and I hesitate to try to introduce new works to a genre that is already under siege. A second, more important reason to shy away from the term "female *Bildungsroman*" lies in the genre's previously mentioned male bias. The effort to unearth examples of the "female *Bildungsroman*" recalls Freud's awkward attempts to account for women in a theory of sexuality based on male development. The very term "female *Bildungsroman*" implies that the novels are only a subcategory of a genre whose "real" representatives are by and about men.

In tracing the evolution of German domestic fiction from 1771 to the 1870s, I show the historical and thematic coherence of a body of fiction by women that has been obscured by traditional literary histories. Although I begin with a brief look at novels by Richardson and Rousseau, and make passing reference to other male writers, my primary focus is on novels by German women. The decision requires a number of disclaimers. First, I do not mean to imply that only women wrote about romance, marriage, and the family; Goethe's

Die Wahlverwandtschaften [Elective Affinities] (1809) is an obvious case in point. Nor can we assume that all women writers were feminists and all men chauvinists; Theodor Gottlieb von Hippel's *Über die bürgerliche Verbesserung der Weiber* [On Improving the Status of Women] (1792) is as "feminist" a work as the writings of Mary Wollstonecraft and Olympia de Gouges.[9] Nor, finally, do I advocate a biological essentialism that assumes *l'écriture féminine* is fundamentally different from texts by men. It would be equally misguided, however, to adopt a gender-neutral approach to texts of this period. It remains a fact of historical contingency, if not biological destiny, that women writers faced different circumstances than men regarding the production and reception of their literary works. Even if women's writing was not essentially different from that of men, it was treated as if it were, as Fanny Lewald discovered when the censor dropped charges against her socially critical fiction when he discovered the author was "only" a woman.

Modern criticism of women writers has often measured them against their male contemporaries. The women write "in the shadow of Olympus,"[10] they struggle to shake off "Goethe's literary paternity,"[11] they come to maturity "as the student of Richardson and Rousseau."[12] Although such comparisons can yield valuable insights into individual texts, framing a broader discussion of women writers in this manner tends to perpetuate the impression that their works are derivative supplements to canonical works of genius, and also tends to obscure the internal coherence of a novelistic tradition that leads from LaRoche to Marlitt. German domestic fiction does not develop in a straight line, but neither does it reproduce a static stereotype. Its variations, mutations, and inversions reflect the idiosyncrasies of individual writers and respond to the vagaries of German history. In the following pages I will map out some of the main currents and counter-currents in German domestic fiction as it develops together with the German fatherland.

The Alexander von Humboldt Stiftung supported research for this project in 1990, 1992, and 1996. My thanks to them and to Professor Rolf-Peter Janz at the Freie Universität Berlin. Thanks also to the German Academic Exchange Service for a grant that enabled me to read from the holdings of the Corvey library at the Gesamthochschule-Universität Paderborn in 1995. Professor Hartmut Steinecke provided invaluable support in Paderborn, and Dr.

Günter Tiggesbäumker led me on a memorable personal tour of the Fürstliche Bibliothek Corvey. The Council for Research in the Humanities at the University of California, San Diego, contributed travel expenses both to Germany and to the University of Chicago, where I used the Lincke Collection of rare nineteenth-century German literature. I would like to thank the many libraries and librarians who helped me gain access to often-obscure materials.

Parts of chapters 1 and 2 appeared in substantially different form in *Impure Reason: Dialectic of Enlightenment in Germany*, edited by W. Daniel Wilson and Robert Holub. Detroit: Wayne State University Press, 1993: 221–41. Parts of chapters 1 and 4 appeared in the *Women in German Yearbook* 12 (1996): 53–69. Parts of chapter 3 were published in *Colloquia Germania* 24 (1991): 27–38, and *Seminar* 28 (1992): 17–32. Parts of chapter 4 appeared in *Carleton Germanic Papers* 24 (1996): 93–108. I am grateful for permission to reproduce this material here.

Special thanks to Jeannine Blackwell, Robert Holub, Dennis Mahoney, and Kenneth Weisinger, who generously supported the project in its early stages. The many other individuals who contributed to the book include Wendy K. Arons, Arnd Bohm, Brent Peterson, Reinhart Sonnenburg, and Erik Thygesen.

I would also like to thank Linda Bree of Cambridge University Press for her initial interest in the project and for her help and patience in shepherding the manuscript through the production process. Martin Swales and the two anonymous readers for the Press provided valuable suggestions for revising my work.

Most of all, I thank Betsy Bredeck for her insight and support in all aspects of the research and writing.

CHAPTER I

Introduction: women, the novel, and the German nation

This book surveys novels by German women over the one-hundred-year period that stretches from the beginnings of a national literature to the founding of a nation-state. Domestic fiction concentrates on traditionally feminine concerns of romance, marriage, and family. In doing so, however, it also addresses matters of public concern otherwise restricted to men: romantic entanglements almost invariably turn on questions of class and money, while depictions of the family address relations between rulers and the people at the level of the state. The novels examined are thus both reflections on private life and commentaries on public politics. They introduce women's voices into a patriarchal state and its literature, and in this sense they are domestic fictions in the fatherland.

My work presupposes a number of insights that have become axiomatic in recent years: that sexual difference and the family are cultural constructs subject to historical change; that the emergence of the middle class in the eighteenth century was directly tied to new attitudes toward the family; that the class-specific sexual revolution coincided with the birth of modern nationalism; that political conflicts can take place in the battle for cultural hegemony as well as on the barricades; and that the novel was a central site in the middle-class struggle for power. I will argue that we must view the history of the German novel in the context of both the history of sexuality and the rise of German nationalism, and – most important – that often-marginalized or -trivialized novels by German women played a central role in shaping attitudes toward class, gender, and the nation.

The belief that women are inferior to men and should therefore subject themselves to their husbands has a long history in Western culture extending back at least to the Pentateuch.[1] Not only was Eve created as something of an afterthought to Adam, she was guilty of seducing him into sin, thus provoking God's wrath: "I will greatly multiply thy sorrow and thy conception, in sorrow thou shalt bring forth children; and thy desire shall be to thy husband, and he shall rule over thee" (Genesis, 3: 16). Christian writers from St. Paul to Thomas Aquinas reiterated these sentiments, stressing women's sinfulness and defining their primary function as vessels for the reproduction of the species. In Germany Martin Luther took issue with the medieval tradition of the Catholic Church by vigorously defending the institution of marriage. In doing so, however, he cut off avenues for women's professional and intellectual development, insisting that they should find husbands, have children, and stay at home.[2] Despite Luther's lasting influence, some opportunities for women outside the home remained from the sixteenth to the mid-eighteenth centuries: Catholic convents and Protestant beguinages provided alternatives to married life; aristocratic women could participate in court culture; actresses found careers in the risky business of the theatre; and, for a brief period around 1730–50, a few women found grudging acknowledgment as intellectuals.[3] For each woman who attained a certain degree of independence, however, many more did not. The price of deviance from the officially sanctioned domesticity could be high, with consequences ranging from social ostracism to death at the stake. Witch burning reached epidemic proportions in Germany and throughout Europe in the seventeenth century, but continued well into the next; the last German woman condemned as a witch was executed in 1775.[4]

At about this time Germany began to undergo social and political transformations that would have a significant impact on private life. Governments based on the personal authority of the local lord [*Herrschaft*] gradually yielded to administrations typical of the modern state bureaucracy [*Verwaltung*].[5] The development gave rise to a new group of university-trained young men employed as civil servants, as the old feudal order based on privilege and birth gradually opened to men with talent and higher education. The men who enjoyed new opportunities for professional advancement also found new means of creative self-expression. Letters, which had once been designed as formulaic business memos, became outpourings of the heart between like-minded friends and lovers. A new genre of confessional literature arose out of religious autobiographies. Moral weeklies introduced readers to new models of sentiment and virtue.[6] Out of these various influences the novel began to emerge as the most popular literary genre. By the 1770s the German novel had begun a period of rapid growth that was to continue, with minor setbacks, throughout the nineteenth century.[7] Entertaining and unpretentious, the novel found a receptive audience in the domestic realm of the family. In the intimate setting of the home family members could read about characters much like themselves. The fiction was thus reassuring in that it represented a familiar reality, but at the same time enlightening, providing isolated individuals with shared role-models and the language to express new ideas.[8] As civil servants for the expanding state bureaucracies, and as the producers of culture written in a common language, finally, the ascendent group of "non-noble élites"[9] began to think of themselves less as subjects of a particular duchy, bishopric, or monarchy, and more as participants in a common German culture. "Germany" as a unified political entity would not exist for another hundred years, but it was already taking shape as an "imagined community" in the cultural productions of the rising middle class.[10]

The wives of Germany's new civil servants did not share their husbands' sense of expanding horizons. When the men went off to work, the women remained isolated at home; the older economic model of the *ganzes Haus* [whole house], where family members worked together with servants in the home, yielded to the modern nuclear family, conceived as a refuge from the masculine realms of business, politics, and the arts.[11] As a result, women who had attained a modicum of independence in the early eighteenth century were once again encouraged to remain within the domestic sphere. The new literary culture played a particularly important role in both reinforcing and transforming the teachings of Luther and the Bible: the subjugation of women that had once been imposed as punishment for Original Sin was now celebrated as the positive fulfillment of their nature. Rousseau became the primary spokesman for the belief that human beings were essentially good in their natural condition, and that only civilization had rendered them evil. In his *Emile* (1762), a pedagogical treatise in novel form in which a tutor raises a young man who eventually meets his ideal mate, Rousseau set out to recover the "natural" distinctions between men and women. Here we encounter what have since become familiar gender stereotypes: the man is strong and active, the woman weak and passive; men have genius, women wit; men use reason, women observe; men are silent, women talk. In Rousseau's view, woman is made for man's delight: she is to raise his children, manage the household, and remain obedient and faithful to her husband – even if he mistreats her. In complying with these demands the woman is not obeying an arbitrary law, but fulfilling her biological destiny.[12]

However reactionary Rousseau's statements about women may seem today, at the time they were an intrinsic part of a politically progressive assault on the Old Regime. The self-understanding of the bourgeoisie was closely tied to its attitudes toward sexuality and the family, which distinguished it from – and made its members feel morally superior to – the aristocracy. While members of the nobility arranged marriages for economic and political reasons, the middle class aspired to an ideal of marriage based on love and sustained by mutual affection.[13] Relations between parents and their children also developed a new emotional intensity.[14] Children were no longer viewed as pawns to advance their parents' social status or financial situation, but were recognized as individuals in their own right, whose personal happiness and professional success was of central concern to their parents. Hence Rousseau's thought resonated positively with the German civil servants whose increased social mobility depended on talent rather than birth, who were beginning to shift their allegiance from hereditary rulers to the German nation, and whose wives remained at home. "The triumph of the nuclear family," as George Mosse has argued, "coincided with the rise of nationalism and respectability."[15] As the most widely read genre in an era of print-capitalism, the novel played a central role in shaping new attitudes toward romance, family, and the nation.

Precisely the link between bourgeois ethics and republican politics became the source of a lasting predicament for women: if all "men" were created equal, then women should have equal rights in the nation, but as paragons of domestic virtue they are also supposed to be invisible in the home. Jürgen Habermas downplays this contradiction when he defines the eighteenth-century public sphere as a realm of "human" equality outside state authority in which members of society could at least begin to develop a sense of collective identity and define their goals.[16] Habermas insists that the public sphere was at least theoretically open to all, but when French women tried to turn theory into practice during the early years of the Revolution, they soon found themselves excluded from active participation in public politics. The Revolution brought liberty and equality to the brothers who rose up against the father-king, as Joan

Landes argues, but not to their mothers, wives, and sisters. "The revolt against the father was also a revolt against women as free and equal public and private beings."[17] Women were to answer their "triple calling" as wives, mothers, and managers of the household economy,[18] while men took care of public affairs. The triumph of the middle class was predicated on the domestication of its women; in Landes's words, "the Republic was constructed against women, not just without them."[19]

Recent studies of the fraternal comradeship emerging out of the French Revolution support the broader thesis "that nationalism favors a distinctly homosocial form of male bonding."[20] The first outburst of German nationalist sentiment in the political realm occurred when the Germans rallied to defeat Napoleon in the Wars of Liberation. The patriotic literature written in the years immediately before Napoleon's defeat suggests that women were to play only a peripheral role in the formation of the German nation. In Theodor Körner's *Leier und Schwert* [Lyre and Sword] (1814), an extremely popular collection of patriotic poems, the primary focus is on male bonding in the effort to expel the French from German soil.

> Doch *Brüder* sind wir allzusamm,
> Und das schwellt unsern Mut.
> Uns knüpft der Sprache heilig Band,
> Uns knüpft *ein* Gott, *ein* Vaterland,
> *Ein* treues deutsches Blut.

Virtuous German women feature as the moral backbone of the fatherland that their sons defend:

> Und Frauenunschuld, Frauenlieb'
> Steht noch als höchstes Gut,
> Wo deutscher Ahnen Sitte blieb
> Und deutscher Jünglingsmut.[22]   (85)

This sort of patriotism in the name of God, family, and fatherland is fairly predictable for inspirational verse written in war. What gives Körner's poetry a macabre fascination is the extent to which he eroticizes war and death:[23]

> Was weint ihr, Mädchen, warum klagt ihr, Weiber,
> Für die der Herr die Schwerter nicht gestählt,
> Wenn wir entzückt die jugendlichen Leiber
> Hinwerfen in die Scharen eurer Räuber,
> Daß euch des Kampfes kühne Wollust fehlt?

Ihr könnt ja froh zu Gottes Altar treten!
Für Wunden gab er zarte Sorgsamkeit,
Gab euch in euren herzlichen Gebeten
Den schönen, reinen Sieg der Frömmigkeit![24]   (89)

Although Körner praises nursing and religion as specifically feminine contributions to the war effort, they seem poor substitutes for
the ecstatic passion of death in battle. The fight for the fatherland is
not just a defense of virtuous women; it is itself an erotic act. This
becomes particularly evident in the final poem of the collection,
which is nothing less than a love song dedicated to the poet-soldier's
sword:

Ja, gutes Schwert, frei bin ich
Und liebe dich herzinnig,
Als wärst du mir getraut
Als eine liebe Braut!
Hurra![25]   (112)

In a logical culmination of this imagery, Körner urges his fellow
soldiers to exchange passionate kisses with their weapons before
plunging into battle:

Drum drückt den liebeheißen
Bräutlichen Mund von Eisen
An eure Lippen fest!
Fluch! wer die Braut verläßt!
Hurra![26]   (114)

At this point it becomes clear that Körner's rigidly heterosexual
division of labor in the war effort serves the primary purpose of
celebrating homosocial bonding.[27] This is not to suggest that either
Körner or his Prussian comrades were homosexuals. It is rather to
demonstrate that the seemingly bipolar gender division between
male and female is actually triangular in Körner's vision. At first
women serve to solidify bonds between men, as soldiers unite on the
battlefield to defend their families at home. In the final poem,
however, women drop out of the picture altogether, as the men make
love to their swords. It is only a short step from Körner's heroes to
the officers of the German Freikorps, whose virulently misogynist
male fantasies have been the subject of Klaus Theweleit's influential
study of fascist ideology. In his view, "the nation has in the first
instance nothing to do with questions of national borders, forms of
government, or so-called nationality. The concept refers to a quite

specific form of male community, one that is 'yearned for' for many a long year, that rises from the 'call of the blood.' "[28] The German men bond together in the nation and on the battlefield, while women serve as little more than brood mares to produce biologically pure sons for the fatherland.[29]

Historical practice has a way of complicating political theory, however, for women never stopped intervening into the fraternal order of the public sphere. The very print culture that contained so many polemics against women's participation in public life opened up new opportunities for them to do so. That an increasing number of women were willing to ignore their domestic "destiny" posed a problem for many self-appointed custodians of culture. What was to be done? Rousseau responded by condemning all women writers as traitors to their sex: "when you enter a woman's room what makes you think more highly of her, what makes you address her with more respect – to see her busy with feminine occupations, with her household duties, with her children's clothes about her, or to find her writing verses at her toilet table surrounded with pamphlets of every kind and with notes on tinted paper?"[30] Following Rousseau's lead, the German pedagogue Joachim Heinrich Campe fulminates against women who neglect their families to seek public fame: "at this unworthy sight the friend of the fatherland's blood boils with indignation, and he would like to crush the pen that has transformed a medium for enlightenment and moral betterment into a vehicle for flattery, vanity, laziness, and lasciviousness!"[31] In neglecting their feminine duties, these women writers also betray the fatherland, arousing the wrath of both the man and the patriot.

Women nevertheless continued to write and continued to publish. By the 1820s, for instance, Carl Wilhelm von Schindel put out a three-volume bibliography of German women writers of the nineteenth century.[32] The women's stubborn refusal to remain silent inspired a different tactic on the part of their opponents, who now acknowledged the existence of their work, but declared it second-rate. The most prominent members of this group were Goethe and Schiller, who developed their theory of the dilettante in large measure to distance their own works of genius from what they considered women's sub-standard literary productions.[33] The tone has shifted from condemnation to condescension, as is evident in Schiller's comments to Goethe regarding Sophie Mereau: "I am really surprised that our women have now learned, in a merely

dilettantish way, to acquire a certain facility of writing that approx-
imates to art."[34] The goal was not so much to silence women as to
keep them in their place as non-threatening colleagues. Even men
sympathetic to women writers granted them a minor role in producing poetry, travelogs, and sentimental fiction for a primarily female
audience, while denying their capacity for political activism or
philosophical rigor.[35] Woe betide those women writers who over-
stepped their "natural" boundaries! "Even if a woman were to
succeed in informing herself about a political question to the point
that no essential aspect of judgment was lacking – which is inconceivable [*sic*!] – her judgment would still always be less mature than
a man's of equal education, because you can only judge clearly and
accurately about matters in which you can be directly involved."[36]
After this prefacing comment, Julian Schmidt launches into a savage
critique of Ida Hahn-Hahn's political novels in his *Geschichte der
deutschen Nationalliteratur im neunzehnten Jahrhundert* [History of the
German National Literature in the Nineteenth Century] (1853). In
Schmidt's opinion, too many German women have abandoned their
instincts and dared to think, but the result is only confusion: "The
logic of women is completely different from that of men."[37]

Increasingly in the course of the nineteenth century, art by and for
women also became the target of a new accusation: that its authors
were primarily concerned with making money, while the true genius
disdained such mundane concerns. Wilhelm Hauff's critique of the
popular writer H. Clauren (Carl Heun) turns on the charge that
Clauren profits from the public's basest instincts with fiction that
draws readers away from worthy German classics by Goethe and
Schiller.[38] Hauff reserves particular scorn for the fact that Clauren's
fiction appeals primarily to women, and it was easy enough to
extend the critique of women readers to the women writers who
reached a broad audience. In an era caught between the conflicting
demands of autonomy aesthetics and the commodification of art,
women writers and their public became both the economic engine
and the bad conscience of the publishing world.[39] By the 1940s
Adorno and Horkheimer could make an easy distinction between
the commercialized art of the culture industry for the feminized
masses and the hard, lonely works of high modernism that could still
resist cultural barbarism.[40]

By this time works by German women writers of the eighteenth
and nineteenth centuries had long since disappeared from public

view. While Goethe, Schiller, and their immediate followers were willing to debate the relative merit of certain women writers,[41] later nineteenth-century literary historians simply ignored their existence.[42] The reason stems from the logic of nineteenth-century canon-formation. As Peter Uwe Hohendahl has argued, nineteenth-century literary historians constructed selective narratives that provided a "cultural identity for the German nation" before actual political unification took place.[43] Critics from Gervinus to Dilthey showed how German literature emancipated itself from foreign influence to attain greatness in the classical works of Goethe and Schiller. Evolution became a central category in these narratives,[44] as the literary historians borrowed the eighteenth-century concept of individual *Bildung* [education, development, formation] and applied it to the nation: "and so the *impulse to shape a new ideal of life* arose at that time," wrote Dilthey of "The Poetic and Philosophical Movement in Germany 1770–1800" (1867), "not just in certain gifted people, but in the educated classes of the nation as a whole – a question about human destiny – about the content of a truly valuable life, about genuine *Bildung*."[45]

Not coincidentally, the term *Bildungsroman* entered general usage at about the same time that Germany achieved political unification. In his 1870 biography of Friedrich Schleiermacher, Wilhelm Dilthey suggests the term for German novels written under the influence of Goethe's *Wilhelm Meisters Lehrjahre* [Wilhelm Meister's Apprenticeship] (1795–96). In Dilthey's view, novels by such authors as Jean Paul, Tieck, Novalis, and Hölderlin portray the development of a young man from uncertain youth to adulthood, as the young dreamer experiences life's vicissitudes to emerge as a productive member of society.[46] If we recall the gendered basis of the bourgeois public sphere, it is hardly surprising that Dilthey focuses exclusively on novels with male protagonists as examples of the genre. Only men could expect to mature into public individuals; women in the classical *Bildungsroman* tend to function either as loving mothers or as erotic adventures for the hero on his journey to self-discovery.[47] In the last decades of the nineteenth century critics began to interpret the genre as Germany's major contribution to the history of the novel; the questers of the *Bildungsroman* exemplified allegedly national characteristics of inwardness and spirituality, and their journey to personal maturation prefigured Germany's movement toward political unification.[48] This tie between the novel and the nation helps to explain the absence of women writers from German literary history. What was true for the individual was true for the nation: if *Bildung* and the *Bildungsroman* were for men only, then the construction of a national literature was also essentially, and not accidentally, masculinist. To paraphrase Landes, narratives of Germany's national literature were constructed *against* women, not just without them. The German fatherland was just that: a nation of patriarchs, a land of fathers, where women – at least in theory – played a subordinate, silent, private role.

In practice, however, women did not remain silent; this book is a study of their contribution to the history of the German novel and the development of the national culture. To a certain extent, at least, domestic fiction served a didactic purpose designed to transform its female reader into another *Elisa oder das Weib wie es seyn sollte*.[49] The heroine of this best-selling novel dutifully renounces her love for one man to enter into an arranged marriage with another. With infinite patience Elisa puts up with her husband's drinking, gambling, and philandering while devoting her energy toward raising the children. Her good example eventually reforms her husband, and she dies having accomplished her mission: "Through her example she taught many women their duties and inspired them to imitation."[50] Not all women were willing to put up with such abuse, however, and not all domestic fiction sought to indoctrinate its readers into submission. Protest abounds in women's fiction, both covert and open.[51] Some novelists showed the degree to which women suffered in their attempts to realize an impossible ideal, while others sought alternative models of feminine assertiveness, creativity, and independence.

Given the proscription against women in the public sphere, novels by German women also reflect on politics to a surprising degree. At times the authors voice their political opinions directly, speaking out against aristocratic abuses or in favor of enlightened patriarchal rule, criticizing revolutionary violence or advocating equal opportunity for all in a unified nation-state. More often than not, however, the women writers address public concerns obliquely through their depictions of the family. As Lynn Hunt has observed, "most Europeans in the eighteenth century thought of their rulers as fathers and of their nations as families writ large."[52] In her view, the Revolution involved killing the father-king and replacing him with a band of brothers in the collective imagination of the French people. Conservative German writers countered with images of benevolent patriarchs whose happy private lives legitimized dynastic authority in the state. German liberals, on the other hand, linked the abuse of paternal authority in the home to corruption in other authority figures, including decadent aristocrats and captains of industry. In other words: whatever the particular political leanings of an author might be, any attempt to draw a rigid distinction between the private and the public proves specious. In fact, German domestic fiction is often at its most political when portraying the dynamics of family life.

In order to get a sense of the historical development of German domestic fiction, it is useful to focus on the century between the publication of Sophie von LaRoche's *Geschichte des Fräuleins von Sternheim* [The History of Lady Sophia Sternheim] (1771) and Eugenie Marlitt's novels of the 1860s and '70s. LaRoche's novel comes at a defining moment in German literary history marked by the effort on the part of a few writers to break free of foreign influence and establish an indigenous literary tradition. While Lessing, Herder, and the young Goethe have traditionally been cited as the pioneers of Germany's national literature, I will argue that LaRoche played an equally significant role in adapting fictional models from Richardson and Rousseau to a German context. Her *Geschichte des Fräuleins von Sternheim* was probably the single most influential work for the next several generations of German women writers. I turn next to a cluster of authors writing "around 1800" at the height of the period still widely known as the "Age of Goethe."[53] Novels by Caroline von Wolzogen, Friederike Helene Unger, Therese Huber, and Sophie Mereau continue the tradition of German domestic fiction established by LaRoche, while reacting to Weimar Classicism, early Romanticism, and the French Revolution. In the chapters that follow I first examine writers of the Early Restoration (*c.* 1815–25), who responded in various ways to the re-legitimation of the old aristocracy and the rise of German nationalism, and then three prominent authors of the *Vormärz*: Ida Gräfin Hahn-Hahn, Fanny Lewald, and Louise Aston. While these writers share common feminist concerns, they vary considerably in their political allegiances, which range from aristocratic conservatism through bourgeois liberalism to radical democracy. I conclude with the novels of Eugenie Marlitt. As the most popular contributer to Germany's most widely read family journal, *Die Gartenlaube*, Marlitt was one of the first German writers who reached a modern mass audience. Her romances expressed moderate views on women's emancipation at the time of Germany's first organized feminist movements, and liberal political sentiments in an era of unprecedented industrial and economic growth. While German university professors in newly established chairs for *Germanistik* were crafting their histories of the national literature from *Das Nibelungenlied* to Goethe,[54] Marlitt was producing "what the Germans really read."[55]

By choosing a cross-section of German women writers from LaRoche to Marlitt, I want to counter the notion that the German *Frauenroman* is an ahistorical, apolitical genre, whose essential elements recur unchanged from the eighteenth century to today's popular romances.[56] German novelists respond in their fiction not only to contemporary literary developments, but also to political change. To highlight the political content of their work I focus on five historical turning points: the waning years of the Old Regime; the first decade of the French Revolution; the immediate aftermath of Napoleon's defeat; the years of political agitation leading up to the March Revolution of 1848; and the decade surrounding Germany's political unification. As I hope to show, the work of each new generation of German women writers differs significantly from that of its predecessors, and not all writers of the same generation respond to historical developments in the same way.

Due to the peculiarities of nineteenth-century German history we cannot expect to find a linear account of the rise of the middle class to political power, nor should we expect steady progress among women from domestic virtue to modern feminism. Germany's struggle toward greater democracy is a story of modest advances met by crushing defeats, from the Mainz Republic of 1793, through the *Burschenschaft* movement of the early Restoration, to the failed Revolution of 1848. The legendary German efficiency manifested itself more in reaction than revolt. The rhythm of German political history in the nineteenth century corresponds roughly to the ebb and flow of German feminist movements during the same time. Periods of political agitation around 1800 and during the *Vormärz* coincided with challenges to sexual stereotypes in the works of writers including Sophie Mereau, Ida Hahn-Hahn, and Louise Aston, while political reaction bred sexual backlash in the Biedermeier and the *Nachmärz*.[57] Here again it is important to avoid sweeping generalizations, however, for there is also room for feminist protest among some writers at politically conservative times, and for a reassertion of traditional gender roles at times of political upheaval.

Individual differences between writers can often be traced to conflicting class loyalties. Sophie von LaRoche inspires a conservative legacy that leads from Caroline von Wolzogen through Caroline de la Motte Fouqué and Annette von Droste-Hülshoff to Ida Gräfin Hahn-Hahn. Each of these aristocratic authors recognizes the need for reform within her own social class, but remains deeply suspicious of the common crowd and hostile to democratic reform. Their attitudes toward Germany vary, but in general they tend to be more loyal to the perogatives of their social class than to the modern nation. An alternative liberal tradition begins with Therese Huber and Sophie Mereau, who write in favor of the French Revolution, and continues in such liberal nationalists as Fanny Lewald and Eugenie Marlitt. Of particular interest is the disjuncture that often occurs between early feminism and bourgeois politics. Because the middle class defined itself in terms of the domestic virtue of its women, feminists had to violate bourgeois ideology in order to assert their rights as human beings. Not infrequently we find women writers looking back to aristocratic models of female assertiveness as a way to escape the strictures of bourgeois domestic virtue. As a result, such writers as Sophie Mereau and Louise Aston provide an intriguing combination of pro-revolutionary political radicalism with pre-revolutionary models of feminist behavior. Conversely, some politically conservative aristocrats adopt bourgeois family values to revitalize their own social class.

The complex interrelation between gender roles and political allegiances in the works of these writers further complicates the history of German nationalism. Historians of twentieth-century fascism often create the impression that nascent German nationalism led inevitably and inexorably toward the Third Reich. As Michael Hughes has observed, however, there were actually two primary strands of German nationalist thought in the nineteenth century, which he terms liberal and romantic nationalism.[58] Romantic or *völkisch* nationalism grew out of German Romanticism, was anti-Enlightenment to the core, and viewed Germany as a spiritual unity linked by bonds of blood to the German soil.[59] Its adherents sought inspiration in such emotionally charged symbols of German unity as the Cologne Cathedral, the Rhine, and an idealized version of the Middle Ages – "invented traditions"[60] that Heine ridiculed mercilessly in *Deutschland: Ein Wintermärchen* [Germany: A Winter's Tale] (1844). Liberal nationalism, on the other hand, emerged from the Enlightenment principles that inspired the French Revolution. Its representatives sought freedom of speech and the press in a unified Germany under a constitutional government of elected representatives. It opposed the practice of hereditary aristocratic rule that had governed the German principalities before Napoleon, and remained a vital force in German politics until the 1870s, despite setbacks in the early Restoration and after the 1848 Revolution.[61] It is to this tradition of liberal German nationalism that many of the women writers examined here contributed, a nationalism compatable with cosmopolitanism (Frölich), that is based on religious tolerance (Lewald and Marlitt), and that includes women in its ranks (Aston). In the increasingly militaristic, anti-Semitic, and misogynist climate that followed Germany's first unification, liberal nationalism represented a dream that was not to be; perhaps the reunification of 1989 offers the Germans a second chance.[62]

I make no attempt to survey all women writers of each period, which would in any case be an impossible task. My goal is rather to strike a balance between breadth and depth, reading enough representative authors to get a sense of change over time and diversity at a given moment, while leaving enough room for close textual analysis of individual works. Because many readers will be unfamiliar with at least some of the novels discussed, I combine analysis with more plot summary than would be necessary when discussing canonical texts. Experts in the field will inevitably miss certain writers; for each noted absence there will be dozens more who have dropped into complete obscurity. I have chosen authors whose novels, with few exceptions, were widely known to their contemporaries, and whose works are at least partially accessible to a modern audience. That some novels are back in print is due to feminist scholars of the past two decades, who have made a concerted effort to rewrite German literary history and to recover works lost to generations of readers. Detailed bibliographies of German women writers and other non-canonical novels now exist;[63] first-rate studies of individual writers and literary periods abound;[64] feminist theory continues to develop.[65] Gains have been made at the institutional level as well, with the growth of university women's studies programs and the establishment of such organizations as *Women in German*.

If the study of German women writers is to remain vital, however, editions will have to become more accessible for classroom use. As Terry Lovell has argued, literary "classics" are consumed for different reasons now than they were originally: "Objects of entertainment at the moment of their production, these works have survived by becoming primarily objects of study. Their sales today do not depend on their capacity still to please. Their market is guaranteed simply by their inclusion on the syllabus."[66] Lovell concludes rather pessimistically that the current boom in gender studies may prove ephemeral unless texts become established as part of the curriculum. In order for this to happen, reliable editions must remain in print at prices that students can afford.

In this context an anecdote might be instructive. In the summer of 1992 I was shopping for books in Berlin's *KaDeWe* (*Kaufhaus des Westens*), that capitalist showpiece erected in a divided city as a temple of conspicuous consumption. Here I quickly found an inexpensive Reclam edition of Sophie von LaRoche's *Geschichte des Fräuleins von Sternheim*, complete with commentary, contemporary sources, bibliography, and an excellent afterword by Barbara Becker-Cantarino. I had less luck trying to find Marlitt's novels. The decidedly unpretentious *Deutscher Literatur-Verlag Hamburg* had recently published her works in paperbacks aimed at a mass audience – to judge by the cover-art and sensational jacket blurbs – but most of these texts were already out of print. Somewhat discouraged, I headed off to the gourmet food floor. On the way I passed through domestics, and there on the sale table, wedged between cut-rate linens and Disney-inspired coloring books, I saw stacks of new, hardback Marlitt editions going for the ridiculously cheap price of DM 5 each.[67] Soon I would leave the store, my complimentary plastic shopping bag bulging with an unexpected windfall.

Within the distance of a few meters I had traversed the chasm that separates serious art from popular fiction: here an inexpensive, first-rate scholarly edition designed for intensive study, there a cut-rate product packaged for speedy consumption. LaRoche's novel has made it into the university; there is even an English translation available in paperback. Marlitt still survives in a different way: as mass-produced entertainment for a predominently female audience, whether in novel form, in film, or on television. Between these extremes the accessibility of the novels I examine below varies considerably. The Georg Olms Verlag has published a series of facsimile editions of women's novels around 1800 complete with critical introductions. The books are useful for the scholar, but prohibitively expensive for classroom use. Other novels, such as Johanna Schopenhauer's *Gabriele*, were once available in quality paperbacks, but have since gone out of print. These works are the exceptions. Most novels by German women during the period must still be read in rare book rooms, if they have been preserved at all; given the economic realities of today's publishing industry, that is where most of them will remain. Perhaps not all, but certainly many more works by German women writers nevertheless should be in print; until they are, the work of recovery is likely to remain a Sisyphean task.

Or perhaps the works do not deserve sustained critical attention. This at least seemed to be my colleague's implication when, after hearing a one-sentence description of my project, he jabbed at me with his forefinger while declaring: "There's a reason why those women are forgotten!" I was confronted with the shibboleth of cultural studies: "But is it any good?"[68] A quick answer to the question might be "yes, some of these texts are really quite good, and the others are at least historically interesting." The response is accurate enough on a casual level, but misleading to the extent that it implies that quality is a fixed, timeless standard. European aestheticians spent two hundred years working to get out of the shadow of antiquity and to recognize the legitimacy of modern poetry; granting unchanging validity to a canon created largely in the late nineteenth century only perpetuates former folly. It is not that we have stopped making value judgments about what we read; we make them all the time. It has become increasingly difficult, however, to pretend that aesthetic judgments are (or ever were) formulated in a neutral space, insulated from material or ideological concerns. In the preceding pages I have given some indication of why women's writing was excluded from Germany's national literature in the nineteenth century; the current interest in women's literature creates a climate that nurtures the study of those same authors. In the analyses that follow I will be less concerned with evaluating the quality of individual texts than with investigating the sort of cultural labor they perform:[69] what new ideas do they disseminate? What do they call into question? How do they shape a sense of community? How do they register the pain of exclusion? At the risk of drawing an old-fashioned distinction between literature and nonfiction, I will argue that the novels have greater subtlety, and greater capacity for irony, than the didactic treatises of a Rousseau or a Campe. The novel would hardly have enjoyed such success and attained such notoriety had it not offered subversive pleasure along with edification.

CHAPTER 2

The emergence of German domestic fiction

INTRODUCTION

The concept of a national literature that expresses the peculiar characteristics of a given people began to capture the imagination of German intellectuals around the middle of the eighteenth century. Lessing fired one of the first shots of the culture wars in his seventeenth *Literaturbrief* of 1759, in which he challenged the Germans to stop imitating the French and start writing authentically German plays. He continued his assault on French cultural hegemony through the following decade, most notably in his *Hamburgische Dramaturgie* (1767–68). Klopstock took up the cause in 1764 with a series of patriotic odes in praise of the German language, German wine, and the old Germanic fatherland.[1] Herder signaled the birth of a new era with his *Journal meiner Reise im Jahr 1769* [Journal of my Journey in the Year 1769], in which he rejected classical norms in favor of the "primitive" genius of indigenous cultures, his own included. By the early 1770s Teutophilia gripped the nation, as a generation of young men began to cast themselves as the new bardic poets of Germania's ancient legacy. Among them Goethe seemed destined to become the Messiah of the new movement, a role he was both willing and talented enough to play. His historical drama *Götz von Berlichingen* (1771) promised that he would answer Lessing's call for a German Shakespeare whose works could establish a national theatre. Earlier that same year Goethe had written poetry of unprecedented lyric intimacy in his "Sesenheimer Lieder," an accomplishment that signaled beginnings of European Romanticism.[2] By the time he published *Die Leiden des jungen Werther* [The Sorrows of Young Werther] in 1774, Germany had completed what nineteenth-century literary historians would hail as its breakthrough to a national literature of international status.

Not everyone shared the widespread enthusiasm for a revitalized national culture. Christoph Martin Wieland was one of the most outspoken critics of "the zeal to give our poetry a national character."[3] In an essay with this title of 1773, Wieland concedes that there is such a thing as "National-Charakter," but goes on to argue that the pseudo-bardic poets of the present are kidding themselves to think that they are one in spirit with their Germanic ancestors. In Wieland's view, the currently fashionable glorification of the ancient bards is a ridiculous affectation at best, and potentially dangerous in that it ennobles "the warlike, bloodthirsty spirit and the patriotic fury of these old barbarians" ["den kriegerischen, blutdurstenden Geist und die patriotische Wut dieser alten Barbaren"].[4] Since moderns can no longer be original in the sense of the ancient tribes, concludes Wieland, why not imitate Greek civilization rather than Germanic barbarism?[5] Bellicose nationalism should be a thing of the past in the age of Enlightenment; the true cosmopolitan [*Weltbürger*] owes his primary allegiance to humanity.[6]

While involved in these debates, Wieland encouraged Sophie von LaRoche (1731–1807)[7] – his cousin and former fiancée – in her work on her first novel, which appeared in two volumes in June and September, 1771. The *Geschichte des Fräuleins von Sternheim* was a great success, going into three editions in its first year and making LaRoche famous overnight.[8] Goethe and J. M. R. Lenz admired both the novel and its author, and the work had a lasting influence on several generations of women writers.[9] For a number of reasons, however, LaRoche has remained considerably more obscure than her German contemporaries. Goethe's *Werther* soon eclipsed *Sternheim*'s early fame, and although LaRoche went on to write many more novels and stories, her didactic fiction seemed old-fashioned in an age dominated by the aesthetics of genius.[10] In addition, she had the personal misfortune to be judged by the standard of her own heroine, as later readers were disappointed to discover that Sophie von LaRoche did not seem as virtuous as Sophie von Sternheim.[11] Probably the single most important reason for LaRoche's low profile in literary history is the fact that she was a woman. Ironically, her works helped disseminate an ideal of feminine domesticity that excluded women from an active role in the production of culture. LaRoche survived in nineteenth-century literary history not as an important writer, but as Wieland's friend, the mother of one of Goethe's early love-interests, and as the grandmother of the Brentanos.[12]

I will argue that the *Geschichte des Fräuleins von Sternheim* is a pivotal work in the history of German literature. LaRoche reworks representations of class conflict and family structures from Samuel Richardson's *Clarissa, or the History of a Young Lady* (1749) and Jean-Jacques Rousseau's *Julie, ou La Nouvelle Héloïse* [*The New Heloïse*] (1761) into the paradigmatic work of German domestic fiction. That LaRoche was influenced by both Richardson and Rousseau is well known, and she makes no secret of her indebtedness to foreign cultures. As the wife of a court councilor, she was expected to be familiar with current literature so that she could entertain guests with scintillating conversation.[13] She probably read Richardson in English, and certainly read Rousseau in French, as she was bilingual.[14] Her own first novel has much in common with the work of both writers. From Richardson, LaRoche adapts the epistolary form and the theme of virtue in distress. She models her villain Lord Derby after Lovelace, and also shares Rousseau's pedagogical intent. LaRoche echoes Rousseau in her critique of the court and praise of simple country life, and she chooses the name Sophie for her heroine at least in part because it recalls the female protagonist of *Emile*.

At the same time, the woman who in the early 1780s would publish the journal *Pomona für Teutschlands Töchter* [Pomona for Germany's Daughters] (1783–84) already targets a German audience in her first novel. Wieland himself, no fan of Germany's nationalist bards, described LaRoche's novel as a present to "all the amiable young daughters of our nation" spread throughout "the far reaches of the German provinces" ["der Provinzen Germaniens"].[15] Wieland defends LaRoche's novel because it promises "to advance wisdom and virtue – the sole great advantages of mankind, the sole wellspring of genuine felicity among your sex and even among mine" (46; 10). *Sternheim* preaches the principles of the European Enlightenment, it is cosmopolitan in taste, and yet tailored to the needs of a German public. As in the case of British domestic fiction, women are to serve as the primary audience for the novel, and they are first to embody the wisdom and virtue of the modern individual.[16] Unlike the British, however, the Germans had no empire and virtually no industry. They also had no legacy of democratic reform that extended back into the seventeenth century, and no cultural center comparable to either London or Paris. LaRoche wrote for a narrow educated elite in a politically fragmented land ruled by aristocrats still enthralled by the fading splendor of France's

Old Regime. In order to appreciate her accomplishment in *Sternheim*, therefore, it is necessary to look at her most important influences from abroad. All three novels – *Clarissa, Julie*, and *Sternheim* – serve as cultural sites for the working out of new understandings of gender and the family. The result is an often volatile mixture of new ideas within old social forms, where progressive and conservative tendencies coexist, and where the characters themselves are often caught up in ideas they do not adequately understand.

RICHARDSON: CLARISSA'S SACRIFICE

Richardson situates *Clarissa* in a period of English history in which capitalism and empire provide new sources of wealth to advance families into the old social hierarchy. While Mr. Harlowe, Clarissa's father, has grown rich by marriage, his two unmarried brothers have accumulated wealth through less traditional ways: the eldest, John, has reaped "unexpected benefits . . . from his new-found mines," while Antony's wealth stems from "his East India traffic and successful voyages."[17] John owns the raw materials for the coming industrial revolution, while Antony profits from the expansion of the British empire. Their combined fortunes provide the means to "raising a family" up the rungs of the social ladder.

The novel's plot hinges on the Harlowes' effort to control the rich uncles' money by using Clarissa as a pawn in the campaign to advance the family fortunes.[18] Clarissa has unexpectedly inherited her grandfather's estate, and her ambitious brother, James Harlowe Jr., realizes that the Harlowes must keep Clarissa's wealth in the family if they hope to gain a peerage. For this purpose he favors an arranged marriage with Roger Solmes, an immensely wealthy but boorish man who has agreed to will his entire fortune to Clarissa or her family. Clarissa refuses to go along with his plan. She insists on love, friendship, and personal choice in marriage in a way that will characterize the new middle class. The enterprising James Jr., for his part, exhibits the aggressive individualism of the same class, but while he seeks social advancement in the public sphere, his sister desires private happiness in marriage. Their conflict is thus internal to the new ideology taking shape, and falls along gender rather than class lines. To further complicate matters, Clarissa's new attitude toward marriage brings with it a heightened sense of the sanctity of the family and paternal authority. Both trends are characteristic of the new morality, but when combined, they produce irreconcilable conflict: if Clarissa is true to herself, she must disobey her father.

While Clarissa craves affection from her parents, they act with ruthless self-interest and a callous disregard for their daughter. Their intractability eventually drives her into Lovelace's control, making the Harlowes indirectly responsible for her rape.[19] To the dismay of her friend Anna Howe, however, Clarissa blames herself for the predicament her family has created. Anna tries to offer Clarissa a more rational assessment of the situation: "The penitence you talk of – It is for *them* to be penitent who hurried you into evils you could not well avoid" (1043). Anna's advice goes unheeded, for Clarissa insists on playing the role of a loving father's guilty daughter. In other words, Clarissa's experience of paternal authority differs from her attitude toward it: Clarissa concentrates her feelings on her father in a way that seems typical of a child raised in an affective nuclear family, even though he is a sickly tyrant and she has received more affection from her grandfather and uncles as a child. In many ways the Harlowe family seems closest to what Lawrence Stone has termed the "open lineage family" of the aristocracy, but Clarissa acts like a child of the bourgeoisie.[20]

The rape functions as the pivotal point in transforming the structure of paternity and Clarissa's relation to it. For Lovelace, the rape is a defeat, an acknowledgment that his attempt at seduction has failed: "There is no triumph in *force!*" (657). Clarissa's initial reaction to the rape follows the sadly familiar pattern of victim's guilt, as she accuses herself more than her rapist: "I hate thee not, base and low-souled as thou art! half as much as I hate myself" (901). In the long run, even the rape pales in significance beside the weight of her father's curse. Again and again she bemoans the curse with an almost obsessive regularity: "Of all the very heavy evils wherewith I have been afflicted, this is *now* the heaviest; for I can neither live nor die under it" (988). Clarissa refuses to blame her family or to make the best of a bad situation and marry her rapist; instead, she condemns herself to death by starvation.

As she is wasting away Clarissa works hard to put the appropriate interpretive "spin" on her decision to die.[21] Of central concern is the way in which the rape affects Clarissa's relation to paternity. After she leaves home Clarissa is certain her family will never accept her back into their midst, and concentrates her efforts on the lifting of her father's curse. When she is gradually convinced of the futility of her efforts, however, she sets off in search of a new person to fill the father's role. The most obvious choice would be Lovelace, and indeed he flatters himself as having been "more than a father to her; for I have given her a life her unnatural father had well-nigh taken away" (518). Belford fears that Lovelace will prove more dangerous than the father he has replaced, and offers himself as a substitute. As her sickness worsens, Clarissa even turns to her doctors as substitute fathers: "Their treatment of me, my dear, is perfectly *paternal!*" (1088).[22] Lovelace sums up Clarissa's almost frantic efforts to find a new family with a cynical but accurate comment: "*Paternal*, poor lady! – Never having been, till very lately, from under her parents' wings, and now abandoned by all her friends, she is for finding out something *paternal* and *maternal* in everyone . . . to supply to herself the father and mother her dutiful heart pants after!" (1082).

Although Clarissa does persuade her father to remove his curse – but not to grant his forgiveness – and she does find some measure of "paternal" protection in Belford and her doctors, she never finds anyone who satisfies her desire completely – until she turns her attention to God.[23] She signals her new resolution in the ambiguous letter to Lovelace that begins "I have good news to tell you. I am setting out with all diligence for my father's house" (1233). Lovelace, who until this time has preyed on Clarissa's penchant for literal truth, falls victim to her figurative language. He hastens to intercept Clarissa at the Harlowes', only to discover that Clarissa has misled him – whether innocently or not remains unclear – by using an allegory: "Read but for my *father's house, Heaven*, said she; and for the interposition of my dear blessed friend, suppose the *mediation* of my *Saviour*; which I humbly rely upon; and all the rest of the letter will be accounted for" (1274).

Clarissa's letter to Lovelace marks a decisive moment in a more general turn of the text toward allegory.[24] The second half of the novel includes several tableaux, carefully staged and described set pieces meant to be read like a Hogarth painting.[25] In such famous images as Clarissa in prison, dressed in what Dorothy Van Ghent sarcastically referred to as "her miraculously dirt-free garments,"[26] Richardson aims less at verisimilitude than allegorical truth. In a similar gesture, Clarissa will eventually give away her clothes and dress herself in virginal white for her death and wedding with God. Increasingly, quotation and literary allusion elevate realistic characters to mythic or archetypal status. Both Clarissa and Belford suggest that Lovelace is either Satan himself or at least involved in a Faustian pact with infernal powers. Clarissa, for her part, assumes at least three different allegorical identities: as Lucretia, she reincarnates the Roman woman who committed suicide after having been raped. As Job, whom she quotes at length in several inserts, she is the long-suffering target of God's inexplicable wrath. Finally, as a Christ-figure, she is the innocent scapegoat whose death atones for the sins of her family.

The primary purpose of the move to allegory is didactic, as Richardson seeks to emphasize Clarissa's virtue and Lovelace's vice. In the absence of an authorial voice, however, it is up to Clarissa to convince the reader of her own exceptional status. We get a key to this process of self-interpretation by examining Clarissa's evolving attitude toward the act of writing. At first Clarissa writes simply to convey information to Anna Howe about recent events in her family. Increasingly, however, Clarissa uses the letters as instruments of self-betterment: "I must write on, although I were not to send it to anybody . . . I have entered into *compact* with myself . . . to *improve* rather than go *backward*" (483). As death nears she bequeaths her letters to Anna Howe and appoints Belford as their editor in an effort to become what Anna Howe calls "a shining example to your sex" (1152). After her death the letters stand in for Clarissa as the public record of a life that has assumed the contours of a cultural icon.[27]

Clarissa leaves a dubious legacy to her future readers and imitators. Her self-imposed sacrifice is both admirable as an expression of her unflinching resolve, and pathetic in its pointlessness. Clarissa becomes a bourgeois saint because she feels guilty about having been raped, and because she feels even more guilty about having been cursed by a heartless father. Rather than accusing her rapist or rejecting her father, Clarissa internalizes injustice and condemns herself. Her death, to be sure, is not completely in vain, for it jolts her family members into awareness of their guilt, and soon leads to their demise.[28] During her life Clarissa never experiences her family's remorse, however, and has to project her desire for a loving family onto her heavenly father. Religion offers her the consoling promise of her "father's house" and provides her with Christ's example of a sacrificial death; thus Clarissa decides to leave this world so that she can find a better one in heaven. Richardson's readers receive mixed messages from the letters she leaves behind:

that someone as noble as Clarissa should feel compelled to die condemns her parents' behavior and the society that produced them; but that Richardson glorifies his guilty victim's starvation as a supremely virtuous gesture of filial piety reestablishes the authority her suicide would seem to undermine.[29] In dying, Clarissa submits to the society against which she protests, winning highest praise for her willingness to suffer for someone else's sins. Subsequent generations of women writers will struggle with an ideology that equates virtue with self-sacrifice, and not all will be willing to embrace suffering and death with Clarissa's serene equanimity.

ROUSSEAU: JULIE'S COMPROMISE

When we turn from *Clarissa* to *Julie, ou La Nouvelle Héloïse* (1762), we find a very different configuration of social conflict. Here it is the woman who outranks the man in a relationship that cuts much more sharply across class lines. Julie D'Etang comes from an old aristocratic family and falls in love with her bourgeois tutor Saint-Preux. At first it seems that Rousseau will write a revolutionary novel, where the inclinations of the heart triumph over class prejudice, and where true nobility is measured in terms of merit and virtue and not on the arbitrary fact of one's birth. Midway through the novel, however, things take a sharply conservative turn. Julie's father thwarts her love for Saint-Preux and arranges an old-fashioned marriage to perpetuate the family name, and after a struggle, Julie betrays her lover and obeys her father. The key to understanding the apparent shift in *La Nouvelle Héloïse* from revolutionary love to resignation for the sake of the status quo lies in the changing relationship between Julie and her father. While Clarissa projects her desire for a loving father into the afterlife, Julie experiences her father's affection at home. In two pivotal scenes, angry confrontations between Julie and her father lead to emotional outbursts that transform the aristocrats into characters who begin to act like members of the bourgeoisie.

When we compare Julie's family with the Harlowes, we note first the marked reduction in size. The Harlowe clan extends beyond mother, father, and siblings to include a grandfather, two uncles, and cousin Morden. In sharp contrast, Julie's only brother has died, leaving her alone with her father and mother in a small family that bears an outward resemblance to the closed nuclear family of the middle class. However, the Baron D'Etang, like Mr. Harlowe before him, does not act like the affectionate, faithful father of the bourgeois family. Quite the opposite; Julie's friend Claire argues that the baron hastened his wife's death by his youthful philandering and his subsequent severity. As the last surviving male of his old noble family, the baron is preoccupied with the desire to preserve his lineage. He finds it unthinkable that his daughter might be attracted to a man beneath her class, and flies into a rage when the English Lord Bomston tries to convince him that Saint-Preux could make a worthy match with his daughter. In a world where individual talent and personal inclination are beginning to assert their authority over birth, the Baron D'Etang remains firmly entrenched in the old ways. Circumstances have reduced his clan to the point where it resembles the nuclear family, but the *pater familias* has not yet accepted the ethos of the new family structure.

The baron's stubborn pride yields in the course of two cathartic confrontations with his daughter. The first outburst occurs when Julie dares to offer a cautious defense of Saint-Preux's character. Her father becomes incensed and begins beating Julie so violently that she falls and begins to bleed. As we learn later, the beating causes Julie to miscarry the baby conceived during her clandestine rendez-vous with Saint-Preux. A reconciliation scene follows this explosion of anger in which the gruff aristocrat melts into a tender father. After supper the baron silently pulls his daughter onto his lap. Julie sits there awkwardly, listening to his stifled sighs, until she decides to break the tension: "I pretended to slip; to prevent myself, I threw an arm around my father's neck. I laid my face close to his venerable cheek, and in an instant it was covered with my kisses and bathed with my tears. I knew by those which rolled from his eyes that he himself was relieved of a great sorrow. My mother shared our rapture."[30]

Despite the baron's sudden emotional outburst, he does not relinquish control over his daughter or forget his loyalty to his heritage. Quite the contrary: the scene ends when he convinces his daughter to agree to renounce Saint-Preux. What changes is the way in which the baron exercises his power over Julie, as he moves from confrontation to coercion. The pattern repeats itself when Julie defies her father and refuses to marry Wolmar. When the baron realizes that his daughter will not give in, he startles her by falling to his knees and begging her not to cause the death of her entire family.

All resistance broken, Julie collapses halfdead in her father's arms, where she stammers in a weakened voice: "'Oh my father! I had arms against your threats, but I have none against your tears. It is you who is killing your daughter'" (French 349; my translation).

Julie's decision to accede to her father's wishes against those of her lover marks the initial resolution of a conflict between two equally "natural" claims. On the one hand, Saint-Preux views Julie's desire for him as a triumph of natural passion over the antiquated demands of social convention. Thus he is offended when Julie repents her love for him: "Have you not obeyed the purest laws of nature? Have you not freely entered into the holiest of engagements?" (82; 100). Later Saint-Preux's ally, Lord Bomston, offers a spirited defense of natural passion against parental tyranny. Julie feels equal loyalty toward her family, however, and chastises her lover for his attempt to make her "an unnatural daughter whose passions could make her forget the claims of her family and whose lover's complaints would make her insensible to her father's caresses?" (60; 72). Julie confronts a dilemma: "Whom shall I favor, my lover or my father? Alas, listening to love or to nature, I cannot avoid driving either one or the other to despair. Sacrificing myself to duty, I cannot avoid committing a crime, and whatever course I take, I am forced to die both unhappy and guilty" (169; 201).

The baron's change from commanding aristocrat to imploring father decides the issue in his favor. On the surface, it would seem that revolutionary sentiment has yielded to a reaffirmation of the established order. Yet that order has been transformed from within, as the D'Etangs begin to act like an affectionate nuclear family. Julie then carries this sentiment into the new family she establishes with Wolmar. As his wife, the mother of his children, and as the head of the household at the Clarens estate, Julie will fulfill the "triple calling" of women in a new program of domestic virtue. Although she remains an aristocrat, she adopts a mode of behavior that will serve as the pattern for future generations of bourgeois women. She does so at considerable personal cost, however, for her marriage to Wolmar requires her to renounce her love for Saint-Preux. Julie says she makes her sacrifice voluntarily, but only after having internalized her father's desires to the point where it becomes difficult to tell where free will ends and coercion begins. The same ambivalence extends to the estate she manages. Wolmar maintains order at Clarens by a technique of indirect guidance, "la main cachée." The trick is to manipulate people in a way that leaves them the illusion of free will.[31] Thus children at Clarens are given the impression that they are acting spontaneously while they are in fact being controlled; Wolmar encourages his servants to perform their duties willingly without granting them actual equality; and Julie even cultivates nature into the semblance of a wilderness.

Saint-Preux receives special attention within the disciplinary regime at Clarens. As Julie's former lover he presents an obvious threat to her marriage with Wolmar, but they encourage him to remain with them as the tutor of their children, whereby Wolmar seems less interested in educating his children than in reeducating his wife and Saint-Preux: "'your mutual attachment had so many praiseworthy things about it that it ought rather to be regulated than destroyed'" (321; 495). With this project in mind Wolmar arranges repetitions of previous scenes of passion. He even leaves the former lovers alone for an extended period, during which they make an emotional pilgrimage to the site where Saint-Preux had once pined for his love. The ostensible purpose of these scenes is to extirpate former passion through a reenactment of the past. The intended cure backfires, however, for the memory of former happiness only serves as a cruel reminder of what has been taken away.[32]

The reintegration of Saint-Preux into the social order he once threatened reveals lingering discontent in Julie's seemingly exemplary marriage. We recall that Julie agreed to the wedding only after two emotional scenes with her father. The intimate exchanges during these two crises have a lasting effect on the baron, who continues to treat his married daughter with tender affection: he keeps watch at Julie's bedside when she has smallpox, falls down the stairs in shock when he hears of her final illness, and is ready to die when she is gone. We see nothing of the same passion between Wolmar and Julie. They have children, but it is difficult to imagine them having sex. In a traditionally arranged marriage between two aristocrats this would not be surprising; conversely, had they been in love from the beginning like Julie and Saint-Preux, we could expect a more affectionate marriage. Instead, Wolmar and Julie enter into a kind of hybrid marriage that attempts to combine aristocratic tradition with bourgeois sentiment. The marriage's foundation rests neither on a calculated arrangement nor on free choice, but on coercion and guilt, as the baron manipulates his daughter into accepting Wolmar. He maintains his aristocratic lineage by acting like an affectionate middle-class father; the resulting marriage bears an outward resemblance to the nuclear family, but lacks its warmth.

While Wolmar conducts one of his many experiments in social discipline with his wife and her former lover, Julie wants Saint-Preux to resume his old roles as lover and tutor in a displaced and non-threatening form. This time Saint-Preux is to educate Julie's children, since Wolmar feels himself unsuited to the task. There is of course something humiliating in this arrangement for Saint-Preux, as he becomes the servant of the woman he once hoped to marry, but it also underscores Wolmar's inadequacy as a father. Julie also wants Saint-Preux to remain for her own sake, a desire she masks under the delusion that former lovers can be good friends. In an effort to keep the situation under control, she encourages him to marry her friend Claire. In this way Saint-Preux would remain in close proximity to Julie without posing a threat to her marriage. Saint-Preux refuses to marry Claire, but he eagerly remains near Julie, thus serving as a constant, teasing reminder of repressed passion.

The latent tension in Julie's marriage becomes manifest on her deathbed. At first Julie's death seems a positive counterpart to Clarissa's virtual suicide. Julie dies after saving her child from drowning. Her death is an affirmation of her maternal role. While Clarissa starves herself in a voluntary renunciation of the world, Julie eats and drinks heartily on her deathbed. Despite Julie's apparent composure in the face of death, however, all is not well. Even before her final illness Julie admits dissatisfaction with her married life: "I am not happy. A secret weariness is creeping into the bottom of my heart. It feels empty and swollen" (French 694; my translation). While Julie attributes her malaise to an overabundance of joy in this instance, she realizes on her deathbed that her continued love for Saint-Preux is the real cause of her unhappiness: "I have been deceiving myself for a long time" (French 740; my translation).

Rousseau's ambivalent ending to *La Nouvelle Héloïse* signals a new stage in the evolution of the family. Both Richardson and Rousseau write about the emergence of the nuclear family in the context of the old social order. Clarissa and Julie function as harbingers of a new ethos, but also as victims of forces still at work from the past. While Clarissa has to project her desires for paternal affection onto God, Julie feels her father's tears and marries his deputy. Wolmar and the baron are not only members of the same social class and generation

– Bomston is fifty years old – but Wolmar even saved the baron's life once in battle. As the baron's surrogate, Wolmar infantilizes Julie, while she deifies him: "My dear Wolmar . . . Oh my benefactor! Oh my father! In giving myself up wholly to you, I can only offer you, as to God Himself, the gifts which I have received from you" (360; 611). In *Clarissa*, religion compensates for the harsh reality of the Harlowe family; in *Julie*, religion sanctifies the new patriarchal order. Wolmar nevertheless remains a distant figure, and Julie struggles in vain to suppress memories of past happiness. During her adult life Julie fulfills her calling as wife, mother, and household manager in exemplary fashion, but in death she reveals the price she has paid in emotional suffering through obedience to paternal authority. She shares with Clarissa the dubious distinction of attaining secular sainthood for her willingness to sacrifice personal happiness.

SOPHIE VON LAROCHE: SOPHIE'S SURVIVAL

Just before Baron D'Etang's violent outburst in Rousseau's novel, the liberal English Lord Bomston offers to divide his fortune with Saint-Preux so that Saint-Preux can marry Julie. True nobility, Bomston argues, lies in quality of character and not the accident of birth. What is denied in that novel takes place at the beginning of Sophie von LaRoche's *Geschichte des Fräuleins von Sternheim*. Colonel von Sternheim, born the son of a German professor, has been ennobled for his achievements as a soldier. "'Your merit, not fortune, has elevated you'" (51; 19) declares the general who grants him his patent of nobility. Sternheim retires near the estate of his good friend Baron von P., where he soon falls in love with P.'s half-sister Sophie. Despite opposition from his family, P. consents to the marriage of his aristocratic sister to the ennobled bourgeois. The happy couple soon has a daughter named Sophie. Unlike either Clarissa or Julie, Sophie grows up in a family that is affectionate from the start. This family serves both as the source of Sophie's values and as the model she hopes to reproduce in her own marriage. Unfortunately, Sophie's parents die young, exposing their innocent daughter to a series of alarming incidents: Sophie is ensnared in a web of court intrigue, tricked into a fake marriage, raped, kidnapped, and left to die in the remote Scottish mountains. Yet Sophie von Sternheim survives to marry a liberal young English nobleman, become the mother of two children, and manage an estate modeled on that of her father. Thus the plot of this German novel differs from its English and French counterparts: whereas both Richardson and Rousseau follow their heroines from love-crisis to death, Sophie von Sternheim moves from birth to marriage.

Sternheim begins with an extended portrait of Sophie's family. On the one hand, as noted, achievement replaces birth as the ticket to nobility. We see not the overthrow of one class by another, but the regeneration of the aristocracy by an infusion of new talent and values. On the other hand, LaRoche constructs a very careful family tree for her heroine that suggests an almost Lamarckian faith in the inheritability of acquired cultural characteristics. Sophie von Sternheim's maternal grandfather, the elder Baron von P., is of the old German aristocracy, but her maternal grandmother is the English Lady Watson. England, from an eighteenth-century German perspective, is the land of Richardson and Shakespeare, moral weeklies and an increasingly democratic form of government; it thus represents a culturally and politically progressive alternative to a decadent German aristocracy enthralled by French fashion. As a professor, Sophie's paternal grandfather comes from the ascendent class of educated professionals that will produce the majority of German writers in the late eighteenth century. We do not hear anything about Sophie's paternal grandmother, but this is quite typical of her class: her identity is contained within her role as the professor's wife. Given this cultural genealogy, it is not surprising that the English aristocrat Lord Derby should describe Sophie von Sternheim as "'an odd mix of the citizen and the courtier'" (113; 123).

Instead of completely abandoning belief in the importance of one's ancestors, in other words, LaRoche suggests that certain individuals are genetically predisposed to superior cultural achievement. Work is nevertheless required, and Colonel von Sternheim sets out to transform his new estate into a model society. As he explains to his wife, had he been born to the aristocracy he might not have applied himself with the same industry to his role as lord of the manor. She goes on at some length in a letter to her mother to report the improvements he has undertaken on the estate, including setting up a poor house and developing pedagogical programs appropriate to different social classes. For all his reforms, there is nothing revolutionary about Sternheim's new social order. Like Wolmar and Julie at Clarens, Sternheim does not seek to overthrow the estate system, but to teach the people "that measure of understanding that they need for the joyful and eager discharge of their duties toward God, their superiors, their neighbors, and themselves" (65; 42).

The colonel shows himself most clearly a member of the middle class in his attitude toward his wife and family. His marriage grew out of mutual attraction, and when he lists his duties, his wife and her family come first. Also typical of the nuclear family is the care he lavishes on his daughter's education. Sophie receives instruction in such academic disciplines as philosophy, history, and languages, but also in music, dance, and "all womanly tasks" (71; 52). Sophie's bond with her father becomes particularly close after her mother dies in childbirth. Sophie is nine years old at the time, and for the next ten years she remains alone with Sternheim. The colonel grooms his adolescent daughter into a replacement for his absent wife. The process begins soon after the mother's death in what might be termed the mirror stage in Sternheim's socialization: father and daughter weep together before the portrait of the absent mother. By the time she is sixteen Sophie has assumed her mother's former position as manager of the estate, and she happily complies with her father's request that she dress up in her mother's old clothing. Mother and daughter share the name Sophie.

The gradual process by which Colonel von Sternheim cultivates his daughter into a reincarnation of her mother shows how great a role socialization plays in individual development. Biology is not enough; Sophie must be carefully trained for her role as daughter, woman, and potential wife. Particularly significant is the fact that she enters puberty after her mother's death, which enables the mother to serve as the idealized image of Sophie's future self without becoming a potential rival for the father's attention. It is difficult not to see an element of barely suppressed incestuous desire when Sternheim admires his daughter playing the role of his wife: "You know, Emilia, that my dear Papa wanted to see me always in my Mama's dresses, and that I too liked to wear them best" (77; 63).

Colonel Sternheim's death leaves the nineteen-year-old Sophie von Sternheim like the cursed Clarissa without an adequate object for the affection she once directed at her father. For a transitional period of one year Sophie lives with the local pastor who becomes her "paternal friend" (78; 64), but then she must leave to live at court with her mother's relatives the Löbaus. While Colonel von Sternheim had brought progressive social reform to his rural estate, the Löbaus live in the corrupt atmosphere of the decadent nobility. LaRoche distinguishes between a progressive nobility that has absorbed middle-class virtues and a decadent *Rokokoadel* mired in the sins of the past.[33] The virtuous Sophie discovers a world of vanity, artifice, and moral turpitude that shocks and revolts her. Sophie's uncle von Löbau has secretly offered his niece as mistress to the Prince as a bribe toward winning a lawsuit. Meanwhile the unsuspecting Sophie becomes attracted to the young Lord Seymour, an Englishman visiting the German court. To make things even more complicated, the rakish Lord Derby finds it an amusing challenge to seduce Sophie von Sternheim before the Prince can carry out his plan. Matters come to a crisis when Sophie attends a ball unwittingly dressed in a costume that identifies her as the prince's mistress. Seymour confuses appearance with reality, rebukes her publicly, and leaves before she can explain. Finally realizing the extent of the Löbaus' treachery, Sophie accepts Derby's offer of marriage and flees. This only makes the situation worse, and only in the novel's final pages do Seymour and his older half-brother Lord Rich rescue Sophie, who begins a new life happily married to Seymour.

Sophie's trials extend from her father's death until her own marriage. As the narrator describes it, we should view Sophie's history as a test of innate character that is to inspire female readers to similar virtue:

We traveled first to the Loebau estate, and from there with the countess to D., where the unfortunate period began in which you will see this most amiable young lady enmeshed in difficulties and circumstances which destroyed at once her beautiful plans of a happy life but which, through a test of her inner worth, made her story instructive for the best among our sex. (76; 61)

In structuring her novel as a test of the heroine, LaRoche draws on the tradition of Pietist autobiography.[34] The protagonist endures a "dark night of the soul" before the work's redemptive conclusion. To an even greater extent than in *Clarissa*, religion in the novel serves to proclaim the values of the nuclear family. It is not God who forsakes Sophie in her time of trial, but her father: "Oh, that my father had remained with me until, with his blessing, my hand was joined to that of a worthy man!" (165; 213). Ironically enough, her father's ennoblement for his bourgeois virtue exposes his daughter to an old-fashioned form of aristocratic vice.

Sophie never forgets her family, however. She carries with her to court a jewel-encrusted locket that contains her parents' portraits and soil from their graves. The locket reappears at important moments in the second half of the novel as well. In her most penitent phase as "Madame Leidens" Sophie sells the jewels from the locket to finance her teaching of poor children. When she is in England she weeps over the portraits together with Lord Rich, himself a surrogate father-figure. The locket eventually confirms her identity and helps rescue her from the Scottish wilderness. Finally Sophie and Lord Seymour kneel on her parents' grave to ask for their blessing in marriage. The locket serves as a reminder of Sophie's origins and her goal in a threatening world, an object that for her has the magic powers of a talisman and the fetish character that recalls her love for her father. Thus LaRoche reworks the religious autobiography into domestic fiction, transforming the spiritual trial in the wilderness into the period when the young woman makes the dangerous transition from father to husband.

Thus described, the *Geschichte des Fräuleins von Sternheim* leaves its protagonist little room for personal development. Yet the wife who stands at the end of the novel has grown considerably from the teenage daughter who loses her father. The novel moves more in a spiral than a circle, as Sophie must earn the virtues she admired in her father. Once again, inheritance is not enough; Sophie matures in a way that anticipates the admonition of Goethe's Faust: "What you inherit from your father, earn it anew before you call it yours" ["Was du ererbt von deinen Vätern hast, Erwirb es, um es zu besitzen"].[35] In this context it is important to note LaRoche's slight but significant complication of Richardson's seduction plot. Clarissa steadfastly refuses to marry Lovelace both before and after the rape, while Sophie von Sternheim does go through a wedding ceremony with Derby. Yet even before she discovers that the marriage is fraudulent, she refuses to have intercourse with Derby, the man she believes is her husband. We must consider three questions when comparing Sophie von Sternheim's predicament to that of Clarissa: why does she agree to marry Derby? Why does she refuse to consummate the "marriage"? And finally, how does she manage to survive the rape, remarry (this time legitimately), and raise a model family?

Although early reviewers complained that Sophie has no compelling reason to accept Derby's proposal,[36] her actions are in fact overdetermined, revealing considerable psychological complexity. Sophie has lost her parents before coming to court, and the pastor who served as stepfather dies shortly after she arrives. She discovers that her remaining relatives are willing to use her to advance their own interests just as Seymour rebukes and deserts her. Derby's offer seems the only honorable way out of a desperate situation, particularly since he has worked successfully to convince her that he is more virtuous than he seems.

Other factors place Sophie's decision in a less admirable light. Derby appeals to her in part because he has half-secretly showered money on a poor family earlier befriended by Sophie. Indeed, the narrator presents Sophie's concern for those in need as one of her most appealing qualities. When she first arrives at court Sophie is shocked both by the extent of poverty among the lower classes and the prince's studied indifference to the plight of his subjects. The sight of a group of pitiable wretches by the roadside moves her to an act of spontaneous generosity: "although they did not beg, I tossed several coins to those standing closest to the road" (90; 84). She displays similar zeal in helping the wife of an unfortunate civil servant. While her charity is well-intended, its very randomness points out its limitations: her actions do nothing to improve the lot of the majority of even those poor families who live near her, much less to change the society that produces such inequity.[37] Moreover, Sophie's charity reveals a rather smug sense of self-satisfaction that opens the door to Derby's machinations. As he puts it, Sophie is one of those women who fall for obvious tricks because they are so convinced of their own moral superiority that they feel immune to seduction. He even goes so far as to suggest that virtue is just a hypocritical form of self-interest. The prize for earthly chastity lies in heaven's sensual delights.

If there is an element of naivety in Sophie's admiration of Derby's seeming virtue, her decision to marry him is motivated by still less admirable concerns, namely revenge against the court and the desire to marry into the English nobility. Since childhood Sophie has displayed an interest in her maternal grandmother's heritage, and Derby capitalizes on this anglophilia by addressing her only in English. While the English language awakens memories of Sophie's mother, it also inspires an ambition for social advancement that contrasts with her mother's willingness to marry below her station for love. "I do not deny it – my love for England and the distinguished rank to which my lord's generosity would raise me; these two considerations also had great attraction for my forsaken

and stunned soul" (164; 212). Her decision to marry Lord Derby
stems from a complex combination of impulses that corresponds to
her nature as a hybrid of bourgeois and aristocratic breeding. Like
the typical bourgeois heroine of the eighteenth century, the innocent
young woman falls prey to aristocratic vice; in fleeing the prince she
runs into the arms of the evil Lord Derby. Yet her decision to marry
Derby is prompted at least in part by an infatuation with aristocratic
philanthropy, the desire for revenge, and a yearning for a husband
who belongs to the English nobility.

Her refusal to consummate the marriage reveals a similar combination of conflicting motivations. Like Clarissa, Sophie von Sternheim
is raped, and LaRoche makes no attempt to minimize Derby's guilt.
Nevertheless, there are certain circumstances surrounding the rape
that render it more complex, if ultimately no more forgivable, than
the rape of Clarissa. Lovelace tells the servants that he is married to
Clarissa, but she knows he is not, whereas Sophie believes that her
marriage to Derby is legitimate. Why then does she resist his
advances? The question obviously bothered LaRoche's editor
Wieland enough for him to add a speculative footnote to the rape
scene: "Presumably because she did not love him, had not been
properly and gradually prepared for such a scene, and, in any case,
was in a frame of mind too different from his to condescend to
acquiesce to a suggestion that seemed motivated more by wanton-
ness than by affection" (171; 223). In part, in other words, Derby
takes the wrong approach: rather than woo her, he demands sex,
and when refused, he rapes her. Wieland also identifies a more
lasting impediment to their marriage when he observes that Sophie
does not love Derby. There is some justification to Derby's reproach
that she has used him as an escape route from the court, although
she does so under duress and without conscious intent to deceive.
Derby even tries to suggest that he has undergone a change of heart
during the marriage ceremony, and later believes that she tricked
him: " 'I have deceived only your *hand* but you, in assuring me of a
love you did not feel, have deceived my *heart*' " (174; 229–30). It is
difficult to summon up much sympathy for a rapist, kidnapper, and
potential murderer, but LaRoche does grant Derby a deathbed
conversion in which he laments his sins in a way that Lovelace does
not. Richardson writes an increasingly allegorical novel that moves
in the realm of moral absolutes; Clarissa is an innocent victim of her
father's tyranny and Lovelace's rape. In contrast, LaRoche allows for

error and correction; Sophie has more flaws than Clarissa, but she is therefore more capable of redeeming herself through penance and hard work. Richardson's blameless heroine finds release in self-imposed martyrdom, whereas Sophie recognizes personal shortcomings and struggles to improve herself in this world.

For example, Sophie moves from random philanthropy to active pedagogy in her treatment of the poor.[38] Already before her rape Sophie supplements her charitable donations to a Mrs. T. with moral advice. In words borrowed from a local pastor, Sophie encourages the woman to work hard, stay within her class, and live modestly. True nobility lies in virtue and talent, and high value is given to cleanliness and education. The tendency for instruction to replace random largesse accelerates in the second half of the novel. While waiting for Derby after eloping, Sophie gives money to the local poor and teaches the innkeeper's nieces. After Derby abandons her Sophie flees to Rosina's house where she first teaches her godchild to read and then establishes "a 'seminary for domestics,' where poor girls could be trained to become good and skilled servants" (179; 238). Sophie's pedagogical impulse continues even in Scotland, where she teaches a child to speak English.

Sophie never seeks to overthrow the social order, but her instruction is revolutionary in that it works to instill in individuals a new sense of social order based on the family. To achieve this goal Sophie employs a particular type of anti-theatrical acting that has parallels in eighteenth-century stage practice. Around mid-century dramatists began to develop a new naturalism in both acting style and staging techniques. The members of the audience, who had once spent as much time observing each other as the spectacle on stage, now sat in darkness and focused their attention on the performance. Actors no longer improvised stock roles, but memorized unique parts within carefully composed dramas. The purpose of the changes was to base the pedagogical effect of the theatre on an emotional identification of the audience with the characters on stage.[39]

We witness an example of just this sort of identificatory theatre in Sophie's pedagogy.[40] While working as a teacher Sophie hears of the family G.'s predicament. Mr. G. has lost his job, and although a certain Mrs. Hill has given them money, the man's pride and his wife's careless nature make mere gifts insufficient. What is needed is a program of reform. Sophie, as Madame Leidens, offers to spend two weeks with the family as a kind of live-in social worker. She begins by talking about her own life, and uses her confessions as a springboard to some general statements about virtue. But then her pedagogy takes a different tack, as she actually plays out the roles expected between Mrs. G., her old friend Miss Lena, and the three daughters. This private pedagogical theatre recalls those scenes from Sophie's childhood when her father coached her in learning to become her mother. In both cases the woman learns to perform gender-specific roles in ways that appear natural. Pedagogical theatre attains its greatest success when the actress forgets she is playing a role.[41]

Central to the new order of the family in the *Geschichte des Fräuleins von Sternheim* is the insistence on separate spheres of action for men and women. Sophie disapproves of her aunt's insistence that she try to curry favor with Countess F., whose husband may influence her uncle's lawsuit. In Sophie's opinion, women should have no say in such public affairs: "I would bring neither my own wife nor the minister's into these matters but rather settle a man's business with men" (79; 66). Sophie tends to defer to male opinion, and she cites with approval the opinions of Count T. on "natural" gender distinctions:

Nature herself, he said, had provided us instruction in this when, for example in love, she made the man passionate and the woman tender . . . In this manner, when each sex remained in its prescribed sphere, both were running the same course, though each in different tracks as it were, toward the final goal of their destiny, without by an artificial mingling of the characters disturbing the moral order. (116; 128)

As Sophie's pedagogical theatre makes clear, however, the new social order rests on a paradoxical foundation of cultivated innocence, for individuals have to be trained to act naturally. An anti-theatrical form of internalized discipline replaces the artificial world of the court, with its operas and costume balls. The new private ethos has clear political implications as well, for by retraining the family, Sophie prepares the father for his role in the state: "Mr. G. himself will supervise the teaching and will conduct their review lessons. Certainly, in time, a man who conducts his paternal duties so faithfully will be entrusted with an office in the service of his country [*Vaterland*]" (184; 247).

While Sophie ascribes wholeheartedly to the view that women should subordinate their opinions to men and restrict their activities to the domestic sphere, other female characters do not quite fit into the accepted mold. One area for feminine independence is the convent. While still at court Sophie makes occasional trips to neighboring estates with her aunt Charlotte, where she encounters the canoness at G. and other noblewomen of her order. Sophie praises Countess G. for her felicity of expression, her modesty, and piano skills; Countess T. W. for her pedagogical talent; and the princess who heads the convent for her serenity and maternal wisdom. Later Sophie agrees somewhat reluctantly to encourage a widow to remarry, but the woman insists on retaining her independence: " 'I simply wish to enjoy the freedom I have purchased with much bitterness' " (188; 254). The woman claims that she has nothing against the institution of marriage per se, but that her own marriage was so traumatic that she has no desire to repeat the experience: " 'my neck is so bruised from my first yoke that even the lightest silk tie would oppress it' " (190; 258).

Sophie respects this decision and admires the women in the convent, but she is not eager to pursue her own independent career. Circumstances leave her no choice, however, and from the time Derby deserts her until Seymour and Rich rescue her, Sophie is on her own. As we have seen, Sophie uses this period to develop more effective means of caring for others; at the same time, she also uses the period to reflect upon herself. During her time at court she sends letters to a friend that record events and her reactions to them. By the time she is isolated in Scotland, however, writing no longer serves the purpose of communication. Somewhat implausibly, Sophie has managed to snatch a roll of paper in the midst of her abduction, and she uses the paper to keep a diary that she is sure no one but herself will ever read. Despite the apparent futility of her effort, Sophie's impulse to write is so great that she continues her diary on canvas when she runs out of paper. When despite all odds Sophie does survive, she treats the letters and diary as a second self, " 'the true expressions of my soul' " (240; 342).

Sophie's autobiographical writings play a role in the novel's resolution, for when she decides to marry Lord Seymour, she gives the original letters and diary to Lord Rich as a kind of consolation prize. Sophie's choice merits a moment's reflection. When first in England it seems likely that she will marry Lord Rich. "My Lord Rich's merits were indeed equal to my father's excellent attributes," reflects Sophie, "my happiness would have been equal to that of my mother. But my involvement, my unholy involvement!" (209; 291).

Tormented by her false marriage and Derby's rape, she feels unworthy of the man who promises to bring her the happiness she once saw in her parents. Once rescued, however, she decides to marry after all. As Lady Summers had pointed out, she can hardly continue as an independent woman; "a woman of your birth and amiability must either live with close relatives or be under the protection of a worthy man" (209; 291). Both Rich and Seymour know of her unfortunate involvement with Lord Derby and brush aside any scruples, and Sophie finally decides "to consent to the union with Seymour as a God-given means to bring my restless wanderings to an end" (239; 341). Unlike Rousseau's Julie, Sophie does not marry the obvious father-surrogate, but opts instead for a younger, more passionate, and at times weaker man, primarily because she has loved him longer and loves him more: "Was he not the man my heart yearned for?" (239; 341). The choice promises to give her greater independence in a marriage based on mutual affection.

The happy marriage represented at the end of the *Geschichte des Fräuleins von Sternheim* mirrors the description of Colonel Sternheim and his family in its opening pages. What Clarissa projected into the afterlife and what Julie realized in flawed form at Clarens finds its most positive fictional representation in LaRoche's novel. Sophie von Sternheim survives her trials, attains a degree of self-reliance, and enters as equal partner into marriage. To this extent, LaRoche grants her heroine a kernel of independence that will flower in some of the less conventional protagonists she helped inspire. At the same time, however, LaRoche produces an equally-influential conservative paradigm of female development based on a reworking of religious autobiography into domestic fiction, where the heroine's dark fatherless night brightens in the arms of her husband. Female independence and potential for growth occur only in the brief period between leaving home and entering into marriage. In leading her heroine to private happiness, LaRoche also pursues a political agenda, as she urges the German nobility to reform itself by emulating English virtue and rejecting French decadence. The middle-class work ethic and family values can revitalize German society without risk of revolutionary turmoil, for Sophie exercises her domestic virtues as an enlightened aristocrat. Significantly, however, LaRoche decides to leave her heroine in England, implying that even her modest proposals for reform have little hope in Germany.

CHAPTER 3

German women respond to the French Revolution

INTRODUCTION

German intellectuals greeted the French Revolution with an enthusiasm that for most soon gave way to horror, as the Declaration of the
Rights of Man led to revolutionary tribunals and mob violence.
Within a matter of months Europe's most powerful country swept
away the feudal order that had structured society for a millennium.
While the events in France did not provoke similar uprisings on the
part of most German subjects against their rulers, they did inspire
intense reflection on the implications of what was immediately
perceived as a watershed event in European history. Could citizens
attain liberty and equality without violence? Could reform mend the
old order and make revolution unnecessary? Because the identity of
the rising middle class was closely tied to its attitudes toward
sexuality and the family, reflections on revolutionary politics were
inextricably linked to issues affecting individuals' seemingly private
concerns. Did fraternity include women, and if not, what role were
women to play in a republic? What was the relation between
patriarchy in the family and patriotism in the nation?

Schiller's "Das Lied von der Glocke" [The Song of the Bell]
(1800) contained one of the most influential German responses to the
Revolution, as subsequent generations of schoolchildren were forced
to memorize his poem. Basing his idealized image of village life on a
strict division of labor between men and women – "Der Mann muß
hinaus / Ins feindliche Leben . . . Und drinnen waltet / Die züchtige
Hausfrau" – Schiller condemns revolutionary French women as
appalling hyenas.[1] Goethe's equally popular epic poem *Hermann und
Dorothea* (1798) portrays domestic virtue with considerably greater
irony. His exiled heroine, who is quite capable of wielding a sword
when pressed by marauding French soldiers, voluntarily submits to a

life of servitude with her future husband and his irritable father in return for a stable home. It was during this same period that Joachim Heinrich Campe's pedagogical treatise, *Väterliche Rath für meine Tochter* [Paternal Advice for My Daughter] (1789) went into multiple editions,[2] while Campe's former pupil Wilhelm von Humboldt published essays "Über den Geschlechtsunterschied und dessen Einfluß auf die organische Natur" [On Sexual Difference and its Influence on Organic Nature] (1794) and "Über die männliche und weibliche Form" [On Masculine and Feminine Form] (1795). Schiller's philosophical treatises also divide aesthetic categories along gendered lines, as he assigns *Anmut* [grace] to women while reserving *Würde* [dignity] to men. On all fronts – literary, pedagogical, biological, and aesthetic – German men sought to establish proper boundaries between the sexes.

These examples do not tell the entire story, however. Not all men, and certainly not all women, were willing to accept the frequently touted gender distinctions at face value. It is impossible to mention Schiller's "Das Lied von der Glocke" without recalling Caroline Schlegel-Schelling's account of the Early Romantics nearly falling off their chairs with laughter when his work first appeared.[3] Theodor Gottlieb von Hippel argued for women's rights in *Über die bürgerliche Verbesserung der Weiber* (1792), while Caroline Schlegel-Schelling, Sophie Mereau, and Therese Huber expressed open sympathy for the Revolution and defended women's emancipation in their letters and literary works. As this brief overview suggests, any attempt to identify a single German response to the Revolution is inherently misguided. We should speak instead of an intensification of debate regarding both political alternatives and sexual politics in an era of unprecedented social change.

In this chapter I will examine the work of four prominent German women writers around 1800: Caroline von Wolzogen, Friederike Helene Unger, Therese Huber, and Sophie Mereau. With the exception of the first volume of Unger's *Julchen Grünthal* (1784), the works were all written after the beginning of the French Revolution, but before the Napoleonic conquest of Germany in 1806. While LaRoche proposes reforms within the old social order, the new generation of women writers reflects on revolutionary upheavals just across the Rhine. The France that was once a symbol of a moribund aristocratic culture now exported images of democratic radicalism that both fascinated and frightened German intellectuals. The work of the writers examined here coincides in time with Weimar Classicism and Early Romanticism, and each woman had personal ties to one or more men associated with these literary movements. The canonical works of the "Age of Goethe" represent only a fraction of Germany's rapidly expanding literary output around 1800, however, and women writers were particularly drawn to the increasingly popular, if still disreputable, genre of the novel.[4] In the following pages I hope to provide insight into the works of individual authors, and in doing so, to demonstrate the obvious but often ignored facts that not all women writers are the same, and that not all domestic fiction concerns itself exclusively with the private sphere. Although their individual responses to the Revolution in France and its reverberations in Germany differ, these novelists share at least one conviction: that the best way to write about politics is to write about the family.

CAROLINE VON WOLZOGEN: FOR A KINDER, GENTLER PATRIARCHY

For many readers of German literature Caroline von Wolzogen (1763–1847) bears the dubious distinction of being the sister Schiller didn't marry. Born into the lesser Thuringian nobility, Caroline von Lengefeld and her younger sister Charlotte lived with their widowed mother in Rudolstadt, south of Weimar.[5] The daughters grew up in a loving family and enjoyed the typical education of their social class. Unfortunately, Caroline's father died when she was thirteen, and three years later her mother persuaded her to accept the proposal of Friedrich Wilhelm Ludwig von Beulwitz. The marriage proved unhappy, and Charlotte welcomed the acquaintance with Schiller as a distraction from the restrictive atmosphere of the local court. The rebellious young dramatist first visited the family in 1787 with Wilhelm von Wolzogen, who later married Caroline after her divorce from Beulwitz. The positive first impression blossomed into friendship during the next summer, as Schiller lived in the nearby town of Volkstädt and visited the Lengefeld family daily. Schiller seems to have been equally attracted to both Caroline and Charlotte, but in the end he chose the modest, quiet Charlotte over her more intellectually gifted older sister.

Relations between the newlyweds and Caroline cooled for some years in the wake of Caroline's divorce and another apparent affair, but by the mid 1790s Schiller and Charlotte were reconciled to her new marriage. Caroline moved to Weimar in 1797 and was in close contact with the leading intellectual figures, including Schiller, Goethe, Fichte, and the Humboldts. At this time Schiller needed more material for his journal *Die Horen*, and turned to his sister-in-law for help. Caroline von Wolzogen had begun writing the novel *Agnes von Lilien* in 1793; Schiller published the first volume in installments in *Die Horen* in 1796–97, and was influential in getting the completed two-volume work accepted by Unger in Berlin. The anonymous novel caused a minor sensation. Friedrich Schlegel suspected that Goethe might be the author; others guessed at Schiller or one of the Jacobi brothers; nearly everyone praised its style. Enthusiasm for the novel soon faded, however, and Wolzogen did not complete her second and final novel for decades (*Cordelia*, 1840). Until its republication in 1988, *Agnes von Lilien* remained a minor footnote to an author remembered primarily for writing Schiller's biography.[6]

Agnes von Lilien contains three interrelated themes: it is a romance that follows the heroine from adolescence to marriage; it is also a mystery, as the eponymous protagonist discovers her parents and the secret of her birth; and, finally, it is a political novel about the restoration of just government to a suffering land. Or perhaps it is best to say that the novel is a fairy tale, in which the heroine discovers she is a princess, marries a handsome aristocrat, and lives happily ever after with her children and loyal subjects. Wolzogen offers a vision of society that harmoniously combines romantic love, the affectionate family, and the patriarchal state.

Agnes von Lilien grows up in the foster care of an elderly pastor in Hohenfels. The principality derives its name from the local hereditary ruler, and is part of a larger, unnamed German state ruled by an aging prince. Agnes experiences the kind of childhood Rousseau considered ideal: far from the court and without money, she learns to appreciate nature under the loving guidance of her stepfather. She receives the usual instruction in modern languages, music, and drawing, but also learns to read ancient Greek and to translate Homer, subjects normally reserved for men. The interest in antiquity reflects the influence of Weimar Classicism, as does the concern for personal development or *Bildung*: "I had a few lessons to get me used to regular work; but at that time my father was unbeknown to me concerned with my education [*Bildung*] all day long."[7] Agnes returns her stepfather's affection enthusiastically, regarding him with an almost reverent awe: "When I became mature enough to compare individuals with one another, I often told my father how vastly superior to all others he seemed to me" (1:4). Like Sophie von Sternheim, Agnes von Lilien goes through adolescence without a mother, which in both cases tightens the father–daughter bond.

The plot gets underway when a mysterious visitor arrives seeking shelter on a dark and stormy night. It is the handsome Baron von Nordheim. In the course of the evening Nordheim and Agnes discover that they are kindred spirits, and it soon becomes clear that they are falling in love. "I was raised properly," recalls Agnes in her narrative, "in the highest purity and chastity of the senses and the imagination; this was the first man with whom I experienced my full femininity" (1:60). In loving Nordheim, Agnes transfers her affections away from her stepfather, as she herself realizes when contemplating her sudden infatuation: "I even left my father gladly, for the first time in my life" (1:66). In fact, Nordheim is old enough to be Agnes's father: she is eighteen, while he is forty, and both comment on their age difference in the course of the evening.

In the four hundred pages that extend from the description of this first evening to the open declaration of love between Nordheim and Agnes at the end of the first volume, the novel proceeds as a conventional romance by introducing obstacles to the protagonists' desires. Agnes soon learns that Nordheim has a long-standing relationship with the Duchess Amalie von Wildenfels; it is even rumored that they are secretly married. Meanwhile Agnes is called away from home to the court, where she becomes close friends with young Julius von Alban. While Agnes encounters Nordheim in seemingly intimate situations with Amalie, he happens upon her and Julius in a series of even more compromising circumstances. For a time events are still further confused when one of the princes at court – who later turns out to be Agnes's uncle – ignores his own marriage and makes advances to his niece.

Wolzogen complicates this plot by combining it with the ostensible orphan's discovery of her biological parents. We eventually learn that Agnes's father was the enlightened ruler of the local community who was forced into exile because of the secret marriage in which she was conceived. Neither she nor her stepfather knows this yet, but the pastor does have fond memories of the prince who left without explanation, and Agnes has cherished the story of his mysterious departure since childhood: "No matter how many times I had already heard this story, I always heard it with the same interest; since childhood it had been my favorite entertainment to hear my father tell about his missing friend" (1:53). It is as if the pastor has programed Agnes with latent memories of her father that are triggered by the arrival of her future husband. As soon as she leaves her stepfather she becomes curious about her biological parents, and before she even gets to court she meets a painter who goes by the name of Charles, but who is actually her father. Without revealing his identity to his daughter, he manages to become her tutor and to arrange a secret rendezvous between Agnes and her mother, who, as it turns out, is secretly living not far from court.

The first volume of *Agnes von Lilien* contains two increasingly intertwined plot strands, as Agnes's gradual discovery of her parents retards her unification with her future husband. Several times Hohenfels's efforts to arrange clandestine meetings between Agnes and her mother inadvertently place her in awkward circumstances that give Nordheim the impression she is interested in other men. The series of misunderstandings climaxes in the melodramatic conclusion of the first volume. As Hohenfels leads his daughter to another meeting with her mother, Nordheim follows behind, concerned for Agnes's virtue. Nordheim's worst suspicions seem confirmed when Hohenfels and Agnes pull into an inn and lock themselves in a room. Nordheim breaks into the room as Hohenfels draws his gun, but Agnes is able to explain that "Charles" is not her lover, and that her heart belongs to another man: "Nordheim lay at my feet. 'Is it possible?' he cried, 'am I the happy man! to be loved by you!'" (1:404). Indeed he is, and the two lovers share their first passionate kiss while the father looks on "as if in a deep dream" (1:408).

Wolzogen constructs the story of the heroine's maturation as an Oedipal rivalry, where the awakening of sexual desire for her future husband coincides with the intensification of her affective bond to her father. The rivalry vanishes at the moment when Agnes clears up the misunderstanding, pointing to something unusual about this particular Oedipal drama. As Northrop Frye once observed, comedy usually involves generational conflict, as the young lovers overcome parental obstacles to their desire.[8] This is not quite the case in *Agnes von Lilien*, as Nordheim at forty is closer in age to the forty-eight-year-old Hohenfels than to Agnes. Moreover, Nordheim deliberately infantilizes Agnes, referring to her as "this lovable child" (1:312), and regarding her with the benevolence of a tender father. Instead of generational conflict, Wolzogen portrays the heroine's simultaneous discovery of father and husband, who after a period of inadvertent rivalry become allies. For a time Agnes is almost passed back and forth between lover, father, and stepfather: when Agnes fears that Nordheim might not love her it is only the thought of the old pastor that keeps her alive, and when Nordheim leaves her, Agnes turns immediately to "Charles" for comfort. Far from seeking to break away from the father, Agnes claims that it is only through him that she learns to understand herself.

Agnes von Lilien moves relentlessly forward in the first volume, drawn by the lovers' desire that is delayed, but not deterred, by obstacles along the way. It concludes with a flurry, as Agnes finishes kissing Nordheim and continues with "Charles" to meet her mother. They arrive at the house to find a noisy crowd gathered. Her father steps from the carriage – a strange man jumps in – two shots ring out – the man holds Agnes down – she swoons and awakens in a small dark room. It is here that we find her in the second half of the novel, which consists primarily of a series of flashbacks that explain the mysteries behind the dramatic events of volume one. Agnes learns that "Charles" is Hohenfels and her father, and that her mother is one of the prince's three children. The prince had tried to arrange a marriage for his daughter, but she resisted and wed Hohenfels secretly. When the outraged prince and his wife discovered their daughter's treachery they sent Hohenfels into exile and reported him dead to the princess, who was pregnant with Agnes. A court minister masterminded a plot to have the child sent to foster parents and declared dead to her mother, but Nordheim's father discovered the infant among coarse peasants and arranged for her to be raised instead by the old pastor.

This would all be ancient history if it were not for the fact that the prince is still alive and still angry at his disobedient daughter. The anger even extends into the next generation, and it is here that we find the connection between the novel's primary plot and the past it unearths. Nordheim's father was Hohenfels's closest friend and confidant. The prince is still trying to keep the marriage between his daughter and Hohenfels a secret, and he mistakenly believes that the old Nordheim passed this secret on to his son before he died. For this reason the prince opposes a marriage between Nordheim and his unacknowledged granddaughter Agnes. With the same minister's help he had organized the ambush described at the end of volume one; now he threatens Agnes that if she insists on marrying Nordheim he will keep her father in prison for the rest of his life. Eventually all turns out for the best: the old prince dies, Hohenfels travels with his daughter back to her stepfather's home where she meets and immediately marries Nordheim. Julius replaces the evil minister at court and Nordheim buys Hohenfels's estate, restoring legitimate government to the land.

The plot moves backwards: the current lovers cannot marry until they resolve the conflict of the previous generation, which entails setting the political house in order. As in a fairy tale, Wolzogen does not reveal the precise setting of her novel, but it takes place somewhere in Germany during the later eighteenth century, and its resolution offers a political vision that stands in clear opposition to both the French Revolution and the increasing bureaucratization of the German states. Early in the novel Agnes visits Nordheim's estate where she admires the portraits of his ancestors. Generation upon generation had filled important government positions, but Agnes notices that the tradition ended with his father and grandfather. As Nordheim explains, the break with the past has nothing to do with their lack of talent, but with the corrupting influence of the French art of government [*französischen Kabinetskünsten* (1:224)]. Nordheim's grandfather retired to his estates where he could better fulfill his patriarchal duties as lord of the manor: "My grandfather was an intelligent farmer and a caring father to his subjects" (1:225). The novel narrates not the coming of something new, but the restoration of the old German aristocracy to its former role in a benevolent patriarchy.

The deep conservatism of the novel explains the ambivalence with which Agnes portrays the prince. By all rights he should be the villain, the unfeeling tyrant who prevented the happiness of his daughter and who continues to abuse his absolute powers by standing in the way of Agnes and Nordheim. At the same time, however, Agnes knows that he is both her grandfather and the legitimate ruler of the country. To oppose him openly would mean going against the bonds of nature and the foundation of the state. Instead of rejecting the prince and his authority entirely, Agnes views him as a basically good individual who has come under the deforming influence of court etiquette and bad advisors. Neither

Agnes nor her father openly defy the man most responsible for their unhappiness. Instead, the obedient granddaughter kneels before the prince and swears she will not marry Nordheim without his permission. Even after the prince dies, Hohenfels plans to honor his memory by keeping his own marriage with Agnes's mother secret. Agnes explains that experience has also taught her "that quiet submission to a number of circumstances is more conducive to the habit of virtue than resistance in some situations" (2:373). Silent tolerance, even of an unjust situation, is often preferable to open revolt.

Wolzogen's conservatism stands in sharp contrast to LaRoche's *Geschichte des Fräuleins von Sternheim*. Both novels portray the conflict between a decadent *Rokokoadel* and a *Reformadel*, and both lead their heroines from a protected home environment through a period of trial at court to a happy marriage. In both novels we find a philosophy that is progressive in the sense that it seeks to reform the corrupt aristocracy, but conservative in that it leaves the social hierarchy intact. Yet there are significant differences as well: by making Colonel von Sternheim an ennobled bourgeois, LaRoche introduces class conflict into the opening pages of her novel, while *Agnes von Lilien* moves exclusively in aristocratic circles. LaRoche's heroine eventually establishes her idealized estate in England, conceding at least indirectly that there is little hope for such a progressive community in Germany, but Wolzogen effectively legitimizes the existing German governments, certainly with an eye toward Weimar. While LaRoche portrays the supreme ruler of the court as a thoroughly corrupt individual, Wolzogen goes out of her way to exonerate the prince.

Wolzogen's conservatism in the political realm coincides with an intensification of patriarchy in the private sphere and a further restriction of the woman's already limited potential for independent development. Sophie von Sternheim is on her own for much of the novel, as first father, then surrogate father dies, and her "husband" Derby deserts and betrays her. She establishes herself as a teacher, travels to England, and survives imprisonment in Scotland without male support. When Agnes first leaves home for court it seems that she will undergo a similar period of forced independence. Separated from her stepfather for the first time, Agnes resolves to be true to herself. As a vulnerable outsider at court Agnes has to resist the pressure to marry Julius, whom she gently but firmly rejects long before she is sure that Nordheim loves her. Meanwhile she counters the threat of becoming financially dependent on the Duchess Amalie by employing her artistic talents as a portraitist. Her career as a professional artist is short-lived, however, as her mother soon gives her a considerable fortune that makes her financially independent. Unlike Sophie von Sternheim, Agnes von Lilien's father is still alive and plays an important role in shaping his daughter's identity. While Sophie chooses Seymour over the older Lord Rich, Agnes rejects a man her own age in order to marry Nordheim. With him she is willing to efface herself entirely, a prospect she describes with an almost religious rapture that recalls her reverence for her stepfather: "To submit to the . . . tall and handsome man, who appeared to me as a godly figure; to live, to feel in him, through him alone – all this filled my soul, and my inward being melted in the power and flux of these blessed images" (1:68). As in *Clarissa*, religious language creeps into the depiction of the family, and in the end Agnes does experience something of an epiphany, as she enjoys the presence of the patriarchal trinity of stepfather, father, and husband at her wedding.

Finally, we should note the increasing subjectivity of the narrative perspective as we move from LaRoche to Wolzogen. Although it contains certain elements of the religious autobiography, *Sternheim* is still written as a multi-perspectival epistolary novel. It unfolds largely as an episodic adventure novel bracketed by the heroine's idyllic childhood and a happy marriage, which gives a sense of closure to an otherwise additive plot. In contrast, *Agnes von Lilien* is constructed as a first-person reminiscence of the heroine to her children. The story unfolds in a series of concentric circles, each containing the next: Agnes looks back on the events that led to her marriage; this romance, in turn, led to the resolution of conflict in the previous generation, which reestablishes the bond between the present government and Nordheim's ancient aristocratic lineage. The movement, in other words, is toward the denial of time, or at least the denial of change in a present that is saturated with past tradition. At the center stands the narrating self, serene to the point of placidity: "Nothing unsatisfied remains in our soul, and the quiet task of a higher *Bildung* continues its uninterrupted course, without being disturbed by the disquieting dreams of an unquenched desire" (iv–v). *Agnes von Lilien* is less about the establishment of a new society than it is about the restoration of the old to new legitimacy. At a time when the French Revolution was shredding the fabric of the existing social order, Wolzogen envisions a world of domestic virtue and enlightened aristocratic rule that stretches seamlessly from the distant past to future generations of German subjects.

FRIEDERIKE HELENE UNGER: JULCHEN GRÜNTHAL'S FATHER FIXATION

Friederike Helene Unger (1741?–1813) was a prolific writer whose works include eight novels, significant translations (including Rousseau's *Confessions* and *Rêveries d'un promeneur solitaire*), and even a popular cookbook.[9] Born the daughter of a Prussian general, she married the prominent Berlin publisher Johann Friedrich Unger in 1785. She worked closely with her husband until his death in 1804, whereupon she took over the business that had published Goethe's *Wilhelm Meisters Lehrjahre* (1795/96) and many works of the German Romantics. Although Unger was therefore at the center of German intellectual life around 1800, her works were largely ignored until the early 1980s.[10] Since then the Georg Olms publishing house has begun reissuing facsimile editions of Unger's novels, laying the foundation for renewed engagement with at least part of her substantial *oeuvre*.[11]

Unger published her best-known novel, *Julchen Grünthal: Eine Pensionsgeschichte* [A Boarding School Story], in 1784. In it she tells of a girl who leaves her doting father to attend school in Berlin. Here Julchen comes under corrupting influences that lead her to various romantic entanglements: when abandoned by a young nobleman she moves in with her cousin Karoline Falk, only to fall in love with Karoline's husband. Falk divorces his wife, marries Julchen, and promptly begins an affair with his servant. Julchen responds by entertaining a Russian nobleman. When Falk flees with his mistress to escape gambling debts, Julchen disappears with the Russian, leaving her distraught father behind. Unger revised the novel in 1787, and again in 1798, when she added a second volume in which Julchen repents of her evil ways and returns to her forgiving father.

The fact that Unger was able to publish three editions of the novel over a fourteen-year period gives a good indication of its popularity. *Julchen Grünthal* received favorable reviews and inspired imitations, most notably Johann Jakob Stutz's anonymous continuation of Julchen's adventures in 1788. Certainly part of the novel's success lay in its topicality: Unger writes a sentimental tale whose primary purpose is to attack the fashionable practice of sending middle-class girls from the country to French boarding schools in Berlin. In the first volume Unger underscores her didactic intent by placing most of the narrative in the mouth of Julchen's father, who uses his own sad experience to advise his neighbors against repeating his mistake. In the course of relating his tale, Grünthal goes beyond the specific polemic against the miseducation of young women to outline the beliefs of the German middle class. Grünthal, whose name means "green valley," views Berlin with the characteristic distrust of the country dweller. He fears that his daughter will come under the dangerous influence of the nobility, and Julchen soon confirms his suspicions by making friends with the flirtatious Mariane von Lindenfels and falling in love with Mariane's brother Louis. As further indication of her slide to iniquity, Julchen forgets to read her Bible and begins reading sensational novels, including *La Nouvelle Héloïse*. Julchen identifies with Rousseau's heroine – who even shares her name, as she points out – and begins to write passionate love-letters to Louis von Lindenfels under its influence. The headmistress of her boarding school, Frau Brennfeld, further poisons her young charge by introducing Julchen to works of free-thinking French *philosophes*. The school even corrupts Julchen's language, as she begins to flavor her formerly pure German with fashionable French words. Thus Berlin occupies the same structural position in this story as the court in *Sternheim* and *Agnes von Lilien*: it is the site where virtuous daughters fall prey to aristocratic vice.

Belief in the family is central to the values Grünthal champions as the antidote to Berlin's aristocratic libertines. Shortly before her early death the repentant Mariane von Lindenfels blames her downfall on her lack of a strong family background: "'I unfortunately never knew my parents; they handed me over to hired strangers at birth, who ruined my first two years of life.'"[12] In contrast to her aristocratic friend, Julchen grows up in a loving nuclear family. Her father takes sole charge of her education until she is ten, instructing her in religion, geography, and history; a tutor teaches her writing and arithmetic, and her mother introduces her to household chores. By the end of her fifteenth year, as Grünthal tells it, Julchen had enjoyed a model education calculated to prepare her for her "calling" as a woman: "I thought that she would be what she ought to be if she became a smart, pious housewife, who was not lacking the intelligence and education to sweeten the life of a sensible man, and to raise her children to be useful citizens of the state" (1:20).

Just before she leaves home Julchen seems poised to play this virtuous role. Her father still cherishes the memory of his innocent daughter as harvest queen in a local pageant, dressed in gleaming white and flanked by her two brothers. As his enthusiastic recounting of this event indicates, Grünthal's affection for his daughter borders on the incestuous.[13] The illustrator Chodowiecki captures something of this latent eroticism in the illustration for the title page of the 1798 edition, which shows Julchen saying goodbye to her father on the eve of her departure to Berlin. Julchen rests her head on her father's shoulder and looks up into his face, while he embraces her with both arms and inclines his head as if for a kiss. Indeed, when Julchen and her father are reunited an observer notes that he looks like her bridegroom: " 'The honest man was as smart and festive as if it were his own wedding day' " (2:206).[14]

This sort of sentiment recalls those erotically charged scenes when Colonel von Sternheim has his daughter dress in her dead mother's clothes. There are, however, also significant differences in the family configurations in the two novels. The early death of the Colonel's wife in the *Geschichte des Fräuleins von Sternheim* enables Sophie to identify with the idealized image of her absent mother without becoming her rival for her father's affections. In contrast, Julchen's mother Lieschen does not die until after her daughter reaches adolescence, creating the potential for considerable intrafamiliar tension. Grünthal draws an ambivalent portrait of his wife that reflects this tension: while he praises her effusively for her love, piety, and skill in directing the household economy, he nevertheless blames her for indirectly causing their daughter's departure from home and eventual demise. In effect, Grünthal splits his wife into the good mother of his child and the bad rival to his daughter's affections. This latent rivalry turns to open conflict when Grünthal remarries. He portrays his new wife as Julchen's evil stepmother who works actively to prevent a reconciliation between himself and his daughter. Grünthal can either have his second wife or his daughter, but he cannot have both at the same time.

Thus we can read the first volume of *Julchen Grünthal* in two different, but related ways: as a polemic against urban boarding schools and as a psychodrama about Oedipal desires and female adolescence. The primary level of the text offers no room for ambivalence: Grünthal sketches a neatly polarized world in which the evil city defeats rural innocence. The psychological text is subtler. At first the conflicting appeal of the city versus the country plays itself out within the triangle of mother, father, and daughter. Julchen is torn between the desires of her father and mother, while Grünthal juggles loyalty to his wife with affection for his daughter. Julchen's departure for the city transforms the external conflict into an internal struggle between the dictates of her conscience and her desire for independence. Just before she leaves home her father instructs her to keep a diary that she is to send home periodically for her parents' inspection. Instead of providing space for self-exploration and self-development, as was the case for both Clarissa and Sophie von Sternheim, Julchen's diary is to function as her "personified conscience" (1:43–44). As Helga Meise observes, Julchen's development involves the gradual internalization of her father's voice as her own conscience.[15] By first moving to Berlin and then fleeing to Russia it would seem that Julchen breaks free of her father's control, but this is certainly not her own view. In her final letter to her father at the end of volume one she interprets the flight to Russia as a self-imposed banishment from the father she is not worthy to confront.

Fourteen years passed before Unger completed her novel, years that saw the coming of the French Revolution and the beginnings of a German nationalist response. During the Napoleonic occupation Unger published *Die Franzosen in Berlin* [The French in Berlin] (1809), in which she sought to rethink the role of women in a society transformed by war,[16] but her continuation of *Julchen Grünthal* already reflects the changed historical situation. The French, who had featured primarily as a corrupting influence on the German aristocracy in 1784, turn into dangerous revolutionaries in the 1798 version. Grünthal had originally encouraged his daughter to marry an upstanding young pastor by the name of Eiche [oak tree], whose name refers to a nationalist symbol; in the revised edition Unger replaces Eiche with a young hothead who sympathizes with the most radical revolutionaries: "*Marat* was his saint, and *Robespierre* still didn't murder enough" (1:182). This *enragé* will walk miles for the latest newspaper from France, and disturbs the troubled rest of Grünthal's dying wife as he pounds the table "in his revolutionary zeal" (1:182). The polemic shifts from class conflict between urban aristocrats and the rural bourgeoisie to an international clash between revolutionary zealots and what are portrayed as morally and physically superior Germans. Hence Julchen's cousin Karoline describes her new husband, Colonel von Auerfeld, as "'a man as tall as a tree, with the strength and character of a genuine old German'" (2:200), and her new friend Minna describes Grünthal as "a man in his early fifties with upright German decency" (2:190). The two men who would have been divided along class lines are now united in their common national identity.

The rehabilitation of the German nobility in the *Julchen Grünthal* of 1798 becomes of central thematic importance in Karoline's decision to remarry. We leave her at the end of volume one having been divorced by her husband for Julchen. Karoline meets the officer Auerfeld by chance, when he falls from a stallion and is carried into her garden house. Auerfeld is smitten by the "'young woman dressed in purest white'" (2:214), but she initially resists his advances because he belongs to the nobility, while she is bourgeois. Auerfeld has to overcome considerable prejudice on her part against the aristocracy before she is willing to get married. Readers familiar with Julchen Grünthal's trials in the earlier editions of the novel are well aware of the dangers such a mésalliance poses to the bourgeoisie, and it is against this background that Unger sets out to justify Karoline's second marriage. Although Grünthal warns his daughter against any association with the aristocracy, he qualifies his critique by adding kind words about the Brandenburg nobility. As a member of this select group, Auerfeld demonstrates his progressive beliefs by conceding that goodness and nobility can be found in all levels of the social order. He goes further to suggest that while the feudal hierarchy may once have reflected significant differences between classes, no such differences remain, "'since education has made the well-to-do classes equal'" (2:229). Echoing LaRoche, Unger suggests that education, ability, and money have forged a bond between the enlightened nobility and the bourgeoisie that will establish a new social order. Like Colonel von Sternheim before him, Colonel von Auerfeld retires from the army to take over his dead brother's estate in the conviction that as head of the manor, he will have a greater opportunity to fulfill his duties to his subordinates. While LaRoche eventually transplants her utopian society to England, Unger follows Wolzogen in proposing a progressive-conservative German alternative to French radicalism.

Part of the new nationalism evident in Unger's revised and

expanded novel is the nascent reverence for a German national literature. In volume one Grünthal distinguishes simply between those who stay in the country and read the Bible and those who go to the city and begin reading inflammatory novels and atheist philosophy. Julchen realizes how far she has fallen when she comes across her mother's Bible, unread and still neatly packed after months in the city, and her reading of Rousseau serves as the catalyst, if perhaps not the cause of her involvement with Louis von Lindenfels. Later Goethe's *Stella* provides the script for marital infidelity between Julchen and Falk. In the second half of the novel Unger hints at a more positive role for German literature. While in Russia Julchen spends a week reading to the Russian Princess Eudoxia from "a valuable collection of German classics in all fields" (2:297). Later the same woman seeks calm after a stormy encounter with her husband by reading Goethe. The attempt proves unsuccessful, but Unger at least raises the possibility that certain works of contemporary German literature can have a positive influence on their readers.[17]

Thus Unger's 1798 continuation of a novel begun in 1784 transforms a didactic tale of lost innocence into a program for social reform, in which aristocrats enter into a positive alliance with the bourgeoisie, and the Germans and their culture take a stand against the French and their Revolution. It is within this context that we need to view Julchen's return to virtue, in order to assess the role of gender in the new social order. Unger makes us wait for some time before satisfying our curiosity about the woman last seen heading toward Russia, however. The second volume begins somewhat disorientingly with a conversation between a new character named Minna Thalheim and a mysterious visitor named "Ida." The reader soon suspects that "Ida" is in fact Julchen in disguise, but before she confesses we hear Minna's tale, which takes up half of the entire volume. Like Julchen, Minna moved to Berlin at a vulnerable age and came under Frau Brennfeld's corrupting influence. Later gambling and infidelity threaten to destroy her marriage, but she and her husband reconcile their differences and discover the virtues of hard work and piety in a country home far from Berlin. On the surface, Unger offers a rather formulaic account of regained virtue that prepares the way for Julchen's return to the straight and narrow. To underscore her didactic intent, Unger italicizes the moral of the story: *"Where virtue and diligence reign, there too resides happiness"*

(2:171–72). At the same time, however, Unger expands on LaRoche's suggestion that one mistake does not preclude a woman's hope for a better future, and that despite literary conventions, life can go on after seduction, infidelity, and – as Karoline's example shows – even divorce.

In her continuation of *Julchen Grünthal*, Unger replaces Grünthal's polemical monologue with a multiperspectival narrative in which "fallen" women can redeem themselves, which led at least one critic to celebrate the novel as evidence that women were beginning to break free of male authority and assert their right to self-determination.[18] Nevertheless, these steps toward the assertion of female independence remain tentative indeed in *Julchen Grünthal*. Like Sophie von Sternheim, Karoline does establish her independence as a schoolteacher, but only for a brief interlude between two marriages. She can remarry primarily because she was never guilty of marital infidelity in the first place, and Minna wins praise only for her model marriage, not for the experiences that led her into iniquity and back to virtue. In both cases Unger commends only those characteristics that coincide with the image of domestic virtue; there is no attempt to affirm female experience independent of marriage or children. Julchen's manipulative friend Mariane von Lindenfels pays the price for her immorality when she dies an early and horrifying death, and the caricatured bluestocking Frau Brennfeld loses her position at the boarding school when she has an illegitimate child with her Jewish tutor.

While Unger devotes considerable attention to a variety of female characters, she eventually brings the primary focus back to Julchen Grünthal. Her father finds her by chance when he, Karoline, and Auerfeld come to visit Minna and her husband. All is forgiven after a tearful reunion that has strong biblical overtones: Julchen features as the prodigal daughter or the lost sheep who returns to the flock. Grünthal strives throughout the rest of the novel to restore his daughter to her former innocence, or, as he puts it, she should "'become as white as she was before'" (2:247). He gets his wish in the final scene of the novel, when Julchen once again plays the harvest queen. But much has changed. In the first scene Julchen really is an innocent, thirteen-year-old country girl. In the second she is a mature woman who has been romantically involved with several men, married, and lived on her own in the most difficult of circumstances. The reenactment of the childish role may whitewash her past sufficiently to please her father, but it amounts to a complete denial of her experiences as a woman.[19]

Before this final scene Julchen writes out a long account of her adventures addressed to her father. Far from representing her "emancipation" through a "confrontation with paternal authority,"[20] Julchen's long confession marks her complete submission to her father's control. In it Julchen completes the process of self-observation that she had begun at her father's urging in her diary. By the end of the novel Julchen has become a pathetic individual tortured by remorse. She actually rubs her face in the dirt at her cousin's feet when they first meet again. At the time Grünthal finds this scene disturbing and orders Julchen to stand up, but he later relates the same incident with some pride to Pastor Eiche: " 'But you should have seen her! As beautiful as an angel, and bent with regret and shame. How she lay her little angelic face in the dust before Karoline, and was unable to lift her eyes to her!' " (2:242). Julchen's guilty conscience reaches neurotic levels, as she accepts full responsibility not only for her own sins – most of which are due more to her guileless nature and to scheming men than to evil intent – but also for events over which she has no control: " 'before you know it she is crying and blaming herself. I think that if hail had ruined my crops she would blame herself for that' " (2:341).

Not surprisingly, this sort of self-abnegation on the part of the heroine has inspired protest. In fact, most recent critics have read *Julchen Grünthal* as a typically palimpsestic novel that hides a subversive subtext beneath its overtly conservative message.[21] To a certain extent, I agree; like anyone who sets out to teach by bad example, Unger runs the risk of making vice seem more interesting than virtue. Unger's cautionary tale offers its predominantly female readers[22] vicarious participation in forbidden pleasures and formulates rebellious thoughts. For example, Julchen's dissolute friend Mariane voices her disdain for " 'the monotony of marriage' " (1:254), and Julchen also dares to suggest that youth is too fleeting to waste with the dull Pastor Eiche. Julchen's romantic escapades in Berlin and her flight to Russia offer the reader glimpses of an exciting alternative to the domestic virtue expected of women. By the same token, these adventures offer only a limited possibility for identification on the part of the reader, as Unger goes out of her way to introduce extravagantly unrealistic twists to the plot. Not only is her heroine whisked off to Russia with a handsome prince, but she later has to escape the clutches of a lesbian lover. Implausibly sensational coincidences find their way into the subplots as well: at one point Minna's philandering husband finds his wife in a brothel when searching for his mistress. Minna herself describes "Ida's" chance reunion with her father as one of those miraculous things that only happen in novels or comedies.

We find a similar ambivalence regarding the status of Julchen's father. At those moments when she inspires clandestine identification, his moral authority is called into question. When compared with LaRoche's Colonel von Sternheim, Julchen's father seems weak and ineffectual. Sternheim takes charge of his estate and dictates his beliefs to a patiently admiring wife, while Grünthal sacrifices his career ambitions for the sake of his marriage. He then goes against his better judgment in yielding to his wife's tearful pleas that their daughter be sent to boarding school, and later claims that he allowed himself to be talked into a second marriage with an unworthy woman. As Grünthal himself puts it, he has never been able to command his fate: "In my entire life I have never yet been able to control circumstances; they have always shoved me here and there without having a say in the matter" (1:128). Symptomatic of Grünthal's weakness is his tendency to blame his wife for his daughter's misfortunes. Indeed, it is tempting to dismiss Grünthal entirely as a lachrymose pedant given to self-pity and tedious tirades.

To do so, however, would be to overlook considerable evidence to the contrary. Although Grünthal appears more than a little ridiculous at times, his concern for his daughter remains consistent. Indeed, he seems to grow in stature in the novel's continuation. Minna describes him as an upright German character who bears his suffering with dignity. He wins Auerfeld's respect, and shows himself capable of revising his opinion of the nobility and forgiving his wayward daughter. Grünthal is a flawed, but essentially positive representative of the new social order, not a throwback to an outmoded conservatism.[23] Even his weakness and sentimentality can be viewed as signs of his "modern" sensitivity; in this he more closely resembles Lord Seymour than Mr. Harlowe, as he holds out the prospect for a benevolent patriarchy.

Grünthal's tender concern for his daughter is part of a broader cultural and political vision, as Unger's novel offers its German readers an alternative to the murderous Marats and Robespierres of neighboring France. At the same time, however, Unger reveals the price extracted from women in assigning them their new domestic virtues. Already in *Sternheim* we saw a partial devaluation of female independence in favor of a protective father or husband, although LaRoche allows her heroine considerable self-reliance and independence in marriage choice. The tendency toward the infantilization of the wife-cum-daughter becomes more apparent in Wolzogen's paean to patriarchy, with its conflation of stepfather, father, and husband. The trend becomes extreme in *Julchen Grünthal*: while Agnes von Lilien marries a man *like* her father, Julchen pretends that she is still a virgin to be her father's bride. From Grünthal's perspective, Julchen's return fulfills a regressive fantasy of Oedipal desire: he manages to discard his wives and concentrate his affections solely on his daughter. Although Julchen feigns ecstasy, her obsessive guilt and denial of the desires that had once made her rebel suggest that the ending is less a wish-fulfillment dream than a recurring nightmare. We leave her where we first found her, as the "virgin" queen compelled to reenact her childhood. In 1940 Thomas Wolfe would come to the melancholy conclusion that "you can't go home again." For Julchen Grünthal and the new paragons of virtue she represents, the real tragedy is that you can never leave.

THERESE HUBER: PATRIARCHY VS. PATRIOTISM IN *DIE FAMILIE SELDORF*

At a time when conduct manuals urged young women to prepare for a life of quiet domesticity, Therese Huber's (1764–1829) unconventional behavior could only provoke outrage. Born the daughter of a Göttingen professor, she married the world traveler and future political radical Georg Forster in 1785. The marriage was fraught with difficulties from the start, as Therese became romantically involved with first the university librarian in Göttingen, and then the Prussian civil servant Ludwig Ferdinand Huber. Forster discouraged neither affair, and even proposed that he, Therese, and Huber should live together in a *ménage à trois*. Instead, Therese left her husband in December, 1792, when he became active in the Jacobin party in the Mainz Republic. While Forster worked to establish the only revolutionary government on German soil, Therese and her children moved to Strasbourg, and later Switzerland. German counter-revolutionary armies besieged Mainz in the spring of 1793, and when it fell on July 23 Forster remained in exile in Paris. He died there in January, 1794, and by April of that year Therese had already married Huber, "amid sharp accusations and almost universal condemnation from the German intellectual community."[24]

Therese Huber went on to publish some half-dozen novels and several volumes of short stories; she also edited the prestigious *Morgenblatt für gebildete Stände* from 1816 until 1823. My interest in this context is in her remarkable first novel, *Die Familie Seldorf* (1795–96). Huber draws on her personal experience and intellectual engagement with the events and ideals of the French Revolution in a novel that combines domestic fiction and political history with a directness unmatched by her contemporaries. The plot centers on the familiar eighteenth-century motif of "virtue in distress," the seduction of a young middle-class woman by a ruthlessly resourceful upper-class villain.[25] The theme recurs with particular urgency in *Die Familie Seldorf*, for Huber sharpens the familiar indictment of the nobility by linking her fictional plot to specific historical events of the French Revolution.[26] Her bourgeois protagonist Sara Seldorf becomes involved with Count L*, an active fighter in the royalist cause. The turning point in the novel comes on the evening of August 10, 1792. At her lover's request, Sara has moved to Paris with their baby girl. As riots break out in the Tuileries, Sara sets off in a frantic search for L*. Swept up in the surging crowd, she sees him emerge from a building with a band of royalists. He fires at the mob in self-defense, but fatally wounds his own child by accident. Sara mistakenly believes that L* intentionally kills their daughter, and soon discovers that he was in fact already married to another woman. Private and public treachery coincide, just as Sara's patriotic neighbor Berthier had warned: "The man . . . is the enemy of his fatherland and a traitor to his people; he who betrays the cause of freedom will not hesitate to sacrifice helpless innocence!"[27]

Sara sets off on a course of personal revenge, and, while disguised as a man, eventually becomes an exceptionally effective fighter in the republican army. By the end of the novel, however, she renounces her role as revolutionary soldier, and retires to a hut built on the ruins of L*'s castle. Here the melancholy woman plans to spend her remaining years in the role of stepmother to the child of L*'s deceased wife, after having rejected the proposal of her bourgeois friend Roger one more time. Thus the novel that delivers a ringing indictment of the bankrupt feudal order ends with its isolated and resigned heroine devoted to the preservation of what remains of Count L*'s legacy.

Sara's ambivalent response to the French Revolution has its direct source in her erotic attraction to L*, which overpowers the mere friendship she feels for Roger. Personal inclination conflicts with patriotic duty. Yet Sara's preference for L* over Roger has its roots in her family history. The novel about contemporary French politics has elements of the *Bildungs-* or *Entwicklungsroman,* in that it examines the growth of the protagonist in the dual context of family and society.[28] Herein lie the deeper roots of the novel's ambivalence: on the directly political level, overthrow of the government means overthrow of the patriarchal order. But Sara's personal development occurs through the internalization of her father's values. The lasting influence of the private father stymies revolution against the public father. Thus the novel ostensibly about the French Revolution includes a critical subtext about the structure of the bourgeois family. Not coincidentally, Seldorf is German: while Huber offers the German reading public a first-hand account of political events in neighboring France, she also addresses private issues that were closer to home.

The novel opens when Seldorf, a recently widowed naval officer, retires with his three children to a town in western France. Huber presents Seldorf as an essentially good individual embittered by his excessive idealism: "raised in isolation, he had only studied people in his own heart, and the ideal that he found here led him onto a path where he remained without companions. He never found in reality the high virtue for which he strove, which he felt was alone worthy of him" (1:11–12). His unrealistic expectations engender inevitably disappointing experiences, as is evident in his troubled relations with women. He has developed his feminine ideal on the basis of one example – his mother: "her memory hallowed her entire sex for him to such an extent that he never made the slightest connection between this sex and the individual female creatures whom he had opportunity to see through his service and through his association with his comrades" (1:16–17). Fixated completely on the ideal of femininity his mother represents, Seldorf fails to grasp that the other women he encounters are even members of the same sex.

This misguided idealism causes Seldorf to indoctrinate his children in rigid sexual stereotypes. One of the first scenes depicts what amounts to a lesson in socialization for the nine-year-old Sara

Seldorf. She accuses her brother Theodor of sharing his father's antipathy toward her youngest sister Antoinette, who, as we later learn, was actually the illegitimate result of her mother's affair with Count Vieilleroche. Theodor stammers a rapid series of explanations to his father: "'Father,' he cried, 'Sara finds me hard toward Antoinette, because I don't – because my heart makes it impossible for me – because we boys certainly like to help, but can't lament and comfort'" (1:5). He eventually excuses personal disinclination with reference to a cultural stereotype: boys don't cry. Seldorf reinforces his son's interpretation of his emotions in his response to Sara: "When one day you are older, you will learn that it would be effeminate if boys and men loved and comforted in a way that is entirely fitting for your sex" (1:7).

Huber's narrator describes the effect of this lesson on Sara in language that complicates the equation of women with nature one finds in many late eighteenth-century texts: "Sara barely understood half of her father's words, for she was very young and naive; but the meaning of these words for which nature has made the feminine heart so receptive impressed itself deeply on this naivety" (1:7). On the one hand, Sara is quite aware that she has received a lesson in sexual stereotypes that do not correspond to reality: she herself has witnessed her brother's care and concern when she was sick, and reminds him that she felt his tears on her face when she was temporarily blinded. On the other hand, the narrator identifies Sara's receptivity to this moral lesson as a "natural" characteristic of the female "heart." She learns, in other words, that women "naturally" internalize social codes that contradict empirical evidence.

Central to Seldorf's understanding of gender roles in society lies the conviction that men should protect women, while women should serve men. He brands any form of deviance from this pattern as unnatural:

The tough, loyal man of iron can only pay homage to the softest femininity; weaklings love Amazons . . . If the woman has no sense for this reward of her charm, she tries to become independent of us, and then she becomes despicable. Nature, which made us stronger than she, cannot bear this independence. (1:26)

The narrator immediately dispels any temptation to accept Seldorf's beliefs at face value by identifying them as potentially dangerous oversimplifications of reality. By passing his prejudices on to his

children, Seldorf sows the seeds of the same tragically flawed
idealism in their lives that has been the source of his own consistent
dissatisfaction.

The result of this upbringing becomes apparent in an incident
that marks a crucial turning point in Sara's life.[29] One day she, her
brother Theodor, and their friend Roger stumble on a starving
peasant family living in a squalid hut. In the previous season the
local landlord had confiscated the farmer's ox and plow after a poor
harvest had left him unable to pay his rent. Left with only a cow, he
could not plant his fields, and thus sank deeper into debt. As
Theodor and Roger enter the hut the landlord is threatening to take
the cow, while the man's feverish wife lies near insanity holding a
starving infant. Huber spares no melodramatic effect in creating a
scene calculated to mobilize moral outrage against the nobility, and
thus to marshal sympathy for the revolutionary cause.

In a subtler way, the incident also serves to characterize the two
boys. Although Roger and Theodor both condemn the oppression of
the peasantry, they differ in their responses to the problem. Theodor
immediately pays the tax collector, gives his remaining cash to the
poor family, and then pulls his sister into the hut to make her witness
the depressing scene. Insensitive to its disturbing effect on her, he
launches into a passionate condemnation of social injustice. Roger
eventually intervenes, leading the shaken Sara out of the hut, whereupon Theodor angrily accuses his friend of callous disregard for the
family's suffering. Roger responds more practically and effectively.
He returns to the poor family the next morning to give them more
money for food and clothing, and then works their fallow fields,
which provides the basis for long-term relief. His actions reflect the
influence of his grandfather Berthier, who has raised Roger to a life
of practical virtue by his good example. In contrast, Theodor's
impassioned but impractical response to the family's plight reveals
the detrimental influence of his father's ineffective idealism: "Theodor's refined sensibility idealized what Roger did merely out of
kindly instinct" (1:75).

The reconciliation between the two friends on the following
evening awakens new feelings in Sara. For the first time she becomes
conscious of the potential sexual component of her attraction to
Roger: "She was now about fifteen years old . . . new ideas developed in her head, which distanced her from him and drew her
towards him, which warmed her heart and made it shy" (1:76–77).

She immediately recalls her father's lessons about the ideal relations of the sexes, and finds reality disappointing in comparison. The sight of Roger polishing off a bowl of milk with a healthy appetite brought on by a day of hard labor repulses her. Instead, she prefers the idle, but aesthetically pleasing image of her handsome brother, who lounges beneath the chestnut tree in the glow of the setting sun. Like Theodor, Sara has been trained to expect reality to conform to her father's ideals. When it does not, she sacrifices substance for surface appeal.

These events take place in the mid 1780s. As the decade draws to a close, the private lives of the Seldorf family become increasingly intertwined with political developments leading to the French Revolution. A common patriarchal structure links the two spheres. From the royalist perspective, the revolutionary rabble drives a wedge between the benevolent king and his loyal subjects. Theodor and L* are willing to engage in any sort of moral outrage in their attempt to restore the order of the Old Regime. The republican Berthier opposes these characters. When we first meet him, the lifelong advocate of the oppressed has retired to a quiet country life, convinced that the times are not ripe for the heroism of the ancients. Nevertheless, his pragmatism makes him receptive to the coming political changes; he gradually realizes that the systematic abuse of power on the part of the nobility has made social reform imperative.

Seldorf takes an ambivalent position between the aristocrat L* and the bourgeois Berthier regarding the coming French Revolution. A German by birth, he is commanded by the French king to fight for democratic freedom in the American Revolution. While Seldorf acknowledges the irony of his situation, he nevertheless eagerly joins the fight. After several years he returns home to discover that his aristocratic wife had been unfaithful in his absence. He conceives a hatred against the nobility, but then assumes the position of father to the community in the role of landed country gentleman near the town of Saumur. Later Seldorf reacts bitterly when his "children" rebel against him: "the people who had been calling me father for seven years wanted to murder the father in his sleep" (1:195). Despite his earlier efforts on behalf of the American colonies, he finds it impossible to embrace the coming French Revolution, not because he disapproves of its goals, but because he feels that this patriotic idealism is also condemned to inevitable disappointment.

While Seldorf wavers between sympathy for the revolutionary

cause and fatalistic conservatism, his children begin to act in ways that he understands as a rebellion against his paternal authority. Theodor goes to Paris against his will, squanders his fortune, and marries the daughter of the man who had cuckolded him. On closer examination, however, Theodor simply repeats character traits of his father. He enters Paris as a dreamer, who, like Seldorf before him has little patience "for the apparently insignificant and often repulsive traits of reality" (1:90). He believes in a revolution led by a select few, and feels himself to be one of the chosen. Theodor drifts into royalist circles, severely compromises his personal integrity in their service, and is finally executed for a cause in which he has long since ceased to believe. Thus there is a certain irony to his lament that his father holds him in chains: on the surface, Seldorf temporarily prevents him from going to Paris, but in the long run, Theodor proves enslaved by his father's ingrained idealism, which leads him into the tragic error of his collusion with the royalist forces.

Seldorf also views Sara's preference for L* over Roger as a personal affront to his paternal authority. The conflict between father and daughter climaxes in the melodramatic scene that concludes volume one of the novel, when the dying Seldorf tries to force Sara to marry Roger. She not only refuses, but sends her father into fatal shock by announcing that she is already pregnant with L*'s child. Thereafter Sara is haunted by the thought that her father has cursed her on his deathbed. Here again, however, Seldorf shares much of the blame for his daughter's presumed betrayal. Both she and her father are seduced by L*, she physically, he politically. Only after L* "rescues" them from the house he has secretly had burned down does Seldorf begin to suspect that he has been fooled. Sara is attracted to the charismatic Count L* just as she had preferred her handsome but impractical brother to Roger; here again, her desires reflect the pernicious influence of her father's early lessons.

Thus the novel presents two patriarchal models that do not neatly coincide. In the political realm of the corrupt patriarchy, benevolent father-figures have become despotic tyrants against whom the people rebel. The seemingly parallel generational conflict within the family reveals a more complicated situation, since the rebellious children have actually internalized the shortcomings of their father. Huber underscores the ingrown nature of the Seldorfs' problems by structuring sexual relations as a form of displaced incest. By agreeing to a marriage of political convenience with the daughter of his mother's aristocratic lover, Theodor reenacts his father's marriage to a noblewoman who ruins his happiness. At the same time, this marriage stands as a displaced and disappointing realization of his desire for his sister. Since childhood Theodor and Sara have viewed each other as embodiments of the sexual stereotypes they have learned from their father. Sara assumes for Theodor the same role as feminine ideal that Seldorf's mother had filled for him. When Theodor reports his marriage to his family, he regrets that his new wife cannot live up to his sister's standards:

I had seen Lady Vieilleroche on a few occasions; and from the moment I thought of her as my wife, Sara's image pressed itself next to hers, and her vestal countenance, illuminated by all the charms of female virtue, seemed to ask me: is this the ideal that is allowed to displace your Sara? (1:236)

While Theodor swallows his pride and consents to this arranged marriage, Sara is delighted to discover in L* the perfect substitute for her brother Theodor: "when L* entered, everything else vanished from Sara's heart; involuntarily captivated merely by the presence of her protective spirit, she ran toward him as uninhibitedly as if her brother were entering [the room]" (1:197). In loving her brother in L*, Sara identifies with values instilled by her father. That is, in the indirectly incestuous relationship of brother and sister we see a secondary level of incest, where their desires repeat the desires of their father. The public conflict between oppressed subjects and the corrupt aristocracy does not coincide with the internalized conflict of the private sphere, where Oedipal bonds unite family members in desires that alienate the subjects from themselves.[30] In killing the king one kills the public father-figure, but revolt against paternal authority in the home becomes complicated when children have adopted the father's beliefs as their own.

This asymmetry between the public and private spheres enables Huber to critique the patriarchal structure of the bourgeois family while seeming to focus primarily on class conflict at the time of the French Revolution. As mentioned above, the novel's turning point comes when Sara discovers that L* has been unfaithful to her and to the country. Yet both before and after this moment of treachery, L* does not act like the typical eighteenth-century villain. Certainly he is no paragon of virtue: he not only deceives Sara, but also arranges for the summary execution of the thugs he hired to turn patriotic celebrations into destructive riots. But how often does a villainous seducer send a chest of monogrammed baby clothes to his victim? It is difficult to imagine Lovelace, Faust, or Valmont doing the same. And why does L* bring Sara to Paris? If he were interested only in sexual conquest, then he could have long since abandoned the dishonored woman. Instead, he wants to enact a clandestine bourgeois marriage with his innocent country "bride" in Paris: "in this place you are my bourgeois wife [*mein bürgerliches Weib*], and, tired by business, by care, I flee to you" (2:81). Sara is to provide him with a soothing refuge from the strains of public life in a role that corresponds exactly to the model found in popular educational treatises of the period.[31] For a brief time L* tries to enjoy "a double sort of existence, in public and in his private life" (2:86). What begins as a confrontation between bourgeois virtue and aristocratic vice turns into a Parisian idyll where the noble L* slips into the role of the bourgeois husband. Of course, he fares better in this arrangement than she, as his private refuge is her prison: "Sara began to feel anxiously lonely: in the midst of people it was as if she were on a desert island, and, due to her ignorance of the surroundings, her timid foreignness, she was more safely locked up in her room than in a prison" (2:79). For the time being, however, Sara accepts her confinement in anticipation of a public marriage.

From this perspective we can begin to see certain parallels between L*'s behavior and that of his frustrated bourgeois rival Roger. On the surface Roger plays the selfless, patient, forgiving lover. Yet his persistence begins to become oppressive: no matter how many times Sara tells him in no uncertain terms that she is simply not interested in him as a lover, he continues to try to win her over. In the second part of the novel his obsession to possess her blinds him to her desires: "he enjoyed a melancholy pleasure in fettering her to himself by all these little means" (2:20–21). The turning point comes when he inadvertently witnesses Sara breast-feeding her baby, which releases long-repressed sexual desires. He resents her for her inability to love him: "He was loyal and without guilt, and yet she was destroying his existence. He only wanted to possess her, hold her for a moment – and then murder her, for he was out of his mind" (2:29–30). With remarkable honesty, Huber probes the latent hypocrisy of Roger's seemingly impeccable virtue: just beneath the surface of his selfless devotion to Sara lies a desire to put her in chains, to rape her, and then to kill her.

Seldorf's earlier marriage to his aristocratic wife reveals a similar pattern of manipulative control. Seldorf had married the much younger, pregnant woman as a favor to his dying friend. As he admits, his relationship to her had been more paternal than marital: "fatherly – yes, fatherly!" (1:248–49). To his astonishment, she cursed him on her deathbed because she resented being handed over to Seldorf without regard for her own wishes. Having been maneuvered into a position where fidelity to her own desires meant being a traitor to her marital obligations, she was left feeling both resentful and guilty about her resentment. Unlike her mother, Sara enters her prison voluntarily, as "love made her into the slave of L*'s will" (1:272). In all three instances, however, relations between the sexes appear as forms of male domination of and potential violence against the woman. The novel contains a double-edged critique: in political terms, L*'s seduction of Sara parallels the abuse of paternal authority on the part of the French nobility. Here the lines are clearly drawn between republicans and royalists, between L* and Roger. Yet L*, Roger, and Seldorf each prove tyrannical in their love. Beneath the familiar tale of decadent aristocrats seducing innocent bourgeois girls lie several variants of a story about bourgeois husbands subjugating their wives. The focus on love out of wedlock as a metaphor for political tyranny shifts to love in wedlock as a form of private oppression.

The unexpected glimpse of Sara's breasts that awakens Roger's repressed passion fortunately does not lead him to commit acts of physical violence against her, nor does he stoop to unspecified "base deviant acts . . . to still the ferment in his blood" (2:32). Instead, he joins the army. Although he has long been sympathetic to the republican cause, the event that puts his patriotic idealism into practice is an incident that triggers his frustrated sex drive. Unable to rule L*'s "love-slave" at home, Roger heads off to subdue the enemy. The war against a perverted patriarchy displaces the bourgeois battle of the sexes. Even the normally sympathetic Berthier sees women as a threat to male patriotism when he supports his grandson's decision with a misogynist tirade: "woe betide, if such a selfish feeling as the one that now struggles in your breast were to unnerve [France's] noblest sons, if our women were to turn them away from their most holy duties, instead of using their power to serve this single great purpose!" (2:38).[32] Berthier blames women for luring French men away from their patriotic duty to the fatherland, whereas Roger actually flees into battle to sublimate his unfulfilled sexual desires.

A number of minor figures in volume two of the novel join the Revolution for similarly questionable reasons. Immediately after L* inadvertently wounds her child, Sara is taken in by a family that has also suffered at the hands of the nobility. The young Nanette has gone mad after having murdered her own starving child fathered by another decadent aristocratic seducer. The courts condemn her defiant brother Joseph to the galleys after he is caught poaching in a desperate attempt to find food for his sister. Upon his release Joseph flings himself into the violent life of a revolutionary, not out of any political idealism, but simply to take revenge against humanity in general: "At another time he would have become a common murderer to avenge himself on the human race" (2:137–38). His brother-in-law Thirion joins the cause primarily out of indignation over the injustice suffered by Nanette and Joseph. Finally, Sara's Parisian neighbor Raimond joins together with Sara to seek personal revenge after his children are accidentally killed in the same skirmish that takes the life of Sara's daughter.

Like Roger, then, these characters join the public cause only after suffering personal misfortune. This in itself does not necessarily undermine the sympathetic portrait of the Revolution in the novel, as the personal sufferings of Nanette, Joseph, and Raimond are symptomatic of general corruption in the state. In the case of both Roger and Joseph, however, revolutionary zeal stands in uneasy proximity to criminal violence: what would otherwise be mere private vengeance now becomes a political cause; what might have led to acts of sexual depravity or even murder now has a "positive" outlet. When the mobs begin to murder, when the half-crazed Sara crawls over bloodied bodies to stab her former lover while carrying a handkerchief soaked in the king's blood, then revolution for even a just cause comes dangerously close to mere chaos.

Sara's own participation in the Revolution goes through two distinct phases. After first learning of L*'s treachery she becomes an avenging fury, setting off on a course of bloodthirsty violence that ends in insanity. After her recovery she becomes a coldly efficient fighter for the revolutionary cause. This development has been viewed as a "purification process," in which Sara learns to place public service over private revenge: "Sara . . . learns to understand her own political action as being motivated solely by personal revenge, which is to say that she understands it as false."[33] However, even when Sara fights *in* the army, she continues to fight *for* herself, which is to say *against* L*: "the names freedom, fatherland echoed dully and without meaning from her empty breast, as if from graves . . . she killed L* in each armed opponent with the terrible hostility that offsets human life against personal misery" (2:249–51). After L* dies Sara fights on more as a cursed soul than as an inspired patriot. Far from marking her entry into a revolutionary community in the army, Sara's military exploits signal her complete alienation from society. She undergoes a gradual process of desocialization in becoming a ruthless killer:

> As every day filled her head with new political follies, so every day a new fiber of her heart died off; in the end even the memory of having been daughter, beloved, wife, [and] mother expressed itself only in more violent outbreaks of partisan spirit on the tribunals of the people's societies. (2:175)

Revolutionary zeal replaces the personal relationships that once linked Sara to society. In the process, she becomes the "unnatural Amazon" her father had condemned when she was a child. The narrator echoes her father's opinion when describing Sara's "un-natural, bloody alliance" with Joseph (2:153), and again in reference to her "unnatural decision to bear arms" (2:250).

It would seem that Seldorf becomes the moral authority in the novel, who speaks for the author in condemning the actions of the unconventionally assertive heroine.[34] However, the opening scene makes clear that what Seldorf terms natural is in fact a simplification and even a falsification of spontaneous emotion in the name of socially sanctioned stereotypes. Sara's education has involved learning to accept these codes as natural, a process that has made her susceptible to L*'s deceptive appeal. With him she plays out the traditional roles of lover, protected wife, and nurturing mother. His betrayal results in "a sudden transformation of her moral being!" (2:143). Convention no longer seems natural to Sara, but she has been so thoroughly indoctrinated that she can no longer make a naive appeal to spontaneous emotions. Instead, she responds by inverting the discredited convention. Her transformation into an avenging Amazon involves not the substitution of the unnatural for the natural, but rather the reversal of one stereotype into its opposite.

Her one remaining connection to others lies in her desire to kill

L*, not in loyalty toward her comrades in arms. She had allowed L*
to control her life in the past; now he continues to do so, as the
longing for his death becomes her sole reason for living. Only Sara's
chance encounter with her brother Theodor after she captures L*'s
coffin and has it burned on the battlefield prevents her complete and
permanent social ostracism. Theodor has already appeared at three
crucial moments in the second half of the novel: first, he prevents
Sara from stabbing L* in prison. Second, she hears his voice in the
graveyard just before she falls insane, and third, she finds him
protecting L*'s dying widow and child with a desperate band of
royalist soldiers. In each case he serves as the tenuous thread that
ties her to the social network.

Upon meeting her brother for the last time on the ruins of L*'s
castle, Sara goes through a physical transformation back into a
woman, "as if with the discovery of her sex its full weakness had
returned" (2:290). Theodor's account of L*'s final days yields an
ambivalent portrait of a man who, despite his glaring flaws, had
loved Sara in a way he could not love his aristocratic wife. Sara's
long conversation with Theodor reconciles her with L*'s memory;
her resocialization is complete when she agrees to care for L*'s
child. Once again she is sister, mother, and – at least in memory –
wife and lover. With this second reversal Sara retires from the army
to live out her life as the stepmother of L*'s child on the ruins of
his castle. Her revolutionary zeal evaporates immediately upon
resumption of her traditional female roles. However, she leads a
joyless existence: L* is dead and her brother is executed within
hours after their reunion, which completes the devastation of the
past few years in which Sara has lost her father, friends, and child.
In the process she has also lost her naive belief in the self-evident
nature of social convention. Her roles as wife and mother have
been emptied of their former significance, as she is married to the
memory of the man who betrayed her, and cares for the child of his
deceased wife.

At this point Roger turns up again, now disfigured by war but still
trying to persuade Sara to marry him. She has rejected his advances
as an adolescent, again when placed under immense emotional
pressure by her father on his deathbed, and yet again when it
seemed that L* had deserted her with her infant daughter, but Roger
refuses to accept defeat. Now in the novel's closing scene Sara rejects
him one more time. Her consistent resistance to Roger's advances

reveals a remarkable strength of character. Even at her most vulnerable, Sara refuses a compromise that social – and also narrative – convention demands.[35] Nevertheless, Sara's self-assertiveness cannot mask the melancholy resignation that has turned her life into a long wait before she can be buried next to L*'s wife. She defiantly spurns Roger only to cling to the remnants of her love for L*, not out of a nostalgic attachment to his royalist politics, but in an attempt to live out a hollow version of their bourgeois "marriage" in the present.

The novel's somber conclusion serves as the final commentary on the double theme traced throughout. The political revolution has been completed. Its soldiers may not always have been motivated solely by their dedication to democracy, their battles may have brought chaos and destruction that will take generations to repair, but the Old Regime has been removed forever. Huber presents us with a more discouraging picture of her protagonist's private life at the end of the novel. Sara's development can be summarized as follows: as a child Sara represses her own spontaneous emotions in favor of her father's dangerously rigid idealism. First Theodor, and then Count L* seem to conform to these ideals. When she discovers L*'s betrayal, however, she has only two options: at first she rejects all culturally acceptable behavior to become an avenging warrior. In doing so, however, she does not find her "true self." Rather, she adopts a masculine role in order to pursue her private war. She remains as dependent on L* in hatred as she had once been in her love. Her only other option is to revert to the discredited feminine stereotypes that bind her to the memory of her deceitful and treacherous lover.

Thus the question of Huber's feminism does not turn on her advocacy or rejection of her protagonist's "Amazonian" behavior. Sara Seldorf stands neither as a warning nor an ideal; rather, she reveals a dilemma. She can either conform to the bourgeois conventions that make her a virtual prisoner of her "husband" in Paris, or else enter the public sphere as a lonely and obsessed virago. While Sara's experiences have taken her far beyond the narrow compass of her "natural" destiny as circumscribed by her father's first lessons, his voice haunts her imagination, determining the path of her transgression and the shape of her remorse.

SOPHIE MEREAU: EXPERIMENTAL FICTIONS

There are times when the German world of letters during the decade or so after the beginning of the French Revolution resembles nothing so much as a soap opera. Everyone knew everyone else, it seems, and partner swapping, whether intellectual or otherwise, was the order of the day. The border between the professional and the personal was quite porous, lending both a tremendous vitality to the creative output and a decided nastiness to factional rivalries. Not surprisingly, the period left a rich lode to be mined by both intellectual historians and biographers, as individuals and ideas, transcendental philosophy and gossip, were inextricably intertwined. Intellectual and creative life was centered in Jena and Weimar, and in the middle of it all stood Sophie Mereau (1770–1806): "At that time she was highly celebrated by everyone with understanding and taste. Wherever she appeared people pressed around her and almost her alone, a thick swarm of admirers, who angled for a word, a smile from her, and around them the onlookers closed in an impenetrable circle."[36]

For the sake of her life alone, Sophie Mereau would deserve to be remembered as one of the most fascinating figures of German Classicism and Romanticism.[37] The daughter of a civil servant in the town of Altenburg, Sophie Schubart reluctantly accepted the proposal of Karl Mereau in 1793, at least in part because marriage to a law professor at the university in Jena granted her access to intellectual circles otherwise closed to a woman. Here she became friendly with Schiller, who regarded her as something of a protégée. He encouraged her writing and helped with publication. Mereau was also Fichte's only female student. Meanwhile she quickly realized that her marriage was a mistake. Rather than endure it in the manner expected of respectable bourgeois wives, Mereau quickly and rather publicly became involved with a student, Johann Heinrich Kipp. When Kipp returned to his native Lübeck, Mereau became involved with another student, Georg Philipp Schmidt, and she soon shocked polite society by traveling alone with Schmidt to Berlin. In 1801 she became the first woman in Jena to demand and receive a divorce from her husband, and only very reluctantly married Clemens Brentano in 1803 when pregnant with his child. Less than three years later she died from complications following childbirth. She was thirty-six years old.

Subsequent generations of literary historians remembered Sophie Mereau only as a curious footnote to the lives of famous men, but during her lifetime Mereau was respected as an author in her own right, producing two novels, two volumes of poetry, numerous short stories, and a considerable body of literary translations. She was also one of the first German women to make a living as a professional writer and editor. The early twentieth century witnessed a brief resurgence of interest in Mereau's work, fueled by both a revival of German Romanticism and the women's movement of the 1920s, but she soon lapsed into obscurity again.[38] In recent years the literary works of Sophie Mereau have experienced a second renaissance, beginning in 1968 with the republication of her literary journal *Kalathiskos* (1801–02). Her first novel, *Das Blüthenalter der Empfindung* [The Springtime of Sensation] (1794), was reissued in 1982; Jeannine Blackwell and Susanne Zantop included translations of two poems and one short story in an anthology of German women writers,[39] and Bettina Bremer and Angelika Schneider have published a critical edition of Mereau's second novel, *Amanda und Eduard* (1803). Despite the recent flurry of interest in Mereau, critical opinion remains divided: while many readers have been delighted to discover in Mereau an early advocate of women's rights,[40] others have questioned the quality of her work. Peter Schmidt observes the "eclecticism" and "dilettantism" in Mereau's collection of stories, poems, and translations in *Kalathiskos*,[41] and Herman Moens raises similar objections in his introduction to Mereau's first novel. He justifies its republication only because its "uneven" quality typifies a broad stratum of (second-rate) literature of the period.[42] Joining the chorus, Christa Bürger begins her study of Mereau's works with a similar disclaimer. Rather than pretending to have rediscovered a neglected literary giant, she sets out to understand the source of Sophie Mereau's persistent mediocrity.[43]

Lack of individual talent is not to blame. Instead, Bürger views Mereau's work in the context of the changing literary institution of the 1790s. The decade witnessed an increasing split between the autonomous works of German Classicism, produced and read by a select few, and the rapidly expanding body of popular literature still indebted to the more directly didactic tradition of the Enlightenment.[44] Women's literature occupied a pivotal position in Goethe and Schiller's reflections on the dichotomization of the public sphere. On the one hand, Goethe and Schiller encouraged a number of women writers, including Sophie Mereau, and published their works in their literary journals. On the other hand, Goethe and Schiller maintained a strict distinction between their own works of art and the inferior productions of the female "dilettantes": "What they write is not trivial literature, but it is not art either. Mediation, not free productivity, is their concern, and the longing for 'something higher' is what drives them on."[45] Selected women writers served a useful, if limited function in Goethe and Schiller's *Literaturpolitik*, in that their works helped to elevate public taste and thus to create an audience for the works of the masters.[46] In Bürger's view, Sophie Mereau both enjoyed Schiller's encouragement and accepted the limitations he placed on the institutional status of her art, producing – depending on one's perspective – either high-class popular literature or popularized German Classicism.[47]

I have recounted Bürger's argument in some detail because it provides a good example of the way in which women writers can be rediscovered and discredited at the same time. What begins as a historical investigation into the bias against women writers ends by adopting Goethe and Schiller's categories as an absolute standard against which competitors inevitably fall short. In the following pages I will take a different tack. I want to view Sophie Mereau as an experimental writer, who works within existing literary conventions to explore gender stereotypes and to produce alternative models of female independence. Her first prose work, *Das Blüthenalter der Empfindung* (1794), makes feminist use of the lyric novel; "Die Flucht nach der Hauptstadt" (1806) does the same for the comic novella; in "Ninon de Lenclos" (1802) she adapts the biography as a vehicle to convey her own ideas, and in *Amanda und Eduard* (1803) Mereau comes to terms with the newly emerging genre of the *Bildungsroman*.

Das Blüthenalter der Empfindung begins when a Swiss man sends his son Albert to Genoa to gain experience. Here he falls in love with Nanette, a beautiful and intelligent young woman. He has admired her from afar, but she disappears almost immediately after their first conversation. Albert and Nanette meet again briefly in Paris, and again in Switzerland, where she tells him her life story. Her parents died when she was very young, leaving her with two brothers, one nearly her own age, and another much older. The older brother spends most of his time plotting to steal the inheritance from his younger siblings. To this end he convinces Lorenzo, the younger brother, to enter a monastery, and encourages Nanette to become a nun. When she refuses he tries to force her to become the mistress of a rich Cardinal. Lorenzo escapes from the monastery and falls in love with a Catholic girl, but when her father discovers that he is a renegade monk, Lorenzo commits suicide. The novel ends when Albert and Nanette decide to escape persecution by emigrating to America.

The plot is admittedly somewhat thin, pieced together from familiar motifs from popular fiction.[48] Characterization remains sketchy, and the story advances by sudden lurches from one country to the next with little concern for realistic description or plausible motivation. But Mereau has no interest in writing a realistic novel. As she explains in the preface, her primary concern is to portray feelings; the plot often serves as little more than a scaffolding from which Mereau can unfold lyric images of youthful sentiments. In this regard her novel has strong affinities with Goethe's *Die Leiden des jungen Werther*, and expresses ideas familiar to readers of Rousseau: praise of youth over age, nature over culture, feeling over reason, and spontaneous love over calculated marriage plans. Yet the novel does more than recycle hackneyed plots and familiar ideas. Its originality lies in the combination of three interrelated topics: the theme of personal development or *Bildung*; an insistence on equal rights for women; and outspoken sympathy for political revolution.

The opening pages of the novel read like the typical *Bildungsroman*, as the hero leaves home to gain experience in the world. At first he is so preoccupied with memories of childhood that he fails to perceive the world around him, but he soon becomes an attentive observer and an active participant in social life. The love for Nanette interferes with his unspecified career plans. When they first meet he spends most of his time in flights of poetic rapture, and her mysterious disappearance flings him into despair. In the months that follow Albert is torn between his preoccupation with Nanette and his public career. Albert's father pulls him out of his despondency when he loses Nanette for the second time in Paris, and when a brief flurry of activity yields again to melancholy, it is the father's death that spurs him into action again. In the end, however, Albert abandons the patriarchal order of the Old World to flee with his lover to the New.

By arranging the plot in this fashion, Mereau offers a feminist perspective on the nascent genre of the *Bildungsroman*. In such works as Goethe's *Wilhelm Meisters Lehrjahre* (1795–96) and Friedrich Schlegel's *Lucinde* (1799), women will be significant only to the extent that they contribute to male development.[49] Here the woman grows out of her subordinate role to threaten, and finally overwhelm the father's ambitions for his son. Nanette breaks completely with the tradition of domestic virtue that would confine women to a subordinate role in the home. Orphaned at an early age, Nanette grew up under the care of an aunt whose pedagogical principle was to let nature take its course: "Nature, she believed, was always good . . . If she prevented evil, she believed that she had done enough; the good, she thought, would come of its own accord" (84).[50] Nanette justifies the aunt's faith in a benevolent nature by growing into an intelligent and forceful individual who refuses to become a pawn in her brother's schemes: "She demanded equal rights with the man whom she wanted to love" (93). When provoked, Nanette rails against the subordination of women in bourgeois society in a series of bitter rhetorical questions:

Where do women have the right to enjoy direct legal protection? Rather, are they not almost everywhere subjugated to the whims of the man? How little consideration is taken even now for their natural rights, for the undisturbed enjoyment of their freedom and their strengths! Are they not more frequently merely *tolerated* rather than *protected*? (96)

Nanette's insistence on freedom as the highest good leads directly to her enthusiasm for the French Revolution, an enthusiasm she shares with Albert – and also Mereau.[51] While in Paris Albert finds himself swept up in the general excitement. At the height of his fervor he hears a familiar voice utter the words "holy freedom!" (38), and he turns to discover Nanette. She must soon flee her evil older brother, however, and when he finds her again in Switzerland, Nanette and Albert decide to escape to America: "A free people lives there; there the genius of humankind enjoys once more its rights, there the new, happy circumstances of a youthful state will give no cause to fear odious reforms for a long time to come" (146–47).

Although there would seem to be a logical connection between female emancipation and political revolution, we have seen that in fact the middle-class revolt against the aristocracy actually tended to work against women's rights. Exactly how it might be possible to combine complete female equality with a new social order based on the subordinate status of women does not become clear in this early work. Or rather, Mereau signals her awareness of its impossibility within Europe by sending her protagonists on a utopian flight to America. She brings things closer to home in the story "Die Flucht nach der Hauptstadt." The unnamed heroine elopes with her lover Albino when her father threatens to force her into marriage with the boorish but rich aristocrat Vincent. She and Albino enjoy several months in B[erlin?] together, before a scheming "friend" named Felix separates them. Felix soon convinces the heroine to stop grieving for Albino, join him and begin a new career as an actress. They travel together to D[resden?], but she soon abandons him when he turns out to be a tyrant. She then takes up with a third lover, but when he dies she returns to B. and is reunited with Albino. He was not in prison, as Felix had led her to believe, but has made his fortune with lucky investments. They return home together, find parental forgiveness and marital bliss.

The most remarkable feature of this story is the heroine's complete lack of remorse. While Julchen Grünthal grovels in the dirt when seeking forgiveness from her father, Mereau's heroine cheerfully defies her parents and enjoys her new freedom: "How boundless was our joy! . . . we felt very innocent because we did not think at all about guilt!"[52] Nothing seems to trouble her for very long; even when her third lover dies she finds it impossible to mourn. As in the case of *Blüthenalter*, Mereau makes no attempt to establish character depth or a realistic narrative. Instead, she draws on the tradition of the novella in a fast-paced tale with sudden, unexpected twists to produce a fantasy in which the heroine experiences multiple partners without guilt and still manages to live happily ever after with her true love. Instead of locating this utopia in distant America, Mereau shifts it to a different social class. The heroine meets Albino in her father's amateur theatre, and later becomes a professional actress with Felix. Although actors and actresses were beginning to gain greater respectability during the late eighteenth century,[53] the theatre still featured as an adventurous realm where characters like the young Wilhelm Meister could have sexual adventures before settling down to a respectable career. In Mereau's story, however, it is the woman who passes through the bohemian world of the theatre on her way to a happy marriage, laying claim to experiences typically reserved for men.

Mereau also uses the theme of the theatre for a light-hearted look at the fluid boundary between role-playing and sincerity in bourgeois society. The heroine first becomes involved with Albino when they play lovers on her father's stage. Acting soon turns into reality: "he told me so often that he loved me that he himself finally felt it and I believed it. Our imagination was kindled ever higher, and soon we were only playing ourselves in the most fervent roles" (381; 140–41). The process repeats itself with Felix later, as play-acting turns friendship to love, and it reverses itself when she receives great applause for her first professional appearance as an actress playing a shy girl: she is so paralyzed with stage-fright that she is not really acting at all.

Mereau's deliberate confusion of reality and fiction continues the critique of female socialization already evident in the work of Unger and Huber. We recall that in LaRoche's novel acting was one of Sophie von Sternheim's methods to train subjects into virtuous family members. The process is based on the deliberate paradox of teaching individuals to act "naturally." The logical way to critique this process of socialization was to stress the discrepancy between the performance of virtue and female experience, as when Julchen Grünthal appears as a virgin in a local pageant after a series of sexual adventures. Eventually it becomes difficult to know what the natural is, as in the case of Sara Seldorf, who can either live in accordance with her father's precepts or subvert them, but who has little room to develop her "authentic" self. Mereau offers a comic reversal of Huber's tragic theme with her two-dimensional lovers who give up the stage in order to play out the roles of husband and wife: "Thus ended unexpectedly in comedy what had started out as sure tragedy. Nothing seemed funnier to us than to remember how we had once left our country as heroes, full of pathos, and now returned, imperceptibly transformed into married bourgeois" (399; 184).

That they are able to return at all has nothing to do with virtue and everything with good luck. Albino invests his gambling profits in overseas trade, and when his ships come in, he buys his way out of the lawsuit that the heroine's father had filed against him. The amoral moral to this comic tale makes a mockery of bourgeois values: "Our parents felt as much honored by us as they were pleased. What they would have otherwise condemned as a reprehensible prank was transformed into the product of a daring and genial spirit – due to our success, which in the eyes of the world justifies any action" (399; 183). By implication, at least, capital investment is simply a more respectable form of gambling, and as long as there is enough money, then morality can look the other way.

While Mereau situates her utopia in America in *Das Blüthenalter der Empfindung* and in the theatre for most of "Die Flucht nach der Hauptstadt," she moves it to the past in her biography of the famous French courtesan Ninon de Lenclos. Mereau's ostensible purpose is to write revisionist history, as she sets out to prove that Lenclos was better than her reputation, although it is easy enough to read the biography as an indirect autobiography, in which Mereau defends her own unconventional life. Yet the detour through biography suggests that Mereau was less interested in personal confession than in experimenting with existing narrative forms to express an alternative feminine subjectivity forbidden by her contemporary society. As a result, the pro-revolutionary, bourgeois writer chooses as her model an aristocratic libertine of the Old Regime.[54] Mereau concedes that Lenclos changed sexual partners frequently, but insists that she remained true to herself and honest with others, and that she was respected and even admired in turn. Lenclos can get away with her unorthodox morality, Mereau suggests, because she always acted in accordance with her own nature: "True to her principles about love, she always followed her inclination, and formed or broke a bond as it suited her pleasure."[55] By appealing to the essential goodness of Lenclos's inclinations, Mereau adopts Rousseau's belief in the superiority of nature to culture. At the same time, however, she subverts Rousseau's belief in "natural" gender distinctions with what he would consider a very unnatural insistence on female autonomy.

Mereau adds a further anachronistic element to her Lenclos biography by importing the dynamics of the nuclear family back into the seventeenth century. Lenclos grows up with a pious mother and a hedonistic father. While her mother denies worldly pleasure for the spirit, her father enjoys sensuality; she models her life on the Bible, while he lives in the spirit of Epicurus and Montaigne. Ninon's father takes great delight in molding his daughter into a woman in a manner reminiscent of Colonel von Sternheim and his eighteenth-century counterparts. But while the typical bourgeois daughter strives to emulate her mother and to marry a man like her father, Ninon de Lenclos has little sympathy for her mother and decides to usurp the paternal role for herself:

I see, she said to one of her friends, that people make the emptiest and shallowest demands on us [women], and that the men have reserved for themselves the right to strive for the most worthy and rewarding things.

From this moment on I will become a man . . . Her morals were the same as those of the most upright men of her time, and she remained true to them. (60)

However radical Lenclos's demand that she be regarded as a man may seem, it does not call for the emancipation of all women from a repressive patriarchal rule. She simply asserts the right of one exceptional individual to reverse existing gender roles. Even this limited revolt is permitted by "the frivolous French character" (58) during an unusual period in their history. On the one hand, then, Mereau insists on Lenclos's right to an unconventional morality, but on the other, she makes it clear that Lenclos's behavior is the product of another time, another country, and that even then, it was not for everyone.

Why should Mereau qualify Lenclos's potential as role-model for women like herself seeking alternatives to domestic virtue? Part of the reason must be to reassure the censor, whether external or internal, that she is not advocating a general revolt among German women against their increasingly restrictive conditions. The disclaimers function as a sort of camouflage that permit Mereau to publish her shocking defense of a courtesan in a journal aimed explicitly at German women. At the same time, she leaves open the possibility that a few women might find in Lenclos's behavior an intriguing alternative to their own lives. Mereau does not want to legislate morality by replacing obligatory virtue with obligatory vice; instead, she insists that women should be free to live in accordance with their own nature, whether it coincides with contemporary morality or not.

The thematic concerns I have traced in Mereau's work receive their fullest elaboration in her second and final novel, *Amanda und Eduard*. Extrinsic evidence alone suggests that *Amanda und Eduard* is Mereau's most ambitious work, as it was written during her most productive years and is her longest prose text. While many of her stories and translations appeared in calendars and almanacs aimed at a popular audience, she first published eight letters of this epistolary novel in Schiller's highly respected *Horen* (1797), while the revised and completed work appeared in a handsome two-volume edition.[56] More important, the novel displays a careful aesthetic structure and convincing character development that distinguishes it from both *Das Blüthenalter der Empfindung* and Mereau's shorter fictional works. Her dual focus on Amanda and Eduard enables her primary achievement: an analysis of gender roles in German society around 1800 in their relation to the concept of *Bildung*.[57] This is not to say that Mereau simply reverses gender roles familiar to the genre to produce a female *Bildungsroman*. Instead, Mereau works within existing conventions to explore their limitations. Both Amanda and Eduard display character traits that correspond to sexual stereotypes of the period: Eduard enters the novel like the typically active protagonist about to complete his personal *Bildung*, while Amanda first appears the passive victim of male oppression. In the course of the novel Mereau develops a critical portrait of Eduard's arrogance, while tracing Amanda's ultimately unsuccessful attempt to realize her frustrated desires. Rather than allowing her initially sympathetic heroine to triumph over her male counterpart, Mereau reveals the insidious persistence of cultural stereotypes that inform, and finally undermine, even Amanda's most rebellious actions.

The text consists entirely of letters by the two protagonists. Amanda writes to her friend Julie, Eduard to his friend and mentor Barton; in addition, Amanda and Eduard write a few letters to each other. The novel begins with Amanda's return from Italy. We learn of her unhappy arranged marriage with Albret and her longing for a more satisfying relationship. At the same time the younger Eduard takes leave of his mentor and sets out into the world. Eventually Amanda and Eduard meet and begin a passionate love-affair that is interrupted when Eduard leaves town at the urgent request of his father. Time, distance, and misunderstandings gradually alienate the two lovers, who overcome their grief and become interested in different partners. Meanwhile Albret dies. Near the end of the novel Amanda and Eduard meet again in Switzerland. They rediscover their love and finally marry, but Amanda dies after a brief illness.

Mereau's second novel has several points in common with *Das Blüthenalter der Empfindung*. The two novels reveal a common indebtedness to Rousseau, expressing faith in the essential goodness of human nature while lamenting the corruption of modern civilization. Both works contain strong statements in favor of women's emancipation, and both make use of such familiar narrative conventions as the mysterious Italian subplot. Perhaps the most significant distinction between the novels lies in their contrasting narrative perspective. Mereau published her first novel anonymously, but signed her preface as "the authoress" [*Die Verfasserinn*]. The first-person narrative that follows would seem to encourage readers to assume they hear a woman's voice, as did Friedrich Schlegel: "At first a young creature [*ein junges Wesen*] appears who is flooded with every possible purple passion. She [*Es*] sits there completely placidly in the grass. I say she, because I was certain it was a girl; but it is supposed to be a boy."[58] While Schlegel's sarcastic comment implies inability on Mereau's part, it is possible to argue that she constructs a deliberately androgynous narrative perspective as a means of reclaiming rights traditionally denied women. Thus before we discover that the narrator is in fact a man, she has him celebrate *human* freedom: "Here I stand, enjoying full health, entangled in no relationships, bound by no prejudices – a free person!" [*ein freier Mensch*] (4).[59] Mereau takes a different tack in *Amanda und Eduard* by choosing the epistolary form to sharpen the distinction between the male and female protagonists. She divides concern between the two principal characters, actually giving greater attention to her heroine in the completed novel: whereas Eduard writes three of the first four letters in the *Horen* fragment, the novel begins from Amanda's point of view.[60] In all, Amanda writes 29 letters, Eduard 19, and Amanda's letters comprise slightly more than 60 percent of the novel.

The *Horen* fragment begins with Eduard's first letter to Barton. Eduard has reached an important turning point in his life, as he has just completed his education and is ready to make his mark on the world. He hopes to transform life's chaos into a higher order, to give form to material, order to accident. Mereau used nearly identical language when reviewing Goethe's *Wilhelm Meisters Lehrjahre* two years later, and included the passage again in the revised 1803 version of *Amanda und Eduard*.[61] Clearly, then, Eduard expresses an important concept for Mereau; indeed, Bürger identifies it as her "poetic credo."[62] In it she formulates the classical notion of *Bildung* derived from Goethe's recent novel and Schiller's contemporary theory. *Bildung* in this view involves not merely organic growth, but the transformation of life into an aesthetic order.

From Eduard's perspective, Amanda serves as a convenient supplement to personal development. The key to Amanda's beneficial effect on Eduard lies in her role as mediator between him and nature. Numerous passages in the novel reflect the familiar three-phase theory of history that views the modern age as a period of alienation between former and future plenitude.[63] Amanda functions as the focal point of the natural order: "In all of nature I saw no other purpose than her; she is the ethereal wreath, into which all beings are woven" (107).[64] In loving Amanda, Eduard feels both at peace with himself and one with the world; when absent from her, the harmony is lost. Eduard thus views Amanda less as an individual than as an aesthetic experience conceived in terms of the German Classicism. Like the viewer of Juno Ludovisi described in the fifteenth letter of Schiller's *Aesthetic Education*, Eduard experiences in his love for Amanda a temporary sense of wholeness in his otherwise fragmented existence. Despite personal rivalry and a differently conceived aesthetics, Friedrich Schlegel shares Schiller's understanding of the feminine; Lucinde plays an identical role for Julius in his early romantic novel.[65]

Amanda's function as an aesthetic object becomes particularly evident in Eduard's last letter in the novel. Here he describes how the artist Antonio helped him rediscover his love for Amanda. Although Eduard is already engaged to another woman, Antonio correctly senses that he continues to lament the loss of his first love. In an attempt to cure Eduard of his malaise, Antonio leads him to a picturesque spot on the Italian coast where he shows him his portrait of Amanda. Before the portrait is revealed, however, Mereau pauses to produce one of several set-piece landscapes that accentuate important moments in the novel. The extended description of the setting far exceeds what is necessary for the continuation of the plot. Rather, Mereau seeks to create the verbal equivalent of a painting that elevates the pleasant setting into a lasting work of art. Amanda finally appears as a portrait within the painting, the exponential intensification of nature transformed into art. As if to underscore the close proximity of verbal and visual arts in this passage, Mereau chose just this scene for the frontispiece to the second volume of the novel.[66]

Antonio's cure succeeds, and Eduard recovers his self-esteem. In his willingness to view Amanda solely in terms of her usefulness to himself, Eduard reveals the arrogance underlying his project of *Bildung*. From beginning to end he feels pity for those inferior to himself: "not one who could have lifted himself up to my feelings. Pity and pride besieged me alternately to such an extent that I could not bear it" (21). His love for Amanda only adds to his sense of self-importance: "Others formed me into a person, but you lifted me up to God; separated from you, I sink even lower, in proportion to my former height" (122–23). Within days of their first separation he becomes so mired in self-pity that he declares that life is all but over for him. He writes to her at great length of his plans to eke out his remaining days in melancholy remembrance of the past, but is so self-absorbed that he forgets to mail the letter.

Eduard's willingness to use Amanda to inflate his already bloated ego combines with a condescending attitude toward her that occasionally approaches that of her husband. At first Eduard would seem to be the perfect counterpart to Albret. He is an accomplished musician and singer, a sensitive individual given to effusive passions, while Albret remains a cold businessman with little time for his wife and no understanding of her needs. Albret treats Amanda like a child, listening to her "with a smile such as one smiles at a child's dreams" (119). "'You fritter away your life,'" he advises, "'and don't worry about serious things'" (65–66). He refuses her the opportunity to become an autonomous individual. "'Those who should not and cannot have ends will always be only means'" (66). Although his tone is gentler, Eduard seeks to use Amanda as just such a means to the end of his own maturation. From the beginning he realizes that women pose a threat to his equilibrium as well as a possibility for self-aggrandizement: "for when the power of a woman is so great that she divides us from ourself, I find her terrible" (86). Eduard's effusive praise of Amanda as the key to nature also functions as a strategy to minimize her potential threat. Thus he occasionally adopts Albret's patronizing tone when extolling Amanda's innocent charm: "You don't know what you are, Amanda, and just this makes you so beautiful!" (135).

While Eduard appears as a proud youth about to begin his career, we first encounter the older and unhappier Amanda long since trapped in marriage to a man she neither loves nor respects. Here Mereau breaks with the tradition of domestic fiction, which usually follows its heroine from adolescence to marriage and leaves her with her Prince Charming at the altar. Mereau's primary concern in this novel is with what happens after the honeymoon is over. As a result, we hear less about Amanda's childhood than we did about previous heroines. Mereau does offer us an important glimpse into Amanda's past when she recalls the events that led to her unhappy marriage with Albret. Already in the *Horen* fragment Mereau had included a brief account of the betrothal. Amanda's father knows Albret as a wealthy business associate; he is delighted when Albret proposes, and finds it inconceivable that his daughter might not share his feelings. Although Amanda describes him as "the tenderest and most beloved of fathers" when he dies, it is clear that he has no sense of her inner turmoil when facing the prospect of marriage to an unloved man. When she finally agrees to the "sacrifice," her father reacts like a businessman who has made a good bargain: "My father was delighted about this transaction and was charmed by these fruits of his education."[67] In the revised novel, Mereau makes Amanda's father much more sensitive to his daughter's feelings. The father has suffered bankruptcy, and Albret's proposal seems the only way to care for his daughter. Instead of the shrewd businessman who cavorts with joy after closing the deal for his daughter, the father now approaches Amanda as a worried old man whose only concern is Amanda's happiness. Like Rousseau's Julie, who serves as the namesake for Amanda's friend and correspondent, Amanda finds the tender father impossible to resist.

The marriage itself grants Amanda a certain amount of freedom. As her father had pointed out, it permits her to continue to live in the luxurious fashion to which she had become accustomed. Her role seems to be that of a diplomat's wife: Albret keeps her at the height of fashion, and she is expected to sparkle at social events. Yet Amanda yearns for the intimacy of a companionate marriage, and, above all, she longs for passionate love. When she realizes that Albret can bring her neither, she is more than willing to accept Eduard's attention. With the disregard for conventional morality typical of Mereau's heroines, Amanda refuses to put up with her unhappy marriage, and feels no guilt about her love for Eduard, whether or not their affair is consummated.[68] As she explains to Julie, love has not come to her in a conventional way in marriage, and thus she has every right to experience it in the form available. As long as she acts honestly in accordance with her own innate being – *Eigenthümlichkeit* (10) – then she has no need to feel guilty. She not only defends her adulterous love for Eduard, but also her later attraction to the Italian painter Antonio: "The assertion that we can love only once, only one single object, is a fantastic, indeed, harmful mistake" (293).

At this point Amanda voices sentiments no different from those of Ninon Lenclos. As we recall, however, Mereau presents Lenclos's hedonism as the natural outgrowth of a bygone culture, whereas Amanda's insistence on her right to enjoy love outside of wedlock stands in deliberate opposition to contemporary morality. Her friend Julie comes close to the feminine ideal of Mereau's own period, having never desired more than a quiet marriage with a beloved husband. Her satisfaction derives from a combination of low expectations and good luck. Amanda wants more and gets less from her own marriage, and is willing to risk disapproval to fulfill her needs. Yet Amanda also has a capacity for brooding introspection that distinguishes her from her cheerfully unproblematic friend Nanette in this novel or from the heroine of "Die Flucht nach der Hauptstadt." Amanda not only champions female emancipation, but also has to confront the consequences of her actions in a more serious way than either the seventeenth-century courtesan or the eighteenth-century actress. The result is a portrait of considerable psychological complexity that explores the limitations as well as the strengths of Amanda's position.

For example, her reflections expose a curious mixture of traditional and progressive elements, as she defends her unconventional behavior by drawing on familiar cultural clichés. Whereas Eduard seeks to impose order on life's fluctuations, Amanda surrenders herself completely to the forces of nature: "I have still rarely thought about our future, and where this might all lead. Do you ask the river where it plans to take its course? It surges omnipotently wherever nature's law and strength command" (157). Thus we find the seemingly radical libertine affirming a series of conservative sexual stereotypes: "Woman's nature is love" (239). Women should be passive, she argues; men should take the initiative. She identifies painting as a typically masculine art form, music as feminine, since men seek clarity and understanding, "while the woman cloaks her feelings in holy darkness, and goes to meet her fate with childlike trust!" (277). In this passage Amanda adopts the same infantilizing tone toward women that she bitterly resents in her husband: " 'Why,' I cried out in pain, 'did you choose a feeling woman as your life companion, when you are unable to appreciate her?' " (66).

Those moments when Amanda's willingness to "go with the flow" of nature result in genuine conflict are of particular interest, for they reveal the inadequacy of her philosophy and the latent conservatism of her position. At several crucial moments in her life she betrays her own self-interest by submitting to male authority. She allows her father to talk her into marrying Albret, despite her instinctive dislike of the man. She then resists her impulse to flee Albret with Eduard, a decision she later regrets. Although she refuses Albret's demands that she deny her love for Eduard entirely, she does give in to his request that she not correspond with Eduard for four months. The most significant challenge to Amanda's *carpe diem* philosophy arises toward the end of the novel when Amanda, now in love with Antonio, rediscovers her love for Eduard at a time when the pleasure can no longer be uncomplicated. Bad timing places their potential reunion at risk. "And that's the way it is: we wait for years for a single moment, and then it takes us by surprise after all" (257).[69] In surrendering herself to her natural impulses, Amanda was able to affirm her love for Eduard at a time when she was still married to Albret. But now her feelings have grown more complex, as she confronts simultaneous, conflicting emotions.

At this point it would seem that Amanda's only logical alternative would be to question the principles by which she has lived. The protagonist of the largely comic novella *Der Mann mit vier Weibern* [The Man with Four Wives] experiences just this sort of crisis near the end of the tale, as he condemns himself for his indecisiveness: "Happy the man who makes a firm plan for his life and then follows it steadfastly; I didn't do it, I passively succumbed to circumstances and became a victim of them."[70] Mereau voices a similar self-criticism in a letter written during the same year in which the novel was published: "I am resolved to remain for now in Weimar. Dear heaven! Before I never knew what making a decision meant, indeed, I often thought that every decision was a sin, and that one must only follow inspirations. How ridiculous!"[71]

By Mereau's own standards, Amanda's response to her dilemma is ridiculous, for she simply bypasses the problem with a reassertion of her original convictions: "No! without consideration for the past and the present, without timid investigation of what is and what could have been, I will now surrender completely to this beautiful feeling, thankfully and freely" (252). This philosophy works well enough for the time being, as she is separated from both Eduard and Antonio. Amanda next writes from the country estate where she had met Eduard, where she is again at peace with herself, happy to love Antonio, and happy to know that Eduard loved and still loves her. "Oh! always let feeling reign, it always chooses that which is true, that which is certain!" (277). Amanda's stubborn faith in her own instincts merely obscures her dilemma; moreover, she casts herself in the familiar role of the woman as the embodiment of nature or the naive, a role that renders any sort of personal development impossible.

While Amanda is willing to love and be loved simultaneously by both Eduard and Antonio, they are not willing to share her. Soon after discovering that they love the same woman, Antonio and Eduard separate, for, as Antonio puts it, rivals cannot be friends. At this point something curious happens: the potential conflict disappears. Before Amanda has to confront both men face to face, she falls seriously ill. Eduard discovers her convalescing in Lausanne, and convinces her to marry him. No mention is made of Antonio until the editor's postscript, which merely confirms that he has vanished. Nor do we hear of Eduard's fiancée Cölestina again; apparently he forgets her the moment he finds Amanda.

Why would Mereau bring her characters to the brink of serious conflict only to avoid the consequences of her own carefully constructed narrative? The most obvious explanation would be that she felt pressured to complete the long-standing project. A certain amount of intrinsic evidence points in this direction. Up until the final fifty pages of volume two, the novel displays a strikingly symmetrical construction. In volume one Amanda and Eduard are introduced separately, brought together gradually, and then separated again. Then in volume two each becomes involved with minor characters: first Eduard flirts with the country girl Agnes while Amanda rediscovers her childhood friend Charlotte; then Amanda and Eduard develop serious interest in Antonio and Cölestina. The disappearance of both these characters in the novel's final pages indicates a desire for a hasty wrapping-up, a willingness to smooth over potential conflict by reducing the increasingly complex constellation of characters to a single pair.

Lack of time may partially explain Mereau's decision not to carry through a complicated narrative structure to a consequential conclusion, but this sort of speculation results in a disappointing, dismissive interpretation of the text. We can produce a more sympathetic reading of the novel by shifting the blame for its problematic conclusion from Sophie Mereau to the society in which she writes. Mereau has a difficult time providing convincing answers because she is asking very difficult questions. It is one thing to argue in theory that every individual has a large number of potential lovers; it is even possible to portray one character passing through a succession of partners; yet it is next to impossible to portray one female character with multiple lovers simultaneously in a serious work set in late eighteenth-century Germany. In earlier works Mereau circumvented the problem by leaving out one of these components. Here

Amanda can either cling to her liberal theory in the absence of both lovers, or choose one and betray her principles; Mereau apparently did not share Georg Forster's belief in the possibility of a happy *ménage à trois*.

The obviously forced conclusion also extends the implicit critique of the protagonists voiced earlier in the text. This critique can be inferred from the way in which Amanda and Eduard rationalize their decision to marry after all. Eduard seems to experience no difficulty: he urges marriage almost as soon as he rediscovers Amanda. Both his brief flirtation with Agnes and his more serious involvement with Cölestina turn out to be temporary replacements for his one true love. Amanda's assertion that each individual has many potential partners does not seem to apply to Eduard. Or does he make things a little too easy for himself? While his devotion to Amanda may seem touching, his untroubled willingness to abandon his fiancée is less than admirable. Once again Eduard, like Albret, is guilty of using women as a means to the end of his own happiness. Cölestina serves as a stopgap that can be discarded as soon as he finds his former lover.

Amanda, for her part, bypasses the problem through a combination of illness and religion. On her way to Lausanne she meets a hermit, with whom she has a series of long conversations. He instructs her in a pantheistic philosophy that reaffirms her own convictions while placing them in a broader context: "Follow your inclinations, if they are true and natural, but honor the Godhead that you feel in yourself tirelessly in your soul, and do not let your spirits be filled with disquiet and dragged down by earthly worries and joys" (289). Faith in one's natural impulses becomes part of a larger cosmic plan, as the individual thereby moves toward reunion with the supreme being. Amanda agrees to marry Eduard in part because her illness has made her too weak to resist, but also because she believes that she has transcended the particulars of earthly existence. She views herself as an incorporeal spirit: "disembodied I immerse myself in the infinite sea of love, where beings are immortal!" (295). Both the sensual appeal of her romantic lover and the social conflict it provoked have been avoided through their transformation into a spiritual experience for the dying woman.

Thus neither Amanda nor Eduard can be taken as the spokesperson for Mereau's ideals. While Eduard has many of the positive characteristics associated with male protagonists of the *Bildungsroman*, he also shows how these same traits stand in close proximity to egocentrism and chauvinism. Amanda makes bold statements in favor of women's rights one minute, while submitting to male authority the next. She both challenges social convention and conforms to cultural stereotypes of the feminine. In the end, the very passivity that has inspired her unconventional behavior makes her incapable of protracted critical self-reflection. From this perspective, the marriage of Amanda and Eduard appears as an act justified by mutual self-deception.

Yet there is a certain integrity to the novel's conclusion that extends beyond its implicit critique of the protagonists. The reunion of the two lovers comes too late; their final days together are tinged with a melancholy that borders on despair. Amanda no longer ponders the complexities of her emotions, not only, as suggested above, because she is avoiding problems, but also because they no longer matter. After all, she dies soon after she marries Eduard, and discovers the consolations of religious mysticism only when she is terminally ill. Mereau's other works also have their dark moments. In describing Lorenzo's state of mind just before he commits suicide in *Das Blüthenalter der Empfindung*, Mereau shows how an ecstatic loss of self in the Oneness of nature can also inspire feelings of dread: pantheism turns to nihilism when Lorenzo loses his faith in the possibility of life after death, and in a benevolent God who cares for his creation. Philipp, "the man with four wives," drifts amiably from one marriage to the next; he finds polygamy disturbing only when he faces execution for the crime. Yet this comic novella also takes a tragic turn: Philipp manages to avoid execution for polygamy and sets off for the South Seas with the only wife he really loved, but she dies before they reach their destination, the ship goes down with all hands, and he spends his last years alone on a desert island. Even Ninon Lenclos has moments of deep crisis in her otherwise unproblematic life. She enters a cloister briefly after the death of her pious mother, and later nearly dies of grief after her son – and would-be lover – commits suicide.

The despondency evident in these passages can be viewed as the third stage in a critical sequence that marks Mereau's life and works as a whole, and which finds its fullest expression in *Amanda und Eduard*. At the first level, Mereau delivers a strong protest against social injustice. Amanda's critique of her husband and insistence on her right to find personal fulfillment typify this aspect of Mereau's feminism. Mereau then distances herself from her protagonist to reveal an ironic awareness of the extent to which Amanda surrenders to the strictures she resists. Finally, she grants Amanda the peace that comes with religious faith, but a peace that hovers near exhaustion and despair. Christa Wolf captures this combination of defiant protest, ironic conformity, and tragic hopelessness in the brief characterization of Sophie Mereau in *Kein Ort. Nirgends* [No Place on Earth]: "Günderrode read Mereau's entire soul in her first glance: guilty, defiant, proud, and despairing."[72] In Mereau's own melancholy self-assessment, circumstances prohibited her from fulfilling her ambitions as a writer:

I found a world inside me that kept me busy, that I wanted to place into reality, a pleasant picture for the onlookers! I only needed calm from without to shape what lay inside me! Fate did not grant me this calm. It forced me into circumstances where everything tortured me, where the cheerful images that lay inside me only struggled out here and there like flowers out of rubble, within which my soft-heartedness held me captive. My peace is a dream, my joy is the laughter of despair, my harmonies are single discordant notes that resound from distant halls of joy through the wasteland.[73]

To an even greater extent than Friederike Helene Unger and Therese Huber, Mereau experimented with fictional alternatives to the domestic virtue increasingly expected of women around 1800. In the process she produced a body of innovative and uncompromising feminist fiction that retains its ability to delight and provoke. Yet passages such as the above express a weariness and despair that go beyond the personal to capture a broader sense of lost cultural opportunity: the French Revolution did not bring political freedom to Germany, nor did it lead to the emancipation of women from patriarchal rule in the home. Amanda's quiescence on the eve of her death contrasts markedly with the defiance that had characterized her life, and the outspoken enthusiasm for the Revolution present in *Das Blüthenalter der Empfindung* is noticeably absent in *Amanda und Eduard*. Sophie Mereau died on October 30, 1806, in the first days of the French occupation that was to last nearly a decade. When the delegates to the Congress of Vienna sat down to piece Europe back together in 1815, they faced a social and political order that had been irrevocably changed.

CHAPTER 4

Liberation's aftermath: the early Restoration

INTRODUCTION

Just a few weeks before Sophie Mereau's death, Johanna Schopenhauer moved to Weimar. Having already enjoyed a certain amount of success as the hostess of social gatherings in Hamburg, the recently widowed Schopenhauer hoped to establish herself in Germany's cultural center. As luck would have it, her arrival came just two weeks before Napoleon's armies defeated the ill-prepared Prussians at Jena and Auerstädt on October 14, 1806. By the next day soldiers were burning and plundering the site of Weimar Classicism. The woman who had come looking for culture suddenly found herself in the midst of a war.[1]

The Germans had watched events unfold in neighboring France since 1789, but until 1806 the actual fighting had taken place only on the western perimeter of their territory. For the next several years the Germans would experience first hand the changes wrought by the Revolution. By the time Napoleon was finally defeated at Waterloo, twenty-six years had passed since Louis XVI had summoned the assembly of the Estates General, and little remained the same. The Napoleonic Wars had engulfed Europe from Gibraltar to Moscow and from London to Cairo. Mass conscription and prolonged fighting had brought the war home to a far greater percentage of the population than was typical for earlier wars. The French had seen their king and queen executed and their nobility sent into exile. For a time Robespierre had led a revolutionary dictatorship that oversaw executions in the name of virtue and terror. The Holy Roman Empire came to an end; churches were turned into temples of reason; even calendars were changed to abolish religious holidays in a new secular society. To individuals who until recently had lived in a world marked by continuity and conformity, the Revolution brought the experience of irrevocable historical change.

One of the most significant – if least intended – contributions of Napoleon to Germany was to inspire a new militant nationalism that began to reach out to the masses. Decades earlier Lessing, Klopstock, Herder, and LaRoche fought a cultural war against French influence in the German states. During the 1790s France represented an alternative political system that provoked intense reflection among German writers, but which remained safely distant from most German lands. After 1806, however, German nationalists had a clear-cut military objective: to expel the invading French armies from their territory. Almost overnight German intellectuals began to respond to the new situation.[2] In his *Reden an die deutsche Nation* [Addresses to the German Nation] (1808) Fichte encouraged the Germans to regain their strength by drawing on their supposedly uncorrupted linguistic and ethnic roots. Kleist wrote a thinly veiled attack on French imperialism in his drama *Die Hermannsschlacht* [The Battle of Arminius] (1808), which celebrates the Germanic hero's defeat of the ancient Romans, and also savage verses urging the Germans to stuff the Rhine with French corpses. A few years later Körner became the most popular of many nationalist poets whose works found wide circulation in German newspapers and journals. It is important not to overestimate the effect of the new nationalist rhetoric, which still reached only members of a relatively small intellectual elite; recent historians have debunked the myth that the German nationalist response to French occupation was either spontaneous or widespread.[3] Nevertheless, the Wars of Liberation did mark the first step toward the widespread growth of national feeling in the German masses, a movement that spread to all social levels by the end of the nineteenth century.[4]

While the efforts of the Vienna Congress to restore the old social order to Europe were outwardly successful, they inevitably generated tensions and contradictions in societies that had grown accustomed to change. In Germany Napoleon's defeat would at first glance seem to have been a great national triumph, and it was celebrated as such. Yet a number of factors complicate the story of the German victory over the "Corsican tyrant." The Napoleonic occupation of German territories had brought political unity to many German principalities, and the introduction of the Napoleonic Code gave German citizens greater civil rights than they had previously enjoyed. These advances, in turn, inspired the liberal Stein-Hardenberg reforms in Prussia. For many Germans the new nationalism was a liberal movement that sought to replace absolutist particularism with a politically unified republic. German student fraternities [*Burschenschaften*] tried to keep liberal ideals alive in the immediate wake of the war, but in 1819 the Prussian government cracked down on dissidents with the draconian Carlsbad Decrees. Seen in this light, the Restoration of 1815 struck a blow *against* German liberal nationalism, as the Congress of Vienna sought to restore the old feudalism to new legitimacy.

The dream of a unified nation returned to the realm of culture, where it received expression in such diverse projects as the completion of the Cologne cathedral, research into German medieval poetry, the publication of German fairy tales and songs, and the cult of the Rhine.[5] One of the most significant media for the development of national consciousness was the literature that emerged during and immediately after the Napoleonic Wars, for it was through their common language that Germans could experience a sense of cultural unity that would take decades to realize politically. After 1815 German literary production quickly resumed the explosive growth that had characterized the prewar years. To an even greater extent than in the late eighteenth century, prose fiction became the dominant literary genre. The number of new novels published annually tripled from 1815 to 1830,[6] while journals and almanacs flourished with the publication of shorter works. As was the case around 1800, this flood of literature triggered a series of conservative reactions by those concerned that the widening base of literary production would lead to a lowering of standards,[7] but others welcomed the new developments. In his announcement of a literary journal in 1818, for example, Ludwig Börne expressed hope that the capitalization of the literary market would actually aid the democratization of Germany.[8]

In this context Friedrich Perthes's short publication on *Der deutsche Buchhandel als Bedingung des Daseyns einer deutschen Literatur* [The German Book Trade as Condition for the Existence of a German Literature] (1816) deserves particular attention. The Hamburg book dealer argues that the publishing industry provides a distribution network that unifies the politically fragmented country. He goes further to argue that the very decentralization of the German territories fosters the growth of German literature:

It is for this reason that we have a universal German literature, whereas France and also England only have a Parisian and a London literature. Thus while in those countries no great writer thrives any longer outside those capital cities, the most splendid intellectual blossoms and the deepest ponderings arise in hundreds of German cities and villages.[9]

The passage is remarkable if we recall Goethe's frequently cited claim in his essay on "Literary Sansculottism" (1795) that the absence of a German capital city hindered the development of a "classical" literature. In contrast, Perthes insists that political fragmentation combined with economic unification contributes directly to raising both the quantity, and the quality of German literary production.

Women played an important role as both consumers and producers of Germany's new national literature, provoking renewed efforts to restrict them to the private sphere. A study of all German novels published between 1815 and 1820 estimates that women wrote approximately one fourth of the texts[10] – far less than the alleged flood of women writers targeted in contemporary polemics, but still more than the stereotypical image of Biedermeier domesticity would lead us to expect. In the following chapter I will introduce works by five of these writers: Caroline de la Motte Fouqué, Henriette Frölich, Karoline von Woltmann, Johanna Schopenhauer, and Annette von Droste-Hülshoff. The first four writers occupy a marginal place at best in current literary histories, while Droste-Hülshoff is better known for her later work. I have chosen works by each author that are set in the historical present or very recent past, and which focus on events that take place primarily in Germany or in revolutionary France. In doing so, I want to correct the common assumption that women writers of the Biedermeier period were interested primarily in private concerns of love, marriage, and the family. The works demonstrate that at least some women writers of the early Restoration used their fiction as a way of coming to terms with the recent Revolution and of seeking orientation in its wake. In doing so they carved out a place in the public discourse that was otherwise denied them by virtue of their gender. Conversely, the novels about the seemingly private spheres of love and the family are often coded ways of commenting on the political situation. Like women writers around 1800, the novelists of the early Restoration occupy a broad spectrum of political positions, ranging from qualified support of the Restoration to absolute rejection of all that it represents.[11] It is in their responses to Germany's political fragmentation that these writers differ most sharply. Nascent nationalism confronts the cosmopolitan legacy of the Enlightenment as authors use their novels to explore conflicting models of collective identity, and to rethink gender roles within these imagined communities.

CAROLINE DE LA MOTTE FOUQUÉ: ROMANTIC NATIONALISM CONFRONTS MODERNITY

Like Sophie Mereau-Brentano, Caroline Schlegel-Schelling, and Dorothea Schlegel, Caroline de la Motte Fouqué (1775–1831) made her way into literary history primarily as a footnote to the career of her more famous husband. Yet she was a prolific author in her own right, publishing twenty novels and several volumes of stories in a career that stretched over nearly three decades.[12] The daughter of a Prussian nobleman, Caroline was actually married twice: first to Friedrich von Rochow, who died in 1799, and then in 1803 to Friedrich de la Motte Fouqué, the popular romantic author of the novella *Undine* (1811) and another dozen *Ritterromane*, tales of chivalry set in an idealized medieval world. Her early work also shows the influence of the romantic period, but the theme that captures her most sustained interest is the French Revolution. A series of historical novels written between 1812 and 1824 provide an ongoing commentary on recent and current events in France and Germany from the perspective of a conservative German noblewoman.

In *Magie der Natur: Eine Revolutions-Geschichte* [The Magic of Nature: A Story of the Revolution] (1812), Fouqué paints a sympathetic portrait of French aristocrats forced into exile.[13] Fouqué makes no secret of her anti-revolutionary sentiments, reserving particular scorn for the revolting masses: "they are the dirty scum spewn out by fermenting thoughts."[14] From the opening image of the quiet Rhône river flowing through a land convulsed with political chaos, Fouqué suggests that the Revolution perverts the natural order of things and creates "vulgar people, who sully the earth with their shame" (101). The mob forces the Marquis de Villeroi out of his ancestral home and sends him fleeing with his twin daughters, Marie and Antonie, into Switzerland and Germany, where they meet other family members and acquaintances. Much of the novel concentrates on the romantic entanglements of the exiled aristocrats, while Fouqué also uses the marquis's obsession with mesmerism and the occult to explore this familiar romantic topos. In the end, the revised French constitution of 1795 enables the aristocrats to return to France. The marquis finds a country that has grown calmer, but even more alienating, in that the new social order has been ratified by law. The result is a profound sense of disorientation in the old aristocrat: "The Marquis felt the push of time's forward progress, but he could not remember where he himself was standing!" (219). With this insight into time's relentless advance, Fouqué identifies an ambivalence that will remain at the heart of her subsequent treatments of the Revolution and its aftermath: while she condemns the Revolution as an unnatural aberration in the order of things, she nevertheless accepts historical change as inevitable and irrevocable: "That which is old will not return" (80). The question for the conservative aristocrat, then, will be how to preserve or rejuvenate old values in a new era without clinging rigidly to an outmoded vision of the past, or surrendering completely to the fashion of the present.

While *Magie der Natur* ends with the final outcome of the revolutionary years still in doubt, *Edmunds Wege und Irrwege* [Edmund's Ways and Byways] (1815) ends with an unabashed celebration of Napoleon's defeat. Fouqué moves the setting of this three-volume novel from France to Germany, and traces the development of the eponymous hero from the completion of his university studies in 1806 until the eve of his marriage in 1814. Yet Fouqué also links the protagonist's personal fortunes to the political events of the Napoleonic years.[15] Edmund is a tall, handsome aristocrat who spends much of the novel in a bad mood. His personal malaise coincides with Germany's national humiliation at the time of the Napoleonic occupation. "Edmund felt the deepest contempt for his age. The external rift split open his breast too."[16] Six years and several hundred pages only intensify the sense of Germany's hopeless situation. Yet by this time Edmund and his compatriots are ready to respond to the Prussian king's call to arms: "A German king calls out to those who have a German heart and German blood" (3:170–71). Napoleon's Russian debacle triggers the chain of events that ultimately end his occupation of Germany. The resolution of the national crisis, in turn, marks the culmination of Edmund's development: "His own fate was resolved together with the task of the time, and the May morning of a new future smiled upon him" (3:221).

On the surface, Fouqué's novel bears a certain resemblance to the tradition of the *Bildungsroman*, as it follows the hero on his uncertain path toward personal maturity and social integration.[17] Like Wilhelm Meister, Edmund becomes interested in a visiting theatre troupe, and like Friedrich of Eichendorff's *Ahnung und Gegenwart* (1815), he is an aristocrat who enters the novel just after leaving the university and gets caught up in the events of the Revolution. Yet the close bond between Edmund and Germany points to an essential difference between Fouqué's novel and the classical *Bildungsroman*, where the goal – at least in theory – is the discovery of one's unique self. Here, in contrast, the protagonist is encouraged to lose himself in the patriotic mission: "The current age demands self-denial for a larger cause. The individual *is obliged* to do everything and *is* nothing" (3:153). This stress on subordination, coupled with an unbridled hatred of the French and a boyish enthusiasm for war as the solution to personal problems, lend an unpleasant taste to Fouqué's novel. Seen as a contribution to the *Bildungsroman*, it has less to do with the humanist legacy of the classical genre and more with subsequent appropriations of the form for a militaristic and chauvinistic nationalism.[18]

Five years after the war's conclusion euphoria yielded to renewed uncertainty, and the sense of common purpose that had briefly united the Germans faded away. "As long as Napoleon was a haunting presence nobody paid any attention to such trivialities," comments one cynical character in Fouqué's *Fragmente aus dem Leben der heutigen Welt* [Fragments from the Life of Today's World] (1820), "then everyone needed everyone else, and people found each other charming. Now the world has what it wanted, and is what it was in the first place!"[19] This unconventional work consists almost exclusively of dialogue between characters living in the historical present. As Fouqué explains in her prefatory comment, segments of the work had appeared independently in the previous year; for publication in novel form she added more material and a narrative frame that gives minimal unity to a desultory text. Whether intentional or not, the open-ended, fragmentary form captures the general mood of modern disorientation that stands in sharp contrast to the triumphant teleology of *Edmunds Wege und Irrwege*.[20]

The central figure Julian, a veteran of "Europe's earnest battle for freedom" (4), has returned home to discover that he feels like an alien in his native land. In a series of conversations, Julian, his old friend Irene, and their acquaintances touch on a variety of topical issues: the state of the current theatre, disobedient children, student Germanophiles, and the emerging Goethe cult. Among the minor characters the mood is one of *Weltschmerz* and general exhaustion. Against these weary misanthropes Julian stands out as the champion of old-fashioned German virtue, who is distressed to find his friends captivated by foreign customs and imported tastes. In one passage Julian singles out an old gardener as the healthy German counterpart to modern decadence: "There is something characteristic about the mindset of the genuine German *Bürger*, something that one never encounters elsewhere, so – how should I put it? – so solid and deep!" (78). Significantly, however, Fouqué does not let Julian have the last word. Irene counters his nostalgia for an idealized past with an insistence on the inevitability of change. Respect for the old has its place, but sentimental yearning for the past cannot be permitted to obscure present needs.

Fouqué concludes this collection of fragments in celebration of peace, love, and nature, but the pervasive mood within the text is far less serene. The same is true of *Die beiden Freunde* [The Two Friends] (1824), Fouqué's last novel about the Revolution. Here again she introduces the motif of the problematic homecoming: the novel begins as young Count Dominique returns to France from England in the fall of 1814 to bury his father on the family estate. Napoleon is in exile, the long years of revolutionary turmoil seem over, and the process of reclaiming the past can begin. Of course, the reader knows that the calm is deceptive: within a few months Napoleon escapes from Elba, rallies his own troops, and resumes his role as the Emperor of France, only to suffer final defeat at Waterloo. It is in the course of this tumultuous year that Fouqué's story of conflict between personal friendship and political beliefs unfolds. The Marquis Alphonse, an outspoken Bonapartist, has been banned from France by the new Bourbon government. In defiance of the ban, Alphonse has secretly entered the country, in part to reestablish contact with his former fiancée Cecilia, but also to work in the underground resistance that will soon topple the Restoration regime. The conflict begins when he requests asylum in the castle of Count Dominique, a cousin and boyhood friend, but also an ardent supporter of the royalist cause. Dominique reluctantly agrees out of loyalty to his friend and concern for Cecilia, whose royalist mother has forbidden her to marry the republican Alphonse. The novel reaches its climax when Alphonse faces execution by royalists on the eve of Napoleon's reentry into Paris. For a moment it seems as though only Dominique can rescue his old friend, and he again faces the choice between personal loyalty and political commitment. In the end Alphonse escapes without Dominique's help, only to die several months later in a hopeless battle against the resurgent royalist army. This time the Revolution is really over. Dominique becomes active in the Restoration government, marries, and returns again to rebuild his ruined estate.

If we look at this novel in terms of Fouqué's earlier representations of the Revolution, we find a far greater degree of ambivalence regarding the assessment of the events. As in the past, her sympathies seem weighted against the Revolution and in favor of the Restoration, yet she goes out of her way to avoid the harsh contrast between good and evil evident in earlier works. The most ardent royalist in the novel is Cecilia's mother, Frau von Harville, and yet she is depicted as a rigid ideologue willing to sacrifice the happiness of her child for the sake of her political designs. In a direct echo of the philosophy expressed in *Edmunds Wege und Irrwege,* Harville insists on an absolute distinction between public service and private desires: "Personal relationships recede ever further, as, increasingly, the interests of politics take complete command" (2:157).[21] In the earlier novel, Fouqué placed these sentiments in the mouth of Frau von Norbert, a commanding matriarchal figure who leads an exemplary life, whereas Frau von Harville emerges fully discredited, "withered, cold, petrified" (3:206). At the same time, Fouqué depicts the Bonapartist Marquis Alphonse as a dashing hero full of the highest, if misguided, idealism. In a letter cited by Harville to prove his treasonous sentiments, Alphonse even utters a ringing denouncement of the entire Restoration that cannot have gone unnoticed by Fouqué's German readers. "Do people really believe," he questions, "tell me, *can* they believe that they can sing us back to sleep with that old lullaby about legitimacy and feudal aristocracy? No, time has long since flown past the heap of dark illusions; no one reaches for the mist of passing clouds. Why the hypocrisy?" (1:105).

Between these extremes stands Count Dominique, a moody aristocrat in the mold of Count Edmund, who proves himself capable of both personal loyalty and public service, and an older baron, who features as Dominique's mentor and the voice of reason in heated political debates. These debates among the royalists turn on the question of whether or not a constitutional monarchy represents an adequate solution for the Restoration government. Those on the right insist that any move toward greater democracy will reopen the door toward revolutionary chaos, but the baron cautions against such reactionary zeal. At times, he contends, one is forced to adjust one's point of view in accordance with experience: "'Insight into the irrevocable teaches our desires to be silent,' he said after a short pause, 'and to follow the tangled path of time with modest selflessness'" (1:125). But in what direction is the "path of time" moving? For large portions of this novel Fouqué exploits the ambivalence of the historical situation surrounding Napoleon's return in a way that again contrasts with the patriotic certainty that pervades *Edmunds Wege und Irrwege*. With the Bourbons in renewed flight and Napoleon not yet back in Paris, the entire social order is suspended. In this situation a Parisian noblewoman scoffs at Dominique's efforts to rescue Alphonse legally from execution: "What is legal at this point in time?" (3:62). Dominique falls into the hands of a Bonapartist lawyer, who voices the same sentiment: "'Today is a day of lawlessness'" (3:130). This time Dominique takes advantage of the situation, shoots his captor, and flees, but we soon find him preaching the virtues of royalist loyalty to an extremely skeptical fisher. "'Yes, that sounds as if it were true,' complained the fisher, 'but when you speak differently with different reasons, that sounds true too'" (3:137).

Fouqué uses the confusion of this specific historical moment to raise larger questions about the general course of history. Napoleon's return seems to signal that history moves in a series of senseless repetitions: "Is the illusion about to start all over again?" (3:116). Yet Dominique insists that Napoleon cannot regain the position he once held: "The wheel of fortune never runs backwards! . . . The same thing does not happen again in the course of a lifetime. Napoleon's hour is past" (3:99–100). In context, this passage insists on the ultimate futility of Napoleon's effort to regain power, but the same historical principle also identifies a central challenge to the postwar government's attempt to restore an essentially feudal order to new legitimacy. As in the past, Fouqué seems to encourage a balance between respect for tradition and understanding of the need for modest reform. In his ability to combine both, Dominique stands as an exemplary figure. "'By heaven, Count,'" exclaims one admirer, "'you are going to summon up a new nobility.' 'Or regenerate the old, responded Dominique,'" a thought that in retrospect seems to

reveal to him "the key to the great secret of the age" (3:159). In her
most optimistic moments, Fouqué proposes a revitalization of the old
feudal order in accordance with the demands of the current time,
but here and elsewhere she reveals an acute awareness of the
inherent difficulties in the project.

Where do women fit into Fouqué's political novels of contemporary events? Most of her work focuses on male protagonists who play
an active role in the public sphere, as we might expect from a
woman whose work deals with the traditionally male concerns of
war and politics. "Dear Edmund," cautions Frau Norbert on the eve
of the German uprising against Napoleon, "the new world will need
men" (3:77). Men, in turn, need their women, but only as foils to
their own development. Three of the novels discussed thus far
conclude with a marriage that promises peace to an exhausted hero.
"The old miracles had disappeared from the earth," writes Fouqué
in conclusion to *Magie der Natur*, "but love created new ones every
day. The magic of Marie's family heritage blossomed in her in such a
unique way that it tied her husband's heart to hers with ever tighter
bonds" (234–35). Edmund seals the German victory over France by
marrying young Agnes, and Count Dominique marries another
woman named Agnes at the end of *Die beiden Freunde*. Yet other
women in these novels play decidedly less conventional roles.
"Antonie is distant from everyone, from me and her sister too" (38)
warns the abbess when her father comes to pick her up at the
beginning of *Magie der Natur*, and the passionate visionary does
indeed stand apart from her fellow exiled aristocrats until she
commits suicide with a dagger on a riverbank – an allusion to
Karoline von Günderrode? – in the novel's final pages. In *Die beiden
Freunde* the demise of the tragic Marquis Alphonse undermines the
health of one woman and the sanity of another. Before Edmund
settles down with his adolescent bride he incurs lasting guilt by
refusing to trust the love of Alinde, a woman trapped in a marriage
of convenience to an older Italian count. Edmund's moral failure, in
other words, arises from the fact that he chooses *not* to continue his
affair with a married woman, hardly the sentiment we might expect
from a Biedermeier author.

Even less conventional in the light of the extreme gender polariza-
tion we noted in Körner's popular lyrics is the extent to which
Fouqué defends the direct participation of women in politics and
war. In an important discussion among the exiles in *Magie der Natur*,

one of the men insists that women have no place in the public sphere, "indeed, they have no other fatherland than the narrow space enclosed by the four walls of their household activities . . . they will never understand politics" (174). Two of the women disagree sharply, pointing out that any number of women have ruled wisely in the past, and insisting that women are biologically capable of any social skill: "'Never,' retorted Viktorine, 'will I be convinced that we are excluded from any sphere of human activity'" (177). Fouqué leaves the argument unresolved in this novel, but Frau Norbert of *Edmunds Wege und Irrwege* provides a good example of a woman whose political activities extend far beyond the narrow confines of her domestic duty. She not only rallies the Germans to fight against Napoleon, but personally organizes the underground resistance. Certainly her aristocratic status gives her access to a much wider range of activity than that of a bourgeois woman. In addition, she remains loyal to her family, whose members fight together for the German cause. It is presumably Frau von Harville's disregard for her own daughter in the name of a higher cause that discredits her political activity in *Die beiden Freunde*, and not her engagement in the royalist cause itself.

The most intriguing case of a politically active woman in Fouqué's fiction is Elisabeth Rochefoucault, the title figure in *Das Helden-mädchen aus der Vendée* [The Heroic Maiden of the Vendée] (1816). Elisabeth – pale, shy, blond, and beautiful – disguises herself as a man to fight with the royalist armies of the Vendée against the Revolution. In doing so she goes far beyond Frau Norbert's discreet efforts to organize future soldiers in an all-male army, venturing into a realm that Sara Seldorf's father had already discredited as "unnatural" for a woman. The topos of the young woman disguised as a soldier recurred frequently in fiction of the Napoleonic era, most famously in the Russian Nadezhda Durova's *The Cavalry Maiden* (1836), but also in Germany. The woman's entry into the male domain "was not necessarily seen as blurring the distinction between the sexes,"[22] yet Fouqué's fictional representations of male and female cross-dressing during the French Revolution *do* seem to reflect considerable cultural anxiety about "natural" gender differences. In the slightly later novella entitled *Laura: Eine Begebenheit aus der französischen Revolution* [Laura: An Occurrence from the French Revolution] (1821), Fouqué includes a vivid description of the women who marched from Paris to Versailles, whom she derides as a "repulsive group of drunken, reeling wenches."[23] Still more shocking is the fact that "men are disguised in women's clothing so that they can commit their crimes all the more safely under this cover" (208). If, from Fouqué's conservative perspective, the Revolution itself violates the natural order of things and causes women to act like men, it is still more perverse to find men dressing up like women to commit criminal acts.

How, then, can Fouqué simultaneously condemn revolutionary "perverts" and glorify her cross-dressing heroine? Most obviously, Elisabeth Rochefoucault fights for the just cause; what for the revolutionaries represents unnatural madness is for the royalist a heroic response to a time that is out of joint. Even so, the female soldier is an exceptional individual, something that troubles Elisabeth in one of her few introspective moments: "why has the unnaturalness of the age thrust me, of all people, alone, onto this forbiddingly steep path?"[24] Precisely this resistance to her potentially unnatural role as Amazon testifies to her mental health, in terms of the gender stereotypes of the period, and Fouqué goes out of her way to emphasize that Elisabeth does not enjoy dressing up like a man. "She wrapped the horse's reins around a low, half-burned branch, and, with trembling fingers and with loud, almost suffocating heartbeats, began the unaccustomed, frequently repellent, change of clothes" (1:88). Once in battle she remains painfully conscious of the potentially transgressive status of her military adventure. An outraged Elisabeth calls out to her fellow royalist soldiers as they begin to retreat: "'Are you men, and afraid of danger? I am a girl . . . is nature so upside-down that France's men crawl away from women?'" (2:195). Another factor that permits Elisabeth's military heroism is her largely personal motivation, namely her passionate admiration for her cousin Prince Talmont. In addition, Elisabeth does not act like the "repulsive wenches" of the lower class. Even in the heat of battle she remains smart in her attractively fitting uniform, and her "fighting" itself seems to consist largely in waving the flag and cheering others into battle.

One interesting question remains in assessing this heroic girl: why does her relationship with Prince Talmont remain unconsummated? The modern reader might assume that their relationship as first cousins would prohibit any romantic entanglement, but this proves no obstacle in many novels of the period. Fouqué gives every indication, moreover, that the cousins are potential lovers. Elisabeth is captivated by Talmont's charm at their first meeting, follows him unswervingly into battle, and shares a quiet moment with him that seals their union: "A ray of higher life shot through them both, and they belonged to one another for eternity" (1:133). Unfortunately for both, Talmont is captured at the end of volume one and executed by a firing squad, leaving Elisabeth to mourn him for the entire second volume. Fouqué could have had the two lovers marry immediately after they declared their love, but I suspect she does not because she needs her heroine to remain a virgin, just as Schiller made Johanna's chastity a prerequisite for her inspirational intervention into military affairs in *Die Jungfrau von Orleans* [The Maid of Orleans] (1801). Fouqué also frees Elisabeth from her feminine duties to a specific man so that she can become a saint for the royalist cause. As one fellow soldier puts it on the battlefield, she represents "France's virginal honor!!" (2:199).

Thus Fouqué's depiction of gender roles displays an unexpected complexity that parallels the occasional subtlety of her political views. As a conservative monarchist she often vilifies revolutionaries and glorifies German patriots and French royalists, but she also recognizes the inevitability of historical change. In reflective moments when her characters are not busy purging their native soil from revolutionary "scum," they often seem uprooted, disoriented, and uncertain of their role in a post-revolutionary world. Perhaps it is Fouqué's recognition of the fundamental instability of the social order that enables her to free certain female characters from the fetters that bind them to their "natural" supporting roles. While Fouqué is hardly the sort of feminist activist who demands equal rights for all women at all times, she does allow a few exceptional women to bend the rules in exceptional circumstances, provided that they remain loyal to their families, act with decorum, and – in the case of Elisabeth Rochefoucault – do not particularly enjoy masquerading as a man.

HENRIETTE FRÖLICH [JERTA]: A COSMOPOLITAN IN KENTUCKY

It would be hard to imagine a more extreme contrast in political opinions than that between the conservative monarchist Fouqué and the radical democrat Henriette Frölich (1768–1833). In her only novel, *Virginia, oder die Kolonie von Kentucky: Mehr Wahrheit als Dichtung* [Virginia, or the Colony in Kentucky: More Truth than Poetry]

(1820), published under the pen name Jerta, the heroine is born in Paris on July 14, 1789, and grows up fervently supporting the republican cause. She idolizes Napoleon, excuses the excesses of Robespierre and the Terror, and criticizes the British and Continental forces that seek to crush the Revolution. With the defeat of Napoleon in 1814 and the return of the Bourbons to power, Virginia flees France and emigrates to America. Here she helps found a utopian community in Kentucky, which realizes the dream of freedom and equality that had been defeated in Europe. The hope this idyllic community represents reflects a correspondingly bitter critique of the post-revolutionary Europe left behind. " 'The people's cause is lost,' " says Virginia, " 'and the cause of the princes is victorious, after twenty years of bloodshed.' "[25] Writing in the reactionary climate of Berlin at the time of the Carlsbad Decrees, Frölich is careful to place her radical views in the mouth of a French heroine far removed from Germany to a distant Kentucky. Yet she manages to make her message to the German readers clear enough. Although she laments the French defeat, she praises the courage and resolution of the German resistance, and hopes that Germany one day might complete the Revolution that the French have abandoned: "May their sense of strength never again fall asleep, so that one day they will perhaps succeed at what France desired in vain" (87). The Kentucky colony stands as a temporary realization of the ideals that Germany should attain in the future.

Given Frölich's uncompromising commitment to revolutionary idealism, it is not surprising that this novel attracted attention in the former German Democratic Republic, where it was republished in 1963. In an enthusiastic afterword to this edition, Gerhard Steiner celebrates Frölich's vision of an early socialist community, and counters the possible charge of escapism to America by pointing out that the proletarian movement in Europe was not yet fully enough developed to permit radical political action at home.[26] Yet in his effort to claim Frölich as an early ally in the movement that led to the formation of a German socialist state, Steiner obscures certain aspects of the text that do not quite fit the mold. If we reverse the historical perspective and view Frölich's novel as growing out of the tradition of German domestic fiction, we see surprising affinities to the conservative ideals of a previous generation in a novel that offers outspoken support of the Revolution.

Virginia's father is Leo von Montorin, a member of the landed aristocracy who abandons his law studies to fight for the American colonies against England. After returning to France he avoids the efforts of his uncle, a count, to place him in a position at court, and retires instead to a small inherited estate. Here he distributes land to the peasants, removes all signs of servitude, and relates to his subjects as a friend and advisor: "The highly educated man, whose scintillating conversation was admired by courtiers, was as simple as these children of nature when he was with them . . . Thus he strode like a demi-god among these oppressed, neglected people, and a new morning broke in this little friendly valley" (20). As the language of this passage indicates, Leo von Montorin rules as a benevolent patriarch, and not as a member of a revolutionary band of brothers. The feudal lord grants favors to his "children," who in turn worship him as a minor deity. When the Revolution breaks out, Leo von Montorin voluntarily gives up all privileges of his estate, and as a result his little valley remains an island of peace while France is wracked with blood and turmoil. For all her support for the Revolution, Frölich suggests that if there had been more nobles like Montorin, the Revolution might never have been necessary in the first place. In this regard Frölich's novel is closer in sentiment to the progressive conservatism of LaRoche or Wolzogen than to the more radical views of Huber or Mereau.

In accordance with his progressive beliefs, Montorin marries for love across class lines. His decision to marry Klara, the daughter of a businessman in Aix, provokes the wrath of his uncle the count, who has his disobedient nephew arrested and imprisoned in the Bastille. The pregnant Klara, in Paris in search of her husband, goes into labor as her brother Victor storms the Bastille. In a burst of patriotism Montorin decides to name his daughter Virginia, after the woman whose death broke the tyranny of the patrician decemvirate and brought freedom to ancient Rome. Given the dramatic – if somewhat implausible – circumstances of her birth, it is not surprising that Virginia should dedicate her life to the cause of freedom: "Could I ever stand to hear people hurl abuse at the 14th of July? . . . No; Virginia, the first-born daughter of freedom, must die in a free land" (29).

The reunited family returns to Montorin's idyllic estate, where Virginia spends her formative years. While she insists that her parents enjoyed an exceptionally happy marriage, she acknowledges that the relationship was not completely free of tension. When Leo von Montorin's wife forbids him to enlist in the revolutionary armies, he keeps a stiff upper lip in her presence, but confides his dissatisfaction to his daughter. While he chafes at his enforced inaction, Virginia understands. Even as a small girl she rejects her mother's puppets in favor of her father's illustrated world history. In her, Montorin finds a malleable subject whom he can mold into his own image, and she responds with boundless love for him and the republican fatherland.

At this point it is useful to recall Lynn Hunt's study of *The Family Romance of the French Revolution*. She interprets the killing of King Louis XVI as a symbolic act that transferred power to the band of patriotic brothers loyal to the French nation.[27] Frölich's novel *Virginia* offers the seemingly contradictory combination of faith in the benefits of enlightened patriarchal rule and open sympathy for the fraternal republican order. The source of this paradoxical blend, in my opinion, lies in the double standard central to republican ideology: the man enters the public sphere as an equal member of the band of brothers, but he becomes king of the castle when he returns home to his family. We observed just this tension between public fraternity and private patriarchy in *Die Familie Seldorf*. Like Therese Huber before her, Henriette Frölich begins from a position of sympathy for the Revolution, but goes on to explore the inherent contradictions of republican beliefs from a feminist perspective.

To a certain extent, Frölich makes her heroine into a tomboy. Virginia identifies more with her father than her mother and has a "manly" appreciation of martial valor. As the proud father puts it, "'there is more Roman spirit and masculine strength in this girl's soul than in many of our comrades in arms'" (95). Identification with her father allows Virginia to participate at least vicariously in the revolutionary struggle. Moreover, Virginia laments the fact that women are remembered in history only as passive sacrifices, not active participants: "Unfortunate woman! The man fights for his opinion and clears a path for himself; the woman is not supposed to have an opinion" (11). Virginia *does* have opinions, most notably in the "masculine" spheres of history and politics, yet she stops short of following the example of Sara Seldorf or Elisabeth Rochefoucault in actually joining the army. "'Women do not belong in battle,'" admonishes her father, "'their participation in martial events is unnatural, and can only be excused when they are forced to do so against their will'" (89). Virginia reluctantly accepts her father's advice, and remains behind when he enlists. The fact that she is a woman excludes her from the political party that promises equal rights for all citizens.

Virginia's deference to her father's authority carries over to her boundless admiration of Napoleon. She astonishes her family by cutting off all her hair when she hears that Napoleon is in Egypt, vowing to remain shorn until he returns safely. She then surprises herself with an involuntary gesture of obeisance when he passes through her village: "I, the born Republican and proud of freedom, equality, and the value of human life, knelt before him, unaware of what I was doing, and laid the little basket with wreaths at his feet" (47). Napoleon leaves her in a state of dazed reverence: "My imagination was silent, but I felt myself penetrated by a submissiveness that, with my liberal education, I did not even feel for my father" (48). In other words, Virginia's Napoleon-worship is a heightened form of her father-fixation. The ambivalence of her feminism in the private sphere shifts now into her attitude toward public politics, and as a result, the staunch believer in human equality finds herself in awe of an emperor.

Napoleon's days as ruler of France are numbered, however, and Frölich intertwines historical events with her fictional character's personal development. While at boarding school Virginia's brother Emil becomes close friends with a young man named Mucius, another fervent supporter of the Revolution who soon meets and falls in love with Virginia. Her father approves of the match, and proposes a formal engagement just before Mucius and Emil enlist. Bad news returns quickly from the front: Emil dies of an infected wound, and Mucius is missing in action and presumed dead as well. Upon hearing of her son's death, Virginia's mother soon dies of grief. Meanwhile Napoleon has been defeated in Russia and the Continental armies threaten Paris. Virginia's father reenlists to defend the fatherland, but it is too late: he is killed in the final battle as the French capitulate in March, 1814.

Left alone in Paris, Virginia undergoes experiences that again recall those of Sophie von Sternheim and Agnes von Lilien. Decadent Paris stands in for the petty German courts that had vexed the earlier heroines, and Virginia is disgusted to see its citizens squander their time on frivolous entertainment when the Republic is in its death throes: "It hurt me, my heart bled" (92). Her father's brother, a royalist count, returns from emigration to Paris. Anxious to consolidate his power in the Restoration government, the count forbids Virginia to mourn for her republican father and tries to force her to marry her cousin. Thus the old motif of the innocent woman imperiled by reactionary Rococo nobles resurfaces in the Restoration, but now they are no longer relics of a feudal past, but rather harbingers of a future that looms as a nightmarish return of the repressed.

Virginia is older – twenty-four in the spring of 1814 – and more assertive than the previous heroines. She outsmarts her uncle, and with the aid of loyal servants and her father's money escapes Paris and sails to America. When the American ship captain falls in love with her, Virginia remains loyal to the memory of her former fiancé Mucius and again insists on her independence. While the captain returns to France in search of information about Virginia's relatives, she embarks on a journey through the wilderness to Niagara Falls. She plans to spend her birthday in private contemplation at the Falls, but happens to run into – Mucius! The reunion is another wildly implausible moment in a novel whose subtitle promises to outdo Goethe by offering "more truth than poetry," but Frölich is clearly willing to sacrifice verisimilitude in the name of political commentary. In finding Mucius on her birthday, Virginia finds a substitute for all that she has left behind in Europe: "he is father, brother, friend to me. And I have my fatherland again, for where Mucius breathes, there is my world!" (150). In private terms, then, we have the familiar pattern in which the woman marries a father-surrogate. Mucius offers Virginia the opportunity to reestablish her childhood paradise. In political terms, Mucius represents revolutionary France and its ideals, now transported to the American wilderness.

Frölich devotes the final quarter of her novel to the description of the community established in Kentucky. It is a deliberately cosmopolitan group, composed of Americans, of both European and African descent, and also British, French, Italians, and Germans. The new republic promises liberty and justice for all, and Virginia often feels as if she is living in the Golden Age or the Garden of Eden. She remains poignantly aware, however, that its very existence is due to the fact that the situation in Europe is unbearable, and likely to remain so indefinitely: "the great struggle is not yet over, not by a long shot; it can go on for generations" (201). The new American government would seem to offer a progressive alternative

to Restoration Europe, but Virginia withdraws from active participation in the new democracy to live in largely self-sufficient isolation
in the wilderness. Gerhard Steiner contends that Frölich improves
on the American model by founding a proto-communist community
where private property is banned.[28] The use of money is indeed
forbidden in the colony, and all goods are shared in common. Yet
the break with capital is not complete: the community keeps the
fortune Virginia inherited from her noble father in case they need
cash in the future, and the property itself was purchased by money
won in the German lottery. Thus the communist colony is possible
only because of money gained from the efficient management of an
old aristocratic estate and from the random luck of the draw.

Within the community itself the treatment of women, blacks, and
Native American Indians is particularly interesting. In describing
Mucius's constitution for the society, Virginia notes proudly that
women are each to receive half a vote in the assembly. This semi-
enfranchisement was certainly more than American women received
for another hundred years, but by the same token, it falls short of
demands for complete legal equality that had already been voiced
during the early years of the French Revolution. In the colony all
children are to be raised equally until age twelve, at which time boys
take up advanced academic courses and ancient languages, while the
girls receive instruction in homemaking, sewing, and weaving. Here
too Frölich envisions a rather half-hearted feminism, which combines a desire for universal emancipation with a Rousseauistic
willingness to restrict women to their "natural" sphere in the home.

One of the more unusual features for a German novel of the
period is the attention directed toward the position of blacks in
America. Near the beginning of her stay Virginia notes that the
European traveler is at first struck by the ethnic and racial diversity
in the country. In keeping with her generally liberal views, Virginia
laments the oppression of the American blacks, but also praises their
diligence and predicts that they will achieve equality in fifty years. A
freed slave named John accompanies her with members of his family
on the trip to Niagara Falls, and later a group of black settlers set up
their own community within the larger colony. When the settlers first
arrive in Kentucky they are overwhelmed with joy: "This moment
made us into *one* people, all differences of color, homeland, education
were annihilated; we all became brothers [*sic!*] with equal rights and
equal duties" (175). Equal in theory, perhaps, but as Virginia has

pointed out just a few pages earlier, the extensive property and cattle granted the black community will enable them to live *almost* on equal footing with the whites ["*fast* uns gleich leben können"] (170; my emphasis). As it turns out, the blacks receive precisely the same sort of patriarchal condescension that Virginia's father has used with his subjects in France: "We treat them as brothers, and they regard the men almost as fathers" (182).

A similar condescension marks Virginia's initial comments about the Native Americans, whom she regards in typical European fashion as noble savages, "children of nature" (147). If we consider that many of her American contemporaries would have branded the Indians as heathen barbarians, however, Virginia appears relatively liberal: "These original Americans that people call primitives are extremely good-natured and their customs shame those of the Europeans" (185). While the neighboring Chickasaw tribe complains of harsh treatment from the Spaniards to the south, the members of the Kentucky colony inoculate them against smallpox. For all her praise of these Native Americans, however, Virginia recognizes that their civilization is in decline. "Forced out by the Europeans and neighboring peoples, by the sword and hunger, reduced by smallpox and intoxicating drink to an insignificant little group, the survivors flee like frightened animals deeper and deeper into barren wastelands" (186). With remarkable prescience, Frölich makes her protagonist aware that the European utopia in the American wilderness will lead to the destruction of the native culture: "At home in our community we play the happy Greek life of the child, but here in these wastelands they mourn for a ruined world" (186).

KAROLINE VON WOLTMANN: COSMOPOLITAN CONSPIRATORS AT HOME

While Caroline de la Motte Fouqué produced a steady stream of novels and stories, Karoline von Woltmann (1782–1847) seems to have needed active encouragement to write at all. She confesses in the preface to her second novel, *Maria und Walpurgis* (1817/18), that she agreed only reluctantly to resume a writing career that had begun and ended more than a decade earlier with her first novel, *Euphrosyne* (1804).[29] Her third and final novel, *Die Bildhauer*, would not appear until 1829. Karoline was first married to the writer and publisher Karl Müchler, whom she divorced in 1804, and then to the historian and novelist Karl Ludwig von Woltmann.[30] It was upon his urging that she began work on *Maria und Walpurgis* in 1813, although the completed two-volume work would not be published until several years later. Like many other novels of the period, *Maria und Walpurgis* follows the romantic entanglements of its two protagonists as they negotiate between their own desires and the machinations of an older generation. What makes the novel remarkable is the way in which Woltmann links the private fortunes of her heroines to the fate of a secret republican society. Whereas Frölich settled her utopian community in the wilds of Kentucky, Woltmann's characters spin the web of their clandestine organization in the heart of feudal Germany.

The novel opens as Maria and Walpurgis, two young aristocrats, journey from the Rhine to Hamburg. There Maria's father, Count Fehr, awaits the two friends with plans to put the final touches on their education. As their carriage passes through the Harz mountains, one of the horses breaks a leg, and they are forced to make an unplanned stop. While waiting for new horses at a nearby inn, the impatient Walpurgis asks the old innkeeper if he will guide them through the spring night to the mysteriously illuminated ruins of the nearby Burg Ilsenstein. Here they stumble upon a meeting of a secret society. This chance encounter changes the lives of the two women. Maria falls in love with an eloquent young man named Alfred, who explains the purpose of the society to its members, while Walpurgis develops a crush on Bruno, another young man, who leads the intruders back down the mountain after they are discovered. By the time they arrive in Hamburg the two women can think of little else than the mysterious strangers and their secret society.

Maria and Walpurgis later discover that Count Fehr not only sympathizes with the goals of the society, but is also its current leader. In his view, humankind is engaged in a gradual process of refinement: "'In the course of history I have seen humanity strive ever upwards from a state much worse than animals to human and spiritual dignity'" (1:191). The task of the society is to aid humanity in its progress toward "truth, freedom, and above all, insight and love" (1:256). The credo combines traditional Christian virtues with Enlightenment optimism. In keeping with the spirit of freemasonry, membership is open to both the nobility and the bourgeoisie.[31] Yet members of the society do not advocate the abolition of class distinctions. They want rather to make people more satisfied with their lot, "to prevent higher education from enticing the lower classes of civil society to go beyond their traditional profession" (1:296). Unlike later writers of the *Vormärz,* Woltmann does not champion the virtues of the lower classes. Indeed, she goes out of her way to underscore the difference between the refined members of the secret society and the uncouth peasants. The meeting on the Ilsenstein takes place on the eve of Ascension Day, and, while traveling through the countryside, Maria and Walpurgis observe people dancing around bonfires in a Christian variation of an older pagan ritual. Although the members of the society also gather around a fire, they maintain a dignified composure. It is their noble comportment, not their noble birth, that distinguishes these men from their crude counterparts.

The concept of an alliance between the aristocracy and educated members of the bourgeoisie for the purpose of improving society without changing its basic class structure corresponds to the ideals of Weimar Classicism, which is hardly surprising, given that Karoline's second husband was a professor of history at Jena, a personal acquaintance of Goethe, and a contributor to Schiller's literary journal *Die Horen.* By the time Woltmann urged his wife to begin work on her novel, however, some twenty years had passed since the heyday of Weimar Classicism, and Germany was about to emerge from several years of French occupation. As a result, the members of Karoline von Woltmann's secret society profess nationalist sentiments that would be alien to the enlightened aristocrats of Goethe's Tower Society. We learn from Alfred's initial speech on the Ilsenstein that the society was founded by Germans, and he takes pains to elaborate their unique qualifications for leadership:

In our districts [*Gauen*], which were never conquered by a more civilized people, *Bildung* developed in quiet succession of its own accord; no violent impulse, no unnaturally grafted branch destroyed its strong stock. Here the native language resounds purely through forest shadows, above meadows, and on mountain heights. (1:31)

The references to the Germans' special status as an *Urvolk* with an uncorrupted *Ursprache* paraphrase ideas found in Herder's *Ideen zur Philosophie der Geschichte der Menschheit* [Ideas Concerning the Philosophy of the History of Humankind] (1784–91) and Fichte's *Reden an die deutsche Nation* so closely that it is difficult to imagine that

Woltmann was unfamiliar with their works. Taken on their own terms, the claims are dubious at best; as E. J. Hobsbawm has observed, "the mystical identification of nationality with a sort of platonic idea of the language, existing behind and above all its variant and imperfect versions, is much more characteristic of the ideological construction of nationalist intellectuals, of whom Herder is the prophet, than of the actual grassroots users of the idiom."[32] Appeals to the uncorrupted purity of the German people and their language become particularly suspect when viewed in the light of the increasingly xenophobic and anti-Semitic *völkisch* ideology of the nineteenth and early twentieth centuries.[33]

Fortunately, Woltmann's secret society is closer in both history and spirit to Enlightenment tolerance than proto-fascist bigotry, and belief in Germany's special status does not inspire a corresponding hatred of things foreign. Membership in the *Bund* soon expanded to include men of all nations, and the German participants show great respect for foreign culture. Count Fehr encourages Maria and Walpurgis to read world literature, Bruno speaks out openly against the fashionable hatred of the French, and Alfred entertains his guests with a decidedly international cuisine. Alfred sums up the position of the society vis-à-vis nationalism and internationalism in the following manner:

The society arose from the German spirit. It strives to mediate between humanity and the nation. For the former it has one purpose, the purpose of the age, its progressive education toward perfection; for the latter may it be a refuge that preserves united everything noble that its members possess individually. (1:30)

By serving as a repository for the nation's noblest qualities, the society nourishes the kernel of a future collective identity. However, nation-formation is not incompatible with a broader cosmopolitanism in the model that emerges from Woltmann's novel. Indeed, the crystallization of national identity, and even the struggle between individual nations, is part of a larger process through which humanity as a whole progresses.

Thus *Maria und Walpurgis* can be seen as an attempt to rethink the legacy of Weimar Classicism and the European Enlightenment in the light of a new German nationalism. Progressive groups of enlightened aristocrats who have absorbed the values of the middle class feature prominently in Rousseau's *Julie, ou la Nouvelle Héloïse* and

Sophie von LaRoche's *Geschichte des Fräuleins von Sternheim,* but in both cases the characters work their reforms within the circumscribed realm of inherited estates. In contrast, Woltmann envisions an organization that cuts across both class and property lines to create the potential for an entirely new form of national government. Franz von Hohenhoff, an intimate of Count Fehr's family and member of the society, touches on this point when he explains to a disgruntled fellow member that under the current system of government, involvement in public affairs is limited to the aristocracy: "Until we get a public sphere in Germany that activates all social circles, no form of culture will be able to make up for the circumstances that annoy you" (1:205). Franz von Hohenhoff's disparaging reference to culture's inability to mask political inequality is an implicit admission that the efforts of Goethe and Schiller to improve German society through aesthetic education have failed. Without planning to do away with class distinctions altogether, Franz nevertheless conceives of a future society in which members of currently excluded classes could have access to the public sphere. In doing so, Franz hints at a national political organization that could eventually supersede the old feudal order, and it is for this reason that the society suffers relentless persecution from the authorities of Restoration Europe.

Before taking up the fate of the society, however, we need first to consider the role gender plays in Woltmann's thought, as evidenced by the bond between Maria and her father. In many ways their relationship bears a striking resemblance to patterns established in earlier novels by German women. Like Sophie von Sternheim, Maria is named after her deceased mother, and, at least to her doting father, she looks just like his former bride. The real purpose of Count Fehr's plan to put the final touches on Maria's education is to perfect her resemblance to her mother: "'I want to see you, her dear image, at work in the same capacities that your mother once filled, as if she had come back to life for me'" (2:41–42). Maria has no objection, for she idolizes her father: "She loved him with uncommon tenderness, she honored the power that he had over her by means of nature and law" (1:45). After her experience on the Ilsenstein, however, the image of the handsome speaker begins to cloud her formerly uncomplicated relationship with her father. Like Agnes von Lilien, Maria is torn between affection for her father and attraction to a potential husband. What distinguishes Woltmann's novel from previous domestic fiction is the way in which she integrates the daughter's dilemma into the larger political concerns of the text.

While Maria has fallen in love with Alfred, her father has plans to marry her to Bruno, the son of his sister-in-law. To make things more complicated, it soon becomes apparent to all that Bruno is in love with Walpurgis. The baroness actually finds Walpurgis person-ally more sympathetic as a potential daughter-in-law, but is more than willing to sacrifice personal desires to family politics and economic gain. Maria not only possesses great wealth, but stands to inherit considerable property. Hence her marriage to Bruno will ensure that the family estates will remain intact. To this extent, Count Fehr's plans for his daughter's marriage reveal the typical concerns of his social class. Thoroughly unconventional, on the other hand, is his second reason for promoting this marriage: Bruno belongs to the society, and in marrying him, Maria marries into the organization. "You know," writes Count Fehr to Franz von Hohenheim after the formal engagement of Maria to Bruno, "that two relationships bind me to the earth, the one to my daughter and the other to our society. Both have now become one" (1:191). Until this point, all descriptions of the society have referred to it as an exclusively male organization, and there is no indication that Maria's initiation into the association paves the way for Walpurgis or any other woman to join. Instead, Count Fehr wants Maria to take over the position her mother once held. In long walks her father tells her "how her mother, who died young, had spent the short years of her life completely in the spirit of the society. She [Maria] enjoyed the highest feeling for a childish heart, the trust of such a father. She felt herself grounded in respect of her mother, and was driven to continue the life-work of the deceased" (1:298). Exactly what her mother did or what Maria's duties will be remain unclear, but it is certain that she is fascinated by the prospect of participating in some way in the organization so enthusiastically endorsed by Alfred, Franz von Hohenhoff, and her father, particularly since in doing so she will become a worthy successor to her mother.

The central conflict of the novel emerges from this marriage plan. Though Alfred also belongs to the secret society, and would thus seem to pose no objection to Count Fehr's wishes, he is not a member of the upper class, and Fehr's sympathy for the egalitarian society does not go so far that he would allow his only daughter to marry a man of low rank. Maria, for her part, experiences the familiar dilemma intrinsic to the ethos of the nuclear family. On the one hand, she loves Alfred and is loath to accept a marriage to another man, particularly one who is in love with her best friend. On the other hand, Maria adores her father and is incapable of disobedience. Her only hope is that her father will change his mind, but until the novel's final pages he remains stubborn. Fortunately for Maria and Alfred, Count Fehr undergoes a deathbed conversion that solves the problem: "'Yesterday I refused to agree to your marriage with my daughter; today I desire it with my whole heart . . . Death is like youth and love, in that it brooks no prejudice'" (2:260). He dies peacefully, surrounded by family and friends, having blessed the union of his daughter and Alfred. Walpurgis is free to marry Bruno, and the novel concludes with an image of Walpurgis "as the blossoming mother of a new lineage" (2:275).

By linking Maria's marriage to the fate of the society, Woltmann introduces politics into questions of love and the family. At stake are two incompatible concepts of marriage: the older aristocratic arrangement for wealth and property competes with the new stress on mutual love and personal choice. Not surprisingly, Woltmann's sympathies seem squarely aligned with the latter alternative. At a wedding attended by the extended family, Franz von Hohenheim speaks of the lifelong commitment and love required of marriage, a sentiment implicitly opposed to the arranged marriages of the aristocracy. Then Woltmann introduces a subplot in which an English sea captain abandons his arranged bride and proposes to Walpurgis. Eventually he encounters by chance the woman he was to have married and, to his surprise, falls in love with her. The moral of the story is that marriage by personal choice is better than marriage by parental design. The count's decision to bless his daughter's marriage to Alfred marks the final triumph of the new ethos, and completes the image of the society. It is not only open to members of all social classes and all nations, but its members must be united with their spouses by love and not family politics. In this way the new family ethos becomes an integral component of the utopian community.

Sadly enough, however, the secret society has been exposed and destroyed by the time of Fehr's death and Maria's marriage. The seeds of destruction are sown on the same night that introduces Maria and Walpurgis to the society and their future husbands. Count Fehr's old servant Herford accompanies them to the Ilsenstein, and is troubled by the implications of what he overhears: "He wanted to know nothing about secret societies. The sovereign was his lord, the management of worldly matters was left to the authorities, that of spiritual matters was left to the consistory" (1:41). The formerly loyal servant begins to spy on his master, and before long feels compelled to report Fehr's suspicious activity to the authorities. Fehr flees to his ancestral estates in Sweden, but the court rules against him and demands that he be stripped of his property. Meanwhile the society's archive has fallen into the hands of the authorities, and its members are forced into hiding.

Woltmann's novel predates the persecution of the radical student "demagogues" that was triggered by the murder of Kotzebue in 1819, yet it gives a good sense of the repressive atmosphere already present in the early years of the Metternich Restoration. Woltmann does grant a kind of bittersweet consolation to the disastrous events that overtake Count Fehr and the society: Fehr loses direct control of his Swedish estate, but he is allowed to sell it to a close friend of the family, and when he dies he is buried on the property next to his wife. Although the society is officially disbanded, many of the members reassemble on Alfred's island in the Baltic Sea. Here he directs a volunteer coast guard, and as luck would have it, he rescues Maria, Count Fehr, Bruno, and Walpurgis from a storm that overtakes them upon leaving Sweden. While assembled on the island, former members of the society have a chance to look back at what they achieved and to speculate about future developments. " 'We formed a republic,' responded the count, 'Perhaps the task that we set as a goal for ourselves will be imposed on a new part of the world' " (2:215). In the meantime he consoles himself with the conviction that the society will remain an inspiration to future generations. Count Fehr's attempt to give a positive interpretation of the demise of the society cannot conceal the damage that has been done, however; just behind the upbeat ending to the novel we sense a depression even darker than that implicit in Frölich's text. Her colony in Kentucky represented hope for a better society already taking shape in America, whereas Woltmann leaves us with an elegiac look at the past and only a vague hope for the future of her utopian community in Germany.

Taken together, the novels by Fouqué, Frölich, and Woltmann support the contention that "the forging and acceptance of national identities" was a tenuous process during the early Restoration, as regional and class loyalties competed with still-nebulous concepts of the modern state.[34] Three distinct models emerge in the novels considered here. In *Edmunds Wege und Irrwege*, Fouqué celebrates Germany's victory over France, but her other works make clear that she does not share the desire of liberal nationalists for a new, republican form of government. At the opposite extreme stands Frölich's cosmopolitanism, which embraces men and women of all nations, races, and social classes. Yet even Frölich's utopian society has its limitations: the colony in Kentucky retains vestiges of the paternalism, misogyny, and racism it seeks to overcome; it does not resolve the misery of Restoration Europe; and it brings destruction to the Native Americans it displaces in the wilderness. Woltmann steers a middle course between these two options, combining national loyalty with cosmopolitan ideals, but she too indicates that in the foreseeable future any hope of realizing the new social order in Germany remains remote indeed.

Of particular interest in the work of these women writers is the role gender plays in relation to politics. In both *Maria und Walpurgis* and *Virginia* the affectionate marriage stands as an integral part of the utopian society. Virginia not only flees Restoration politics, but also the attempt of her aristocratic uncle to force her into an undesired marriage, and love eventually triumphs over class prejudice in Woltmann's novel. Yet by championing the bourgeois concept of marriage these women take on the burden of domestic virtue that will exclude them from participation in the new republic.[35] Liberal politics in the state go hand in hand with conservative gender stereotypes at home; conversely, it is the politically conservative Fouqué who grants certain aristocratic women relatively greater room for public action in her novels. In doing so, she continues a tradition of the feminist aristocrat that leads from Sophie Mereau's Ninon Lenclos to Ida Hahn-Hahn's Gräfin Faustine among the next generation of women writers.

JOHANNA SCHOPENHAUER: GABRIELE'S RENUNCIATION

In the midst of one of his bitter quarrels with his mother, Arthur Schopenhauer predicted that his philosophy would still be read long after her works had been forgotten. In the long run he was right, of course, but in 1819 it was Johanna Schopenhauer's *Gabriele* that captured the attention of the literary world, while *Die Welt als Wille und Vorstellung* (1818) languished on the shelf. Johanna Schopenhauer (1766–1838), who had arrived in Weimar with such dramatic timing in 1806, was already fifty-three years old when she published her first novel. The daughter of a prosperous Danzig merchant with business connections from Moscow to Paris, Schopenhauer grew up in a cosmopolitan household of republican sympathizers. The gifted child learned Polish, English, and French in addition to her native German, and shared the enthusiasm of both her father and husband for the American and French Revolutions. Her literary career began with translations, a biography, and descriptions of her travels to England and France after the death by apparent suicide of her husband in 1805. In Weimar she quickly established herself as a fixture on the cultural scene with her literary teas, and won Goethe's support by defending his decision to marry Christiane Vulpius. Years later Goethe returned the favor with a positive review of *Gabriele*, and it is largely her association with him, together with her famous son, that kept the memory of her person, if not her literary works, alive. As is the case with so many of the writers discussed in this book, it is only in the last two decades that the works themselves have begun to attract attention again.[36]

Both Frölich and Woltmann envision families in which fathers treat their daughters with love and respect, and cosmopolitan republics where men and women from different social classes join in affectionate marriages. Both authors are also aware, however, that their alternative communities could not survive in Restoration Europe, and both threaten their protagonists with the perils of the old world order. Although Virginia's father is a paragon of virtue, his brother embodies all the evils of an unregenerate aristocracy; Maria's otherwise kind father has a streak of stubborn pride regarding his daughter; and Virginia, Maria, and Walpurgis all narrowly escape arranged marriages. The latent negativity of Restoration society just beneath the happy endings of these novels resurfaces with a vengeance in Johanna Schopenhauer's *Gabriele*. In this novel there are no imagined international communities; the tyrannical father does not have a change of heart; and the daughter suffers and dies in the worst of all possible arranged marriages.

Gabriele grows up in isolation on her father's estate. Her mother Auguste provides affection and instruction in the usual feminine skills of languages and music, while her father, Baron von Aarheim, remains forbiddingly aloof. Embittered by the results of a court intrigue that cut short his career as a young man, the baron soon retired into self-imposed exile on his last remaining property. He marries in an effort to sire a male heir, but Gabriele remains his only child. Still further embittered, the old baron becomes obsessed with alchemy, convinced that he can regain his lost wealth and power through magic. He only succeeds in exploding one wing of his castle, however, and decides instead to force Gabriele to marry her distant cousin, Moritz von Aarheim, in order to keep the family name and estate intact. Although Moritz is a ridiculous fifty-year-old fop whose idea of a hobby is to collect deformed animals, the obedient daughter says yes, unaware that her father would have killed her with a capsule of poison gas had she refused. Satisfied that he has put his house in order, Baron von Aarheim kills himself instead.

As in the pre-revolutionary novels by Richardson and Rousseau, the heroine's relationship to her father stands at the emotional center of *Gabriele*. Yet significant differences obtain: Baron von Aarheim is every bit as rigid as Mr. Harlowe, but he is the last of an old aristocratic line, not a member of a newly rich family of entrepreneurs trying to marry its way into a British peerage. In this regard Baron von Aarheim resembles the Baron D'Etang, but he undergoes no change of heart in the face of his daughter's plight. Rousseau shows us an old aristocrat learning to act like a member of a loving bourgeois family on the eve of the Revolution; Schopenhauer depicts an obstinate patriarch who clings to the memory of power in the Revolution's aftermath. In a setting that shows the influence of Gothic fiction, the father becomes an ogre who haunts a dark castle and offers his daughter the alternative of the slow torture of an unhappy marriage or the quick death of poison. Patriarchal power, once a benevolent alternative to absolutist abuse and revolutionary terror, has become monstrous in the Restoration.

Gabriele's mother Auguste dies when her daughter is only sixteen, and after her father's suicide two years later Gabriele is left alone with her new husband. She is able to derive comfort from a surrogate family that provides at least some of the affection she is otherwise denied. Gabriele's father had sent her to spend the winter with his sister, the Countess Rosenberg, immediately after her mother's death. The young Gabriele finds aristocratic society dazzling and disorienting, but two figures come to her aid: Ernesto, a German artist who had once been a private tutor to Gabriele's mother in Rome, offers his services as her "fatherly friend" as soon as he hears of her arrival, and she gladly accepts. He will remain loyal to her throughout her life out of a sense of "genuinely paternal, true love for the orphaned daughter of the woman whose memory still shone like a bright star on the distant horizon of his long-departed youth."[37] Frau von Willnangen fills a similar maternal role for Gabriele. As it turns out, this close relative of Countess Rosenberg's husband married the man that Auguste once loved, Ferdinand von Willnangen. Auguste's father had disapproved of the liaison and separated the young lovers; after his death she had felt compelled to marry the tyrannical Baron von Aarheim. Frau von Willnangen was able to experience the loving marriage that Auguste was denied, and now the widow decides to take Gabriele under her wing as a surrogate daughter. To complete the pattern of exchanges, Frau von Willnangen has named her own daughter Auguste in memory of Gabriele's mother. Richardson's Clarissa had compensated for her unyielding earthly parents by anticipating a tender union with her heavenly Father; Gabriele derives faint comfort from the traces of her mother's past.

Gabriele's tendency to seek partial compensation for denied happiness continues throughout her life. While in the care of her aunt, Gabriele becomes infatuated with Ottokar, a handsome aristocrat in his late twenties. He dashes her hopes, however, when he accepts an administrative position in Rome and reluctantly agrees to an arranged marriage to another woman. Gabriele's own coerced marriage only completes an already bleak picture. Yet she manages to survive for at least several years with dignity. The key to her success, as she sees it, lies in her ability to acquiesce to the inevitable: "I am satisfied, for I am resigned" (204). The concept of renunciation [*Entsagung*] is of course central to the work of the late Goethe, and his influence permeates Schopenhauer's novel: her characters display Werther's sentimentality, share Wilhelm Meister's interest in personal development or *Bildung*, and experience the sort of marital discord depicted in *Die Wahlverwandtschaften*. In its stress on resignation Schopenhauer's novel also anticipates *Wilhelm Meisters Wanderjahre, oder die Entsagenden*, the first version of which appeared in 1821. *Gabriele* in turn inspired so much domestic fiction that the critic Wolfgang Menzel declared that "all novels for women are also necessarily novels of renunciation [*Entsagungsromane*]," a tendency he decried as "bizarre" and "sick."[38] In the case of *Gabriele*, at least, we might question whether or not *Entsagung* is the proper term, if thereby we mean the renunciation of desire. Gabriele does not so much give up her desire as she displaces it into the imaginary realm, and it is this displacement that enables her to survive an otherwise impossible marriage.

She learns the trick from her mother Auguste. Although deeply saddened by the loss of her first love, Auguste accepts her lot and later teaches her daughter that quiet patience is a woman's highest duty. Nevertheless, Auguste retains the memory of the man she once loved: "the transfigured image of the lost lover still lived hidden deep in her heart, flooded by the eternal radiance of youth, like the picture of a saint in a dark grave illuminated by an eternal light" (17). Years later Gabriele explains that she follows her mother's example in coping with the loss of Ottokar: "Only now do I understand the true meaning of my immortal mother when she taught me: 'Love is the source of unspeakable bliss all by itself, without hope, without reciprocation, even without desire'" (205–06). Gabriele is seemingly content to survive her miserable marriage by projecting her desires onto an idealized image of her one true love. "Gabriele had learned from her [mother] to consider them [the innumerable, unnoticed sacrifices] to be the destiny of her entire sex, but also to bear the unavoidable with grace" (26). To everyone's astonishment, Gabriele not only survives her marriage to Moritz von Aarheim, but actually matures into a strikingly handsome, universally admired woman.

Schopenhauer uses Gabriele's superhuman resolve to underscore her status as a paragon of German virtue. At one point she is forced to flee estates along the Rhine when the invading French set up field headquarters in her home. For the most part, however, Schopenhauer comments on current events indirectly by developing contrasting images of feminine behavior. While visiting a spa with her friends Gabriele meets Adelbert, a young German veteran who is recovering slowly from a wound received in battle against the French. He had been engaged to his childhood sweetheart Hermine before the war, but when he returned on crutches, the fickle woman rejected him and ran off with a French officer. All seems to turn out for the best when Adelbert eventually recovers and marries Frau von Willnangen's daughter Auguste: "Delighted, he pressed the dear creature to his breast, who offered him the bourgeois crown of domestic bliss braided with roses of love as a reward for his struggle for the fatherland and honor" (202). Echoing Schiller's paean to

"The Dignity of Women,"[39] Schopenhauer cites the common view that the woman exists to supplement the man, and to compensate for his sacrifices for the common good. Unfortunately, however, Adelbert encounters his former fiancée later in the novel. Hermine, now completely corrupt, is masquerading as a French lady while her husband is off at war in one of Napoleon's armies. Adelbert reacts at first with outrage when he finds the woman who had once betrayed him, but she soon manages to seduce him and ruin his marriage before returning in disgrace to Paris.

The entire episode serves to highlight Gabriele's Germanic superiority. While the traitorous Hermine – ironically named after the old Germanic hero – abandons her fiancé and apes the manners of French society, Gabriele adheres to simple German traditions. When her husband Moritz, who is incapable of completing a sentence in German without a few French, English, or Italian phrases, tries to import maids from London and Paris, Gabriele refuses: "She completely forbade the foreign servants, because they were inappropriate in a German household" (187). Her aunt, Countess Rosenberg, has gone to Paris and adopted French fashion with a stunning, but slightly alienating result, "that in its way could not quite be reconciled with German sensibility and German custom, whereas Gabriele's constant unpretentious kindness always made an agreeable impression on the mind, the senses, and the heart" (247). Not surprisingly, Hermine is a brunette, while Gabriele is a blond, and when the two first meet Gabriele's "golden hair hovers around the dark locks of the Marquise like a radiant halo" (233).

While Hermine destroys her former fiancé, Gabriele sets out to purify Hermine's former admirer, a handsome but dissolute Hungarian noble, Count Hippolit. Only twenty years old, handsome, and rich, Hippolit has a basically good character corrupted by bad experiences. Neglected as a child by his father, deceived by his guardian uncle, and jaded by his precocious experiences with women, Hippolit soon recognizes that Gabriele is a woman of a completely different sort than he has known. He soon falls passionately in love with her and fights a duel for her sake. When the married woman realizes the extent of his infatuation, however, she sends him off on a journey to regain his composure. He returns transformed into a responsible adult. It has often been said that *Gabriele* can be read as a "female *Bildungsroman*,"[40] and it is true that she undergoes a process of maturation, measured in terms of the progression from her adolescent infatuation with Ottokar to her maternal concern for young Hippolit. In this particular episode, however, Gabriele serves in the more traditional role as agent to the *Bildung* of the man. Hippolit, in turn, idolizes his mentor and begins to view her as a supernatural being. Her ethereal beauty overwhelms him when he watches her walk in her white dress: "the light blond hair, shimmering in the red glow of evening, surrounded her head with the halo of a saint" (298).

Despite Hippolit's willingness to turn Gabriele into a Germanic saint of feminine resignation, Schopenhauer makes it clear that all is not well in her world. Gabriele is ready early on to resign herself to an unhappy marriage, taking solace in the memory of Ottokar, but the older Ernesto is concerned that the impressionable sixteen-year old is willing to give up love for the rest of her life for the sake of what may well be a mere infatuation. Gabriele's later love for Hippolit reveals an unmistakable degree of self-deception at work in her seemingly most noble impulses. It is an open secret that Gabriele's relations with her husband are distant at best, and Hippolit has already declared his passionate love, yet Gabriele thinks nothing of inviting him for an extended stay at her isolated castle. At first the narrator presents this decision as an admirable extension of Gabriele's guileless character. In the end, however, Gabriele is forced to acknowledge that she indeed feels more passion than maternal love for Count Hippolit and, in realizing this, she loses faith in her mother's most treasured lessons: "Indeed, she finally had to admit to herself, despite all inner resistance: it was love that she felt, hot, glowing love that she now recognized in her torments, and oh how vastly different from those ideals with which her gentle mother, who was dedicated to unconditional submission, had filled her young heart in early childhood!" (369–70).

With this admission the entire ideology that has canonized Gabriele crumbles. If Schopenhauer had not allowed her heroine to grasp the falsity of her mother's beliefs, then the novel would offer an implicit affirmation of the corrupt patriarchy that forces Gabriele into her predicament. Baron von Aarheim's tyranny would become a necessary evil that allows his daughter to fulfill her destiny through feminine self-sacrifice. Gabriele's final insight makes such a reading of the novel impossible. She is not only the victim of her father's injustice, but also the victim of her mother's insistence that she should put up with it. In response to those who view *Gabriele* as an

Entsagungsroman, I suggest that it is an *Anti-Entsagungsroman*, a novel that denounces both female resignation and the abuse of paternal authority that makes it seem necessary. For Gabriele, sadly, the insight comes too late. Wasted by the strain of her illicit passion, she fades away to an early death. She does confess her love to Hippolit at the last minute, and her husband conveniently dies to open the possibility for a new beginning, but Schopenhauer denies her readers this happy ending. After a life in service of a flawed ideal, Gabriele can no longer rebound with youthful resiliency; resignation has become a bad habit, and she carries it with her to the grave.

ANNETTE VON DROSTE-HÜLSHOFF: LEDWINA'S LETHARGY

Until a few years ago, Annette von Droste-Hülshoff (1797–1848) was liable to have been the only woman writer that most students of German literature knew. Exactly how Droste-Hülshoff's works attained canonical status, while so many of her contemporaries were forgotten, is itself an interesting question.[41] Part of the reason is that Droste-Hülshoff had the equivalent of a good agent and a good publicist: her friend Levin Schücking encouraged her to write during her lifetime, edited her work when she died, and wrote the first Droste-Hülshoff biography. Soon afterwards Paul Heyse and Hermann Kurz included *Die Judenbuche* in their influential anthology *Deutscher Novellenschatz* (1876). In addition, Droste-Hülshoff's work did not seem particularly threatening: she was not an outspoken feminist, at least not in the sense of such *Vormärz* authors as Fanny Lewald, Luise Mühlbach, or Louise Otto-Peters. Nor could the aristocratic Catholic be accused of political agitation. In one satirical poem Droste-Hülshoff ridiculed nationalist enthusiasm for the completion of the Cologne cathedral with the suggestion that the new building could be used by future generations to pray for the souls of those who had desecrated the church by turning it into a political symbol.[42] While others stormed the barricades, Droste-Hülshoff quietly produced a body of introspective works rooted in her native Westphalian soil, so the story goes, seemingly content to bend her near-sighted eyes to little objects and to reproduce local knowledge.

Such an image of the poet depends on a highly selective appropriation of her works, including *Die Judenbuche*, the poetry of the "Heidebilder," and a few other frequently anthologized poems. Consistently ignored until recently is the early novel fragment

Ledwina.[43] Droste-Hülshoff began writing it in approximately 1819, and then seems to have set it aside in the winter of 1825–26.[44] Little is known about the composition of the text, since it falls into the period between 1820 and 1825 for which we have almost no record of the poet's life. The fragment depicts an aristocratic family in a rural Westphalian setting. Here the widowed Frau von Brenkfeld lives with her four children: two older daughters, Therese and Ledwina, a son Karl, just returned from the university, and a child named Marie. Karl expects a visit from a certain Steinheim, who may or may not be interested in Therese. In any case, Steinheim never appears. Instead, the handsome but consumptive Count von Hollberg becomes a patient in the house after causing the drowning of a local boy who tries to guide him across the nearby river at night. On the following day, the Brenkfelds receive a tedious visit from a neighboring aristocratic clan, and here the fragment ends.

With its primary focus on the private lives of family members, the novel belongs to the genre of domestic fiction. Droste-Hülshoff evokes a claustrophobic world governed by the strictest etiquette that struggles in vain to stifle seething passions. Nothing is quite what it seems: Frau von Brenkfeld has trained herself to control her body and voice in all social situations, but her fluttering eyelids give her emotions away. Therese, desperately hoping that Steinheim cares for her, says nothing in public, but steals off into the bushes at night to weep. Each gesture, each word, each silence prompts interpretation: does Steinheim's failure to mention Therese in his letter indicate lack of interest or the opposite? Karl and his mother keep up a lively conversation that bores both of them in the desperate attempt to avoid talking about the drowning that occurred just hours earlier. And the game has high stakes as characters suffer deep emotional wounds from stray comments, often delivered casually with no intent to harm: "and thus the conversation went on – in sharp strokes, often unjust, always missing the mark – between people one would have to consider to be good."[45]

Although Droste-Hülshoff gives every indication that the events described in *Ledwina* take place in the present, she makes no explicit mention of the political situation during the early Restoration years, nor does she comment on the recent Napoleonic Wars. Her depiction of the family in *Ledwina* does, however, offer a coded critique of Restoration society.[46] If Frölich and Woltmann lament the failed Revolution, Droste-Hülshoff joins with her fellow aristocrat Fouqué in recognizing that even the Restoration will not bring back the old patriarchal order. The fragment sounds an elegiac note for a culture that is quickly fading away: servants are no longer as loyal as they used to be, children no longer respect their elders, and Ledwina complains that her family has lost touch with its ancestors.

The most significant indication that corruption has settled into society lies in the repeated motif of the dead father. Herr von Brenkfeld died eight years ago; he is remembered as a well-meaning, but financially irresponsible individual who left his family and others he had tried to help under a crushing burden of debt. When Count von Hollberg arrives everyone is at first impressed by his uncanny good looks, but it turns out that he is flushed with fever and dying of a disease that has already killed the rest of his family. Here again, the father is to blame: by dragging "consumption into the family," he has poisoned his "entire lineage" (506–07; 2:136). Nor are the lower classes immune to fatherly weakness: the old servant Franz has died shoveling snow for Ledwina, leaving his impoverished widow and son behind, and even the macabre tale told about a toothless woman who saves her old teeth so that she has something to rattle in hell, concludes by observing that she has gone mad in the wake of her husband's bankruptcy. *Ledwina* thus presents an image of society in decline, suffering from financial, moral, and even biological degeneration, where widows struggle to hold together broken families, and where young men of the next generation are either callously indifferent to their mothers' sacrifice, as in the case of Karl, or are themselves fated to die young of accident or disease.

Thus described, *Ledwina* sounds like a naturalist novel *avant la lettre*, introducing themes of social and environmental determinism that Droste-Hülshoff will also include in *Die Judenbuche*. Yet the eponymous heroine adds a lyric, even visionary component that looks back to both Romanticism and the Gothic novel, and anticipates images of drowning and dismemberment found in expressionist poetry. Ledwina is sick, and probably dying. While her sister Therese still hopes for the man who will rescue her from the stultifying atmosphere of her family, Ledwina has given up. Although she still goes through the motions of being the obedient daughter, Ledwina spends much of her time detached from her surroundings. Whenever possible, she slips away from family gatherings to walk alone by the river, and she lives in accordance with her own private rhythm, eating breakfast when others eat dinner, napping during the day and pacing her room at night.

During these periods of solitude Ledwina experiences dreams and visions that illuminate fears and desires beneath the carefully modulated tones of polite society. The novel begins, for instance, by following Ledwina's reflection on the river's surface as she walks upstream. She then turns to gaze "upon her own image, as the curls fell from her head and drifted away, her dress tore to shreds, and her white fingers disintegrated and floated apart, and as the cramp quietly began to yield, it was as if she were dead, and decay were dissolving, eating its way through her limbs, and each element were tearing away its own" (481; 2:105–06). The image repeats itself later that night, when Ledwina awakens from a dream to see the reflection of the river across her body in bed: "She observed this for a while, and the longer she did so the more ghastly it seemed; the idea of a water sprite changed to that of a corpse submerged in the river, being slowly consumed by the water" (500; 2:128).

The most obvious reason for Ledwina's morbid visions is that she is mortally ill; the first image of her dissolving body coincides with an agonizing cramp. The pain tyrannizes Ledwina, breaking both body and spirit, a torment she hates so much "that she would gladly have let all her life's energy, which was glimmering out a spark at a time, flare up and expire in a single blazingly brilliant day" (484; 2:109). Yet Ledwina's own premonitions of death by water seem to provide a supernatural connection to the deadly landscape outside her window. Her second vision awakens her just in time to hear the boy Klemens fall into the river and drown, and the peasants refuse to search for the body when they hear that he is the river's first victim of the year. Here the ancient folk superstition captures the mood of modern Biedermeier society, which slowly decays above a swamp that demands the occasional human sacrifice. Even the willow leaves remind Ledwina "of beautiful but weakly children, their hair bleached by a single night of terror" (492; 2:119).

In addition to registering personal and cultural mortality, Ledwina's visions of watery death and dismemberment may well have a sexual component. The second vision accompanies a sense of "burning heat in her body" (500; 2:129) that may be just a fever, but could signal arousal. After all, there is an old literary topos familiar from both Shakespeare and the German Romantics of death linked with the loss of self in sexual intercourse; Thomas Mann would still

get considerable mileage out of the association between illness and
eroticism on the Magic Mountain. As both Brigitte Peucker and
Irmgard Roebling have observed, moreover, Droste-Hülshoff frequently uses images of a doubled self to explore transgressive realms
of female sexuality and writing.[47] In Peucker's view, Droste-Hülshoff
uses the Ophelia motif of the drowning woman as an allegory of
poetic creativity. In a complex procedure, Droste-Hülshoff first
purges herself of the demonic other by projecting it onto nature, so
that she can then allow this other to speak with nature's voice:
"Herein revealed, then, is the close alliance of the poetic impulse
and the death wish . . . But one must equally stress that the gift of
the Ophelia figure to Droste-Hülshoff is renewal and vitality."[48]

I will return to the question of female creativity in *Ledwina* in the
discussion of her dream in a moment, but at present I would like to
interject a note of caution against reading Droste-Hülshoff's appropriation of the Ophelia motif in terms of "renewal and vitality."
Bram Dijkstra has assembled an entire catalog of images that testify
to the nineteenth century's necrophilial fascination with Ophelia
and other drowned women. Far from symbolizing feminist protest,
in his view, the mad or drowned Ophelia fulfills "the nineteenth-
century male's fondest fantasies of feminine dependency."[49] Seduc-
tively beautiful, but safely dead, Ophelia stands as an extreme
embodiment of the cult of the invalid woman. Droste-Hülshoff
actually brings out the implicit violence against women in this image
by having Ledwina's watery reflection seem to rot and fall to pieces
as she watches. The river not only brings death; it attacks its victims
with a sadistic pleasure. In the novel's most horrifying image,
Ledwina identifies with the drowning boy, his head and hair
entangled in thorns, his bloody limbs beaten "by the waves in cruel
rhythm. He was still alive, but his strength was gone and he could
only wait in ghastly mortal fear until the pounding waves had torn
out his last hair" (511; 2:141).

Taken together, then, Ledwina's fascination with water arouses
multiple associations: of personal mortality and social decay, of
erotic excitement and terror. At another point she startles her family
by imagining the desert as a kind of ocean, in which the clouds are
pillars of fire [*Glutsäulen*], the flowers flaming serpents, and trees
lions and tigers. The burning desert ocean offers an exotic, erotic
alternative to the domestic virtue demanded of women in Biedermeier society. And yet, these brilliant images have their dark side as

well: when the setting sun bathes the leaves outside her window in golden light, Ledwina sees "a sinister image of captivity within a scorching flame, which one strives to escape constantly but in vain, for one's foot is rooted in the tormented earth" (497; 2:125). Like the water, the sun tortures its victim, permitting neither flight nor oblivion. Once again, Ledwina's tormented body inspires mental images of death and decay, images that also characterize the fetid state of Restoration society. At the same time, physical illness brings with it a heightened sense of the body and its erotic needs. Given the strict taboo against the open expression of female sexuality during the Biedermeier period, however, it is not surprising that its evocation inspires guilt expressed in sado-masochistic fantasies.[50] It is in this context that we can speak of Droste-Hülshoff's feminism: not a demand for equal rights, but a look into the deformations, self-denial, and even self-hatred engendered in a society that represses all its members, but especially women. Indeed, Ledwina's illness is not an aberration from the norm, but a metaphor for the fate of all women in a patriarchy turned sour.

With this in mind we can turn in closing to Ledwina's dream. In the early evening Ledwina slips into restless sleep, and dreams that she is visiting a graveyard where "the one she loves most in the whole world" (499; 2:127) is buried. She watches in horror as her double digs frantically in the upturned soil. Suddenly the ground gives way and she falls into the grave of her beloved. She presses the dead hand to her lips and buries her head in the rotting body, but feels no fear. She resolves to stay in the grave until she dies, but then a child appears next to the grave selling flowers, just like in a theatre. She buys all the flowers and fills the grave with them, and is delighted to think that she might reconstruct the decomposed body out of flowers and bring it back to life. She awakens feeling "rather calm, but unbearably hot" (500; 2:291).

Droste-Hülshoff is careful not to identify Ledwina's beloved other than to say it is human; it could be either a lover or a double. The dream starts as a nightmare, but ends as a wish-fulfillment. Just when it seems most horrible – when Ledwina falls into the open grave – things take a positive turn. Ledwina loses all sensation of fear, night turns to day, and miraculous snowflakes fall through the hot air. The dream thus works through the fears and frustrations revealed in the other visions in the text. On one level, the dream enables Ledwina to confront her fear of death. The beloved figure in the grave is herself. In embracing the corpse she accepts her illness, accepts her mortality, and has a comforting vision of a resurrection, whether this means a cure and return to health, or some sort of religious afterlife. On another level, however, the beloved is a sexual partner – whether male or female is unclear – and the embrace in the coffin is a sexual fantasy. Previous images of potential passion return to torture the subject: the river beats its bleeding victim against the shore, and burning pillars in the desert become flames around the martyr's stake. Here, too, sexual union involves embracing a putrefying corpse. Yet in the dream what should be terrifying becomes a source of otherwise forbidden pleasure. We are in the realm of a Catholic mysticism of the sort captured so well by that Protestant Novalis: "Hinüber wall ich, / Und jede Pein / Wird einst ein Stachel / Der Wollust sein" ["I pilger beyond and every pain will one day be a sting of ecstasy"][51] or of Droste herself, "Wollüstig saugend an des Grauens Süße" ["Sucking voluptuously on horror's sweetness"].[52] For a brief moment, at least, Droste-Hülshoff allows her heroine to dream of a world where death can regenerate life, and where pain becomes a source of pleasure; a somewhat masochistic utopia, to be sure, but one that captures, as if in a reflection, the suffering and decay that gnaw at the edifice of Restoration society.

CHAPTER 5

Feminists in the "Vormärz"

INTRODUCTION

The Restoration came to a sudden end on February 24, 1848, when angry mobs stormed the Palais Royal in Paris and forced King Louis Philippe to abdicate. Uprisings spread to the Austrian empire and into Germany, and within a matter of weeks Prince Metternich had been driven into exile. In Berlin matters came to a head on Saturday, March 18, as crowds gathered to hear the king order the convening of a general assembly.[1] In her novel *Revolution und Contrerevolution* (1849), Louise Aston captures the sense of delight and near disbelief among the people gathered to hear the king's proclamation, but the mood changes abruptly when soldiers advance into the throng in a menacing gesture that reminds people where they are: "Prussia was a police state, but even more, a military state."[2] Aston's protagonist Alice watches in horror as two soldiers approach a harmless bystander "and suddenly – whether by accident or on purpose she could not tell – discharged their rifles" (2:75). Savage fighting breaks out, and we soon find Alice standing on the barricades, "fully armed with a musket and a sword." Her friend Ralph offers to bring her to a safe haven, but Alice has no patience for his condescension: "'Bah, do you think I'm a coward, even if I am a woman? Say "du" to me, for here we are all comrades'" (2:99). What had begun with the peaceful transition of power from the king to the people had become a bloodbath, a turn of events that presaged the fate of the 1848 Revolution as a whole. A National Assembly did in fact convene in Frankfurt, but the Prussian king refused to ratify its constitution. By the summer of 1849 Prussian troops had crushed the last pockets of revolutionary resistance. But what caused the revolution to break out in the first place, and what was Aston's heroine doing on the barricades in Berlin?

Crop failures and an international fiscal crisis triggered the outbreak of the March Revolution, but pressure for reform had been building for decades. Between 1815 and 1848 Germany underwent profound changes.[3] The industrial revolution, which had begun already in the previous century in England, finally began to affect Germany during the 1830s. The combination of the factory system of production with capitalist speculation created the potential for great wealth among the manufacturers, but also unprecedented poverty in a new social class: the fourth estate, the urban proletariat. Berlin expanded with astonishing speed, while a decline in infant mortality spurred slower, but still significant population growth throughout Germany. The publishing industry continued its explosive expansion, fueled by greater literacy rates among the German public, technological innovations that produced faster presses and cheaper paper, and the spread of commercial lending libraries.[4] Steamships plied the Rhine and railroads connected cities in a matter of hours that had been separated by days. Everything seemed to move faster, as the social transformations begun by the French Revolution and the Napoleonic Wars accelerated into the breathless pace of modern times.

Only the Restoration governments seemed impervious to change. When news of the July Revolution of 1830 reverberated in Germany, however, radicals who had cut their teeth in the *Burschenschaft* movement of the immediate postwar years began to clamor for democratic reform in an increasingly politicized literature. Autonomy aesthetics was out, *Tendenzliteratur* was in; Balzac and Dickens were on the cutting edge, Goethe was passé.[5] The novelist Fanny Lewald included a typical defense of politically engaged art in her novel *Eine Lebensfrage* [A Vital Question] (1845). "A novel that does not stand in a precise relation to the time in which it was written will rarely be a successful work."[6] The historical novels that had been in fashion in the 1820s are not intrinsically bad, her protagonist concedes; in countries where people rule themselves the poets have the leisure to summon up the past. "At the moment, however, I do not think it is the time for [historical fiction] in Germany" (108). When rulers fail, poets must take over: "as long as the people are not permitted to express their opinion freely, the poet must speak in images for them, and explain in images what the nation needs and demands" (109). Because novelists reach the broadest audience, it is their particular responsibility to address matters of pressing national concern.

In the 1830s a group of writers who became known as Young Germany [*Junges Deutschland*] began to speak out against aristocratic abuses of power, to question the authority of the Church, and to express concern for the plight of the poor. When Karl Gutzkow allowed one of his characters to defend atheism in *Wally, die Zweiflerin* [Wally, the Doubter] (1835) and Theodor Mundt advocated the "emancipation of the flesh" in *Madonna: Unterhaltungen mit einer Heiligen* [Madonna: Conversations with a Saint] (1835), the government had had enough: their works, together with those of Ludwig Börne, Heinrich Heine, Heinrich Laube, and Ludolf Wienbarg, were forbidden.[7] Discontent with the political situation in Germany continued to fester, however, and the following decade saw the emergence of a new group of politically engaged authors. While the Young Germans had all been men, some of the most outspoken authors of the 1840s were women, including Louise Aston, Ida Hahn-Hahn, Fanny Lewald, Louise Mühlbach, and Louise Otto-Peters. In their novels they not only addressed issues of particular interest to women, such as arranged marriages and the possibility of divorce, but also matters of public concern, including religious freedom, factory labor, and national unification. Political activism on the part of men was suspicious enough in the reactionary climate of the Restoration, but considered outrageous on the part of women, who were after all supposed to be tending hearth and home in domestic tranquillity. By publishing politically engaged novels, and by demanding what to many seemed an intolerable degree of freedom in their personal lives, these women writers gained unprecedented notoriety and provoked a sharp backlash of resentment against a new caricature, the emancipated woman.

Despite – or perhaps because of – their notoriety, the German women of the *Vormärz* suffered the same neglect as previous generations of women writers in literary history. That the *Vormärz* writers today enjoy at least more widespread name-recognition than those of the early Restoration is largely due to the work of a single critic, Renate Möhrmann. Her study *Die andere Frau* [The Other Woman] (1977) reintroduced forgotten writers to German literary history, and her collection of reprinted texts published in the following year made at least some of the obscure material available to contemporary readers. Written at the height of the "second wave" of the German feminist movement, Möhrmann makes it clear from the outset that she considers her archival research an active intervention into her own situation in the 1970s. "The views that some of the women writers of the Metternich Restoration held more than 125 years ago are in fact not only dusty documents of emancipation. Some of what is up to date today can already be found there in nuce."[8] Not surprisingly, then, Möhrmann tends to approach literary texts with what might be called an excerpt mentality, as she highlights proto-feminist passages in novels, while downplaying the extent to which overall context often qualifies individual emancipatory statements.[9] By concentrating primarily on novelists of the *Vormärz*, moreover, Möhrmann emphasizes their novelty while minimizing their indebtedness to previous generations of German women writers. Yet it is often by inverting traditional configurations of the family and femininity represented in earlier domestic fiction that the novelists of the *Vormärz* establish their own radicality. Conversely, the persistence of gender stereotypes and family pressures often hinders their attempts to break free of the past.

In the following chapter I examine three of the most prominent German novelists of the 1840s: Ida Gräfin Hahn-Hahn, Fanny Lewald, and Louise Aston. As in previous chapters, I make no effort to provide a comprehensive survey of all women writers of the period,[10] or even of all of those whose novels address contemporary issues in a way that is typical of the *Vormärz*. My selection is motivated in part by practical concerns: at least one novel by Hahn-Hahn, Lewald, and Aston has been reprinted in its entirety in recent years, while works by such other authors as Louise Otto-Peters or Luise Mühlbach remain accessible only in special collections or in reprinted excerpts. Hahn-Hahn, Lewald, and Aston were all well known to their contemporaries, and their works share similar concerns for women's rights and a willingness to tackle political issues at time of widespread discontent. As in previous generations of German women writers, however, the differences that separate these authors are at least as great as the causes that unite them. If they had not happened to have fallen in love with the same man, the blue-blooded Prussian aristocrat Hahn-Hahn would have had little in common with Fanny Lewald, the liberal bourgeois daughter of a Jewish merchant. While Lewald lived at home with her family until she was in her thirties, Louise Aston was a pub-crawling "Amazon" in Berlin whose political sympathies lay with the extreme left wing of the democratic radicals. Taken together, Hahn-Hahn, Lewald, and Aston indicate the range of personal and political viewpoints within the ranks of women writers of the *Vormärz*. In their novels they rework literary tradition to address contemporary issues affecting women, families, and the nation on the eve of Germany's belated revolution.

IDA HAHN-HAHN: THE CURSE OF THE IDLE RICH

Ida Gräfin Hahn-Hahn (1805–80) was one of those rare individuals who managed to offend just about everyone.[11] To conservative men she seemed an unnatural Amazon filled with a "sick craving for emancipation,"[12] while the liberal Fanny Lewald attacked her as a self-indulgent aristocrat indifferent to the plight of the poor.[13] To be sure, Hahn-Hahn remained popular with her contemporary readers, and continued to find supporters after her death, but here too critics have tended to pick the Hahn-Hahn sympathetic to their cause and to disregard less palatable aspects of her life and work. To Catholics Hahn-Hahn offered a reassuring image of a repentant lost soul, who, after her conversion to Catholicism in 1850, repudiated her earlier works and produced a series of novels in praise of family and the Church.[14] More recent critics have embraced the feminist Hahn-Hahn, while downplaying her political conservatism and ignoring her later work.[15] In doing so, they divide Hahn-Hahn's career neatly into a progressive youth and a reactionary old age.[16] Even in her early writings, however, Hahn-Hahn remained loyal to her own aristocratic class and staunchly opposed to the democratic reforms advocated by other writers of the *Vormärz*. I would like to focus on the combination of political conservatism and feminist radicalism that gives Hahn-Hahn's early novels their peculiar flavor. *Gräfin Faustine* [Countess Faustine] (1841), *Zwei Frauen* [Two Women] (1845), and *Sibylle* (1846) reveal a growing complexity in the portrayal of the heroines' development and an increasing attempt on Ida Hahn-Hahn's part to situate personal growth in the context of broader economic, political, and ideological developments affecting the German aristocracy in the 1840s.

Hahn-Hahn establishes Countess Faustine's unorthodox character by subverting the conventions of German domestic fiction. The typical novel tends to focus on a young woman moving from father to husband, and from childhood to motherhood, a pattern that recurs – with significant variations – from LaRoche's *Sternheim* through Wolzogen's *Agnes von Lilien* to Schopenhauer's *Gabriele*. In contrast, Hahn-Hahn's heroine has little in the way of a family life while growing up and soon abandons her first husband for another man. Orphaned at an early age, she and her sister Adele were entrusted to an aunt, who promptly placed them in a boarding school "and paid no attention to them until they had grown up."[17] Coerced into marriage with a brutal drunkard, Faustine falls in love with Baron Anastas Andlau. She flees to Italy with Andlau after her husband seriously wounds him in a jealous rage. As the novel opens we find Faustine living openly with Andlau in Dresden. Her former husband is dead, but she resists remarriage. As the narrator informs us, Faustine has won public acceptance for her unconventional behavior by force of her personality, yet it is easy to imagine the shock and perhaps clandestine delight such a figure would have caused readers weaned on the traditional romance.

Of central importance to the novel is Faustine's insistence on her right to the sort of self-fulfillment usually considered a man's prerogative. She strives to emulate her namesake in a restless pursuit of knowledge and experience. "I was always particularly interested in my godfather, Faust . . . I always wanted to discover my own fate in this restless striving, in this thirsting and longing for satisfaction" (175). In rapid succession Faustine dazzles society with her wit and charm, travels throughout Europe and the Near East, and wins fame and fortune as an artist before vainly seeking spiritual peace in a cloister. She combines her unconventional life with outspoken criticism of the traditional marriage. While visiting her happily married sister – whose chief delight lies in stockpiling linen for her daughters' dowries – Faustine mocks the idea that it is natural for men to consider themselves lords of the earth, destined to be served by women: "'And the one half of humankind was supposedly created to be brutalized by the other?'" (49). Faustine insists that she does not want to reverse the existing gender hierarchy: "'No, I only want men to treat them [women] as their equals and not like purchased slaves'" (50). Reacting against the sort of stifling domesticity her sister embraces, Faustine insists on her right to abandon an abusive husband and to seek happiness with other men. In this regard she resembles the male figure who, as Renate Möhrmann aptly puts it, consumes women like snacks to fuel his quest for self-fulfillment.[18] Faust seduces and then abandons Gretchen with little remorse in Goethe's play, and Faustine also leaves a trail of corpses in her wake. Having fled her husband with Baron Andlau, she then leaves Andlau for the dashing Count Mario Mengen. The heartbroken Andlau eventually dies of the wounds inflicted by Faustine's first husband. Meanwhile the younger brother of her sister's husband falls in love with her, and, when he finally realizes that his love is unrequited, shoots himself in the head while sitting next to Faustine on the couch. Small wonder, then, that he should liken Faustine to the Czech Queen Libusa, who discarded her former lovers through a trap door into the Moldau.

As female Faust and *femme fatale*, Countess Faustine is far removed from the bourgeois ideal of domestic virtue, and yet she fails in her quest for self-fulfillment. The reason lies in the very quality of genius that sets her apart from her contemporaries. Genius is something you either have or you do not: "you [can] never *become* a genius . . . you have to *be* one by nature" (26). For Faustine, genius has no gender ["das Genie [ist] geschlechtslos"] (155). Despite this claim, Faustine's faith in the romantic concept of innate genius plays into feminine stereotypes that limit her potential growth.[19] Faustine acts only in accordance with her nature, "according to mood, out of passion, out of inspiration," never according to principles (17). "She was completely and undividedly one, not in pieces, not fragmented; that gave her clarity" (19). Seen from the outside, Faustine's clarity of purpose follows nature's enigmatic rhythms: "There was something unfathomable, mysterious, simple in her, something of the primitive vigor of life in nature" (221). Faustine thus exhibits the same sort of contradictory characteristics evident in Sophie Mereau's Amanda. While her natural spontaneity allows her to flout social convention, her radicality depends on a proximity to nature that denies her the potential for intellectual growth or mature decision-making. Thus the independent woman finds herself unable to resist Mario Mengen's insistence that she renounce Baron Andlau and marry him: "the moment ruled her, the present triumphed; she forgot the past and did not think of the future" (199). Andlau finds her impulsive behavior both devastating and exasperating: "Will she remain a child forever?" (206). Predictably, Faustine finds no lasting satisfaction with either Mengen or her own art; the vitality that has consumed others eventually turns inward and she destroys herself.

Hahn-Hahn returns to the theme of dissimilar sisters in *Zwei Frauen*. Once again inverting the pattern of the traditional romance, Hahn-Hahn begins with the joint honeymoon of the twin sisters Aurore and Cornelie. Aurore's husband Herr Friedrich von Elsleben soon settles into his role as a *Landjunker*, while Count Eustach Sambach retires from a diplomatic career to his estate in Altdorf, where he plans to live the life of a patriarch with his young wife Cornelie (he is close to forty, she nineteen). Just a few pages into the novel Hahn-Hahn makes it clear that her protagonists will find little happiness in their respective marriages: "Three years have passed, and Aurore is bored in Elsburg, and Eustach is bored in Altdorf."[20] Aurore, who had entered marriage as a vivacious young woman with hopes of sharing intellectual and emotional concerns with her husband, finds herself shackled to a relentlessly cheerful boor interested primarily in hunting and horses. Despite her protests, Elsleben insists on addressing her as "kitty"[*Miezchen*] (1:19). In an increasingly desperate effort to escape her claustrophobic circumstances, Aurore becomes a doting, overly protective mother to the children she produces at regular intervals, only to discover that motherhood alone cannot satisfy her needs. A brief attempt to begin a book club fails when she puts George Sand's *Lelia* on the reading list: half of her neighbors are unable to read French, and those who can find the novel shocking. Aurore comes close to having an affair with an army captain who fancies himself a poet, and eventually turns into a religious fanatic. Nothing works. She dies young, just after writing a chilling letter in which she condemns her pointless existence: "In love I yearned to the point of exhaustion – in vain! In religion I prayed to the point of exhaustion – in vain! For husband and children I worked myself to the point of exhaustion – in vain! Now I'll have to die too – in vain!" (2:224).

While Aurore spirals downward toward despair and death, Cornelie develops into a mature and independent woman who eventually finds happiness. Initially quiet and even simple in comparison with her sister's brilliance, Cornelie uses the first years of her marriage to broaden her knowledge of literature and the world. During this period she looks to her husband for guidance, and for a time he enjoys cultivating his innocent bride into a sophisticated aristocrat. Already as a young woman, however, Cornelie shows signs of independence that do not sit well with her husband. "'So you are already thinking?'" he comments sarcastically when she ventures an opinion on the concept of free will. "'Why shouldn't I think? Am I not a human being?' 'Of course, darling, of course you are . . . but only incidentally; mainly you are a woman'" (1:33). Despite her husband's scorn, Cornelie insists that each individual –

"whether it be man or woman" (1:189) – be allowed to develop his or her innate potential for the sake of general human progress. People today concern themselves with the emancipation of the slaves, the Poles, and the Jews, she continues, but "who thinks about women? Nobody! So they have to think about themselves – and that, and only that will lead to the best result" (1:189).

Faustine voices similar feminist views, but proves incapable of sustained character growth. In *Zwei Frauen* the model has shifted from a Faustian striving to a process of development more typical of the *Bildungsroman*. Here again, Hahn-Hahn reverses the patterns of previous writers, as her heroine grows away from rather than into marriage. She soon breaks free of her husband's tutelage, and he quickly loses interest in his patriarchal idyll. Lack of character and a life spent in the most fashionable circles of European society tempt Eustach to resume his old ways, and he soon begins an affair with Madame Antoinette Orzelska, a capricious Polish beauty in the old aristocratic mold. When the pregnant Cornelie receives proof that her husband has been deceiving her, she declares independence: "'You are free – but so am I, Eustach, so am I'" (2:39). After the birth of a son Cornelie plans to separate from Eustach and return to her father, only to receive news of his death. This would have been a last resort in any case, since she had never been particularly close to her father. His timely demise actually buys Cornelie her freedom by granting her a substantial inheritance. She moves with her son and her faithful servant to Switzerland where she lives in quiet retirement. Here she at first resists the advances of her loyal friend Prince Gotthard Callenberg and then has a brief affair with a young doctor named Leonor Brand. Unlike Faustine, however, who allows Mario Mengen to dictate the terms of their marriage, Cornelie sends Brand away when she recognizes that their love has no future. Eventually her estranged husband dies and Cornelie marries Callenberg on her own terms to attain "internal equilibrium with the external circumstances" (2:234). Although her sister's unhappy fate was probably more typical of the life that awaited women of her social class, Cornelie's development suggests that at least some women could escape the sense of utter futility that clouds Aurore's final moments.

Hahn-Hahn does not write historical novels in the manner of Caroline de la Motte Fouqué, but she does set her works in the historical present and alludes to contemporary events. *Zwei Frauen* begins in 1826 and continues into the 1840s. Like her fellow Prussian aristocrat Fouqué, Ida Gräfin Hahn-Hahn introduces characters who resist revolutionary change, although in Hahn-Hahn's work it is the July Revolution of 1830 in Paris and the November Revolution of the same year in Poland that serve as points of reference. For example, Prince Gotthard Callenberg concedes that the French Revolution was in its origins just as "grandiose" as the German Reformation, but he derides the July Revolution as an overly democratic event that has debased the character of society. While he cautions Cornelie against any association with French radicals, she nevertheless provides Leonor Brand with letters of introduction to friends in Paris, and later even declares that communism is "a natural and justified opposition to the currently dominant and oppressive power of wealth." In her opinion, a third revolution will inevitably follow the Reformation and the French Revolution " 'and that will be the most ferocious, because it will be driven by hunger' " (2:170). But Cornelie hardly looks forward to the triumph of the proletariat; instead, she castigates the greed that is undermining the old social order.

In this context Leonor Brand plays the role of an upstart bourgeois who gains social status at the cost of his soul. Born to the middle class and raised in abject poverty, Brand is convinced that money inevitably brings happiness. For this reason he envies the aristocrats, ignoring the fact that many modern nobles possess little more than their titles. Eventually Brand's rich uncle dies and names his nephew heir on the condition that he marry his uncle's illegitimate daughter. This Brand does, only to discover that he has lost his integrity and Cornelie in acquiring a fortune and a remarkably stupid wife. By use of such characters Hahn-Hahn updates the general sense of aristocratic decline found in the works of Schopenhauer, Droste-Hülshoff, and Fouqué around 1820 to fit the new period of capitalist expansion in the Germany of the 1840s. She leaves us with the image of an old aristocracy that no longer has the financial basis for power; a new plutocracy that degrades the old institution; and an increasingly hungry populace moving toward bloody insurrection. Hahn-Hahn's assessment of German society is less revolutionary than apocalyptic, less hopeful than despairing.

Cornelie also refers to the Revolution when speaking of women's social status. " 'Women now find themselves in exactly the same relation to men as did the Third Estate to the old aristocracy *before* the French Revolution' " (1:183). In order to specify the nature of

Cornelie's feminism more precisely, it is useful to consider the role played by her husband's mistress, Madame Antoinette Orzelska. She exhibits the libertinism of an Old Regime aristocrat, and it is perhaps not coincidental that she should share a name with Marie Antoinette. Oddly enough, however, Orzelska also turns out to be a fervent supporter of liberal politics. Her father fought under Kosciusko, and her brother under Napoleon. When news of the July Revolution breaks out she returns to Poland, excited by reports that the Poles are again flying republican flags. Several months later Orzelska returns bankrupt and in poor health. She accepts Cornelie's generous offer of support, becomes a house guest with the married couple, and promptly begins an affair with Cornelie's husband.

Sophie Mereau once borrowed the figure of Ninon Lenclos from the Old Regime to provide a model for female emancipation for German women around 1800. Hahn-Hahn, in contrast, clearly distances herself from Orzelska's behavior. Her heroine Cornelie may be unconventional in her demand for women to have the same growth-potential as men, but she hardly advocates sexual promiscuity. With the exception of one weak moment with Leonor Brand after having lived for several years apart from her husband – "'I was [weak] . . . because I wanted to be weak!'" (2:197) – Cornelie restricts her sexual activity to marriage. Her goal is not sexual license but a mutually fulfilling partnership, and only her husband's clandestine affair drives her away. She even nurses him when he shows up with failing eyesight years later in Switzerland. In the light of Cornelie's exemplary behavior, Orzelska's immoral actions appear both as a throwback to an older form of aristocratic libertinism and as an implicit reference to the Young Germans' call for the "emancipation of the flesh." Faustine had already derided such notions as "the right to bestiality" championed by "a literary clique" (110), and Cornelie proves no more sympathetic to such immoral behavior. By making Orzelska into a Polish patriot, moreover, Hahn-Hahn suggests that sexual license is akin to an abhorrent form of revolutionary politics.[21] Hahn-Hahn's likening of her contemporary women to the pre-revolutionary Third Estate stops short of a demand for a complete transformation of either the family or the state. She envisions significant progress for women, but only within marriage and without toppling the existing social order. Cornelie stands as a model of an unconventionally independent woman who is neither a happy housewife nor a libertine, and who eventually finds a suitable husband. Just how tenuous her achievement is becomes apparent when we turn to the protagonist of *Sibylle* (1846).

Ida Hahn-Hahn subtitled *Sibylle* "an autobiography" [*Selbstbiographie*] and here as elsewhere in her *oeuvre*, she blurs the line between fiction and autobiography.[22] Taken on its own terms, *Sibylle* could be termed a *Bildungsroman* composed as a fictional autobiography, which traces the heroine's life from childhood to maturity. Unlike Faustine, Sibylle does undergo significant character development, as she grows from a spoiled child-bride into a mature woman who keeps close control over her emotions and her money. Despite her progress, however, Sibylle is not happy; indeed, in her own increasingly bitter assessment, her life has been a miserable failure. We leave her on the brink of death, and the fictive editor introduces her memoirs as the sad "remnants of an existence that ran aground too soon."[23] Hahn-Hahn constructs her narrative as a riddle, then, inviting us to understand why a woman who seemingly had everything – intelligence, beauty, money, lovers, children – finds herself incapable of love, religious faith, or self-esteem.[24]

Like previous Hahn-Hahn heroines, Sibylle spends her adolescent years without a father or any close family ties. She is born as the youngest of three children to a rich Prussian heiress and a Catholic nobleman who moved from his native Franconia to his wife's estate on the Baltic Sea. In early childhood Sibylle identifies most closely with her older brother Heinrich, but he returns from a brief tour of duty in the Napoleonic Wars infected with a disease that in short order kills him, his sister, and his father. The mother suffers a severe nervous breakdown, leaving the thirteen-year-old Sibylle to fend for herself at an age when a Sophie von Sternheim could look forward to another seven years of paternal supervision. Within little more than a year Sibylle has become infatuated with her sister's former fiancé Paul, whom she marries on her fifteenth birthday: "And so I was still almost a child, having barely reached puberty, and already a bride" (1:43).

The newlywed plunges into life at a reckless pace that takes her from Germany to France, from there to Italy, and on to England, Spain, and Switzerland. She squanders money in Paris, collects art in Florence, and enjoys a sensual idyll with Paul in Sorrento, only to discover that she does not love him. She finds his doting affection pitiable, and manipulates him to her advantage, causing him to neglect his diplomatic career and fritter away his fortune to satisfy her whims. At her most decadent moment we find Sibylle stretched out on a hammock on her private yacht, smoking Spanish *cigaritos*, rattling castanets, and accepting burning kisses from Count Otbert von Astrau, a poet-cum-ladies' man in the mold of Mario Mengen. Astrau is called away on urgent family business before things get more serious, and in any case Sibylle was merely testing her own seductive powers on a subject that remains indifferent to her. When Paul dies suddenly after a brief illness, however, it is Astrau who seduces Sibylle into marriage. She soon discovers that her new husband is a compulsive gambler who has married her at least in part to manage his money and pay his debts. Like Cornelie, Sibylle eventually leaves her husband when she learns he has been keeping a mistress. She returns to her estate, where she becomes the unresponsive object of her former music teacher's love. After firmly rejecting his advances Sibylle moves to Switzerland with her now-adolescent daughter, only to inspire passion in a young man whom Sibylle had hoped might become her son-in-law. Her dejected daughter dies of grief, leaving Sibylle to wander aimlessly around Dresden, broken in spirit and in health, and anticipating an early grave.

Sibylle attributes her unhappy adulthood to a series of shocks that interrupt her normal course of female development at three crucial moments. The first is when she loses her entire family just at the onset of puberty, leaving her as a precocious but spoiled child in charge of an estate. Raised in virtual isolation with an exalted sense of herself, Sibylle develops correspondingly unrealistic expectations of suitable men, resulting in inevitable disappointment. The second key moment comes when she goes on a whirlwind tour of Europe just after getting married for the first time. In retrospect, Sibylle feels that a few stable years as a housewife might have compensated for her lost youth: "Simple warm care of the emotions and a sphere of activity restricted to household duties and regulated work is the natural, and therefore the healthiest atmosphere for female development. – But instead of leading me into his house, Paul put me into his traveling coach!" (1:55). The third disruptive moment in Sibylle's formative years occurs just after the birth of her daughter. Motherhood promises to give a sense of discipline to the profligate teenage bride. She nurses her own baby and is at peace with herself until

Paul suddenly dies, her milk dries up, and she is again isolated in Engelau, "without family, relatives, friends; restricted entirely to myself" (1:137). Thus Sibylle interprets her own life in terms of the absence of the traditional support structures that guide female development: had she had a supportive family during adolescence, a period of quiet domesticity in early marriage, or uninterrupted maternal bonding with her daughter, then she might have enjoyed a happier adulthood. As it is, she finds herself incapable of loving the men who love her, bored by motherhood, and consumed by self-reproach on both accounts.

Sibylle's guilty self-censure stands in an odd relation to her unconventional self-assertiveness. Like previous Hahn-Hahn heroines, she is also a Faustian feminist. In a bitter correspondence with her estranged husband Astrau, Sibylle admits that she is imperfect, but insists that her shortcomings are symptomatic of the subjection of women in general: "Since women are treated like children, they cannot act as adults" (2:25). Sibylle demands that women have the right to full development of their innate talents, and rejects any notion of their innate inferiority. She manages to escape the limitations imposed on most women due to her unusual strength of character, but also her social class and her money. In addition to buying her independence, Sibylle's wealth and status also allow her to satisfy what might be termed her sporadically voracious appetite for knowledge. When left as a near-orphan with her incapacitated mother, the ten-year-old Sibylle decides to take charge of the family property and learn everything about it. After her first husband's death she returns to Engelau and quickly turns it into an efficiently managed estate. Having mastered the typically masculine tasks of property and financial management, Sibylle decides to give herself the appropriate education when she returns home for the third time after leaving Astrau in Italy. "But a course in chemistry, physics, or astronomy did not seem at all serious enough for me; instead, I wanted to be educated like the men with ancient languages and mathematics" (2:3). After hiring the appropriate tutors Sibylle puts herself on a grueling round-the-clock schedule for the next three years: "there wasn't a minute that was not allocated to a task . . . my house really seemed like a penal institution" (2:8).

Not surprisingly, Sibylle breathes a sigh of relief when her self-imposed sentence is over: "No more studying and reading! – was *one* main desire; no more boredom! was a second" (2:40). The boredom that plagues Sibylle points to a deeper sense of dissatisfaction with life that goes beyond a distaste for Latin and mathematics. As she suggests, part of her unhappiness stems from a series of unfortunate coincidences that disrupt her normal female development at crucial stages in her life: adolescence, marriage, and motherhood. The recurrent cycles of frenetic activity followed by lethargy and depression indicate that Sibylle's dissatisfaction is not only gender-specific, but class-specific as well. The inherited wealth that enables her to escape restrictions placed on less fortunate women brings with it the curse of boredom that afflicts the idle rich. "So I made and received visits," writes Sibylle of her winter in Venice, "I had soirées, I took a box in the *Fenice*, I had myself introduced at court . . . and I was terribly bored" (1:189–90). That this sort of pointless life should lead to boredom is not surprising, but Sibylle's intermittent bouts of self-discipline in Engelau leave her no more fulfilled. Greater knowledge produces only greater boredom, and even the experience of running her estate produces no lasting satisfaction.

To an even greater extent than in *Zwei Frauen*, Hahn-Hahn moves from her protagonist's personal frustrations to analyze problems confronting the entire German aristocracy. As a young woman Sibylle visits England, where she develops an appreciation of the local form of government. The English aristocracy has retained its vitality, in her view, because it is an "organic institution" that accepts talented men into its ranks regardless of their birth. "In Germany the nobility has not chosen to adopt this noble and wise course of action, and has become completely debased by [offering] patents of nobility for sale" (1:78). The fact that money rather than talent provides access to the German nobility has two dire consequences: it not only demeans the aristocracy, but it also breeds resentment on the part of the masses: "If they can't rise – well then, they drag downwards! This development debases both halves. Because *everything* is supposed to be *in common* [*allgemein*], it becomes *common* [*gemein*; base, vulgar]" (1:78). Hahn-Hahn's characters again express the concern of blue-blooded aristocrats who fear that new capital degrades the old social order.

Sibylle returns to her analysis of the German aristocracy when she spends time with Count Wilderich Wildeshaus, a young East Frisian nobleman. Wilderich features as a representative of the old landed German aristocracy who is sickened by the "anti-aristocratic trend" of modern times (2:227–28). As a representative of the old school,

Wilderich feels that it is his duty to be the "head of a family for his subjects" (2:227). His despair stems from the fact that he lacks money to care for his wards and that his social class makes it impossible for him to learn a trade and work for a living. When he expresses his horror to Sibylle at his cousin's marriage to a rich banker's daughter, Sibylle repeats her earlier argument that the English nobility has remained vital precisely because of its willingness to absorb new talent – and new money – from worthy individuals of low birth. Sibylle then goes further to suggest that it is not merely personal obstinacy on the part of the German nobility that has rendered it obsolete, but the transformation of the old feudal estates into a modern state bureaucracy: "'You are all the first farmers on your estates and nothing more. You are no longer lords at all! The government – that is the lord! It tells you precisely what to do. You should have no illusions about it: noble peasants, that's what you are'" (2:233). Like it or not, money is the only way to achieve the independence he craves: "'Nowadays it is impossible to acquire wealth without commercial or industrial speculation'" (2:234).

Through Sibylle, then, Hahn-Hahn offers a clear-eyed assessment of the economic and political changes wrought by capitalism and an expanding state bureaucracy that render impossible the sort of benevolent patriarchy that had once attracted conservative writers. What in the work of Sophie von LaRoche had seemed a progressive alternative to a decadent Rococo aristocracy now looks like a hopelessly inadequate response to nineteenth-century social and political change. For this reason Sibylle urges Wilderich to travel outside Germany and to give up his provincial adherence to outmoded beliefs. Hahn-Hahn would like to see the rebirth of the old aristocracy through new money; in doing so she distances herself from the anachronistic pride of the young *Landjunker*, but also from liberal calls for a republican nation-state. Writing just two years before the German National Assembly convenes in Frankfurt, Hahn-Hahn makes her protagonist highly skeptical of nationalist sentiments. Sibylle claims that she has experienced pride in her country only when listening to a Beethoven symphony. Otherwise she finds nothing to celebrate in the current state of the nation. Sibylle has largely exhausted her energy by the time she makes these statements and has fled to self-imposed exile in Switzerland; despite her admonitions to Wilderich, she seems largely resigned to witness the further degeneration of the old social order and its bankrupt ideology.

With increasing intensity Sibylle's personal sense of *tedium vitae* broadens into a preoccupation with the transitory nature of all life: "Nothing lasts!" (1:274). The discovery of Astrau's infidelity reminds Sibylle of "the nullity of everything that people call happiness" (1:282). This overwhelming sense of the pointlessness of human existence even drives the Protestant Sibylle to flirt with conversion to Catholicism. The idea first occurs to her when visiting her father's brother, a bishop in Würzburg, but he insists that she lacks the emotional stability to make such a serious decision. Much later Sibylle returns to Würzburg on her way to Switzerland. This time she throws herself into theological studies, although she is tormented by the religious doubt that typifies the modern age. In the end, the very skepticism that compels Sibylle to search for stability in the Catholic Church makes it impossible for her to convert: " 'But I, my father – born to Protestantism and come of age in a time of protest – I have only the capacities that it [Protestantism] inspires: I understand your church, I kneel before it – but . . . I do not believe in it' " (2:183–84). Within four years Ida Hahn-Hahn would find the faith that Sibylle lacks and convert to Catholicism, yet her heroine of 1846 finds no such consolation. Her overwhelming sense of this world's vanity rivals that of a Gryphius or a Hofmannswaldau, but she lacks the transcendent faith of the Baroque authors: "I was dying of the general transitoriness. And the end of everything – was death!" (2:211). Sibylle begins her autobiography under the sign of death: "Slowly and with great torment life recedes from me and I know it" (1:5). She concludes on a similar downbeat, presumably dying in mid-sentence: "I have not lived through my heart; it takes its revenge, and I die of my heart —" (2:302).

FANNY LEWALD: REPUBLICAN, FEMINIST, JEW

In 1847 Fanny Lewald published a novel entitled *Diogena* under the transparent pseudonym of Iduna Gräfin H. H. The viciously witty text lampoons what had become standard features of Ida Hahn-Hahn's early fiction. Like Faustine, Diogena amasses knowledge, experience, and men with frightening speed, only to discover before long that she too is unhappy. Frenetic activity alternates with crippling boredom in a life that grants Diogena no lasting satisfaction and destroys the lives of others. " 'Have a look at the life of my mother and my Aunt Faustine,' " summarizes Diogena to Prince

Callenberg (the son of the man who had followed Cornelie so patiently throughout *Zwei Frauen*), "'we are the incarnation of today's restlessness, emptiness, and idleness; we are the female Eternal Jews, we are cursed, we are tragic figures, vampires.'"[25] By the time Diogena is seventeen years old she has divorced one man, driven another to suicide, and caused yet another to die in a duel for her sake. She takes to the road in hope of better fortune, traveling first to the Near East and then to North America, where, inspired by Cooper and Sealsfield, she hopes to find a healthy alternative to European civilization. Dressed in a fetching costume as an Indian maiden, Diogena enters the wilderness to find a suitable mate. She offers herself to an Indian chieftain over a haunch of venison, only to discover that he will expect her to do all the work around the wigwam before he discards her for a younger woman. "Oh, what remained of my hopes! What of Cooper's ideals did I find in this horrible reality?" (168). After a last trip to China Diogena ends up where Lewald clearly thinks she belongs: in a madhouse outside Paris.

Critics have speculated that Lewald's parody was motivated by personal jealousy, since both she and Hahn-Hahn were romantically involved with the same man. Professional rivalry may also have played a part, since Lewald and Hahn-Hahn were two of the most widely read German women writers of the 1840s.[26] Taken on its own terms, *Diogena* reveals fundamental differences between the two writers regarding both women's issues and politics. Lewald portrays Diogena as the worst sort of aristocratic snob who is indifferent to the plight of the lower classes. To her horror, Diogena discovers that her first husband – from the highest nobility, of course – turns out to be a closet liberal: "his principles of humanity, his ideas about equal human rights seemed crazy to me" (39–40). In Lewald's view, it is Diogena who is insane: "Her madness is the product of an intellectual trend among idle women of the aristocratic world" who have "created a theory of feminine selfishness which has now reached its highpoint in German women's literature" (178). Mistakenly convinced that the world does not understand them, these women remain blind to their own egotism. By the time we have finished *Diogena* it is abundantly clear that Lewald finds Hahn-Hahn's work stylistically pretentious, politically reactionary, and detrimental to the feminist cause.

Parodies are by their nature unforgiving, so we need not belabor the point that Lewald fails to do justice to progressive aspects of Hahn-Hahn's work. Personal animosity aside, it would in some ways be difficult to find two more dissimilar writers: the one, a Protestant aristocrat raised on ancestral estates, the other, the eldest daughter of a Jewish businessman brought up in the city of Königsberg.[27] While Hahn-Hahn remained deeply suspicious of the lower classes, Lewald supported the 1848 Revolution enthusiastically and championed the rights and values of middle-class workers in her fiction. Despite their differing political allegiances, both Hahn-Hahn and Lewald wanted to liberate women from their narrowly defined roles in nineteenth-century society. The combination of class-specific beliefs and experiences with a common feminist agenda resulted in different sorts of internal tensions in the works of the two writers: Hahn-Hahn's aristocratic heroines lack close family ties, which grants them a degree of independence absent in the writing of the politically liberal Lewald, who grew up in a loving, but stultifying bourgeois home. Hahn-Hahn's characters draw strength for feminist assertiveness from the same social background that colors their political conservatism, while Lewald's liberalism stems from the same middle-class environment that subjects daughters to paternal authority.

In a touching moment in her autobiography, Lewald gives her father a copy of her first novel, which he promises to read in bed before falling asleep. Several days later Lewald is relieved when he gives the work his stamp of approval, despite several outspoken passages against the sort of arranged marriage that he had once tried to force on her. This episode from Lewald's autobiography characterizes the mixture of protest and acquiescence that runs throughout the novel itself. *Clementine* (1842) tells the familiar story of a young woman pressured by her family to accept an arranged marriage to an older man. Although the heroine acknowledges that the Geheimrath von Meining, age fifty, is an upstanding citizen and one of the most respected medical doctors in his field, Clementine remains loyal to the memory of Robert Thalberg, a man now in his late twenties like herself, who had once seemed certain to marry her. Although he has long since broken off contact, Clementine remains faithful to his memory and speaks out strongly against marriages of convenience: "'The marriages that I see contracted daily are worse than prostitution.'"[28] Clementine insists that she has nothing against marriage itself: "'I do not hate marriage; on the contrary, I respect it so much that I fear I will debase it and myself if I conclude the holy bond unfeelingly'" (15). Just a few days after taking this strong stance, however, Clementine bows to family pressure and marries Meining after all.

Clementine speaks boldly, but acts obediently, a pattern that continues throughout the novel.[29] Three years after their marriage, Meining receives an invitation to move to Berlin, which he accepts without consulting his wife. Although Clementine is happy to return to the city where she was born, she finds his failure to ask her opinion insulting: "Her husband treated her like a child whom one loves very much, whom one wants to spare all grief – but she was not a child, she was his wife, who wanted to share his worries with him, and who interpreted his reticence as condescension" (42). A rare quarrel follows, during which Clementine laments her husband's reluctance to speak of his life before marriage and his insistence that she remain silent about her own past, but in the end she takes back all protest: "'Don't be angry, my love, if I was wrong, and remain fond of me! Just tell me what you want, you strict master, and I will obey'" (46).

Clementine's oscillation between self-assertion and submissiveness recurs when she reencounters Robert Thalberg in Berlin. He soon realizes that he had been foolish to abandon Clementine for a brief fling with an actress years ago, and before long the two old friends are more in love than ever. Clementine struggles to repress her desires, but when caught off guard in Meining's absence she declares her love for Thalberg, and they exchange passionate kisses. Mention of her husband's name brings her to her senses, however, and by the next morning Clementine renounces Thalberg forever. A concluding flash-forward shows Clementine two years later, still married to Meining, and consoled by the knowledge that Thalberg once loved her. Thalberg, having given up any hope that Clementine will request a divorce, has taken her advice and married a pert blond teenager.

Small wonder, then, that *Clementine* should prove a disappointment for feminist critics in search of a consistent polemic against patriarchal abuse. *Clementine* is most notable for its glaring inconsistencies, whether understood negatively as a loss of nerve or sign of immaturity in the fledgling writer,[30] or – more generously – as a reflection of the tension between feminist outrage and guilty self-censorship felt by Lewald and many other nineteenth-century women.[31] The conflict is both against external restrictions and against an internalized voice of authority that censors protest and turns it into guilty acquiescence to acknowledged injustice. As Regula Venske has observed, *Clementine* reveals an ambivalence that recurs throughout Lewald's *oeuvre*, which oscillates between criticism of patriarchy and "her respect and admiration of paternal strength."[32] It seems unduly harsh, however, to conclude that Lewald's indecisiveness resulted in "her failure as a writer." Literary works that express contradictory impulses are often more interesting than self-confident polemics, after all, and I wonder whose interests are served with a rating system that (once again) dismisses "the literary triviality"[33] of a neglected woman writer. *Clementine* performs valuable cultural labor both by articulating feminist protest and by revealing its enemies, both without and within. Lewald's development as a novelist lies not in her move toward a more consistent feminist stance, but in the expanded scope of novels that begin to address broader political issues.

Lewald's second and perhaps most famous novel *Jenny* (1843) breaks new ground by linking the question of women's rights to Jewish emancipation.[34] At the center of the novel stands the wealthy Meier family. The son Eduard, a handsome and accomplished young doctor, would have qualified for a position as the director of a major clinic had the government not barred Jews from such positions of authority. Already as a schoolboy Eduard had been outraged to learn of the discrimination he would face as a German Jew, and he experienced first-hand the anti-Semitic "Hep-Hep!" disturbances of 1819.[35] Like many young men of his generation, Eduard joined the initially liberal *Burschenschaft* movement and was imprisoned for his subversive beliefs. Doubly marked as a Jew and a liberal, Eduard had considered emigration, but love of family and the fatherland kept him at home. The action in the novel begins some fifteen years later when Eduard faces a new crisis: he has fallen in love with his Christian patient Clara Horn. Eduard's easiest option to solve both his personal and professional difficulties would be to convert to Christianity, but he refuses, not out of religious faith – the Meiers are an enlightened family of secularized Jews – but out of loyalty to the Jewish people. "'Is it possible to tear yourself away from your people?' he asked himself, 'can I separate myself from my people for my own pleasure, because they are unjustly despised, because they are oppressed? Never!'"[36] When the government rejects his request for a "mixed marriage," Eduard reluctantly gives up hope. Clara marries another man, while Eduard remains single and works for constitutional reform that will prohibit discrimination against the Jews.

Eduard's sister Jenny also falls in love with a Christian, the young theologian Reinhard who had been Eduard's fellow *Burschenschaftler* at the university and who has taken a position as Jenny's tutor. As a woman it is assumed that Jenny will adapt to her future husband's beliefs, and unlike Eduard, Jenny does agree to convert to Christianity.[37] Repressing both her own religious skepticism and her witty, sophisticated personality, Jenny tries hard to become the pious and docile Christian Reinhard expects in a wife. She allows herself to be baptized, but balks when Reinhard requests that they take communion together. In a courageous letter Jenny confesses her lack of faith to her fiancé: " 'I don't believe that Christ is the Son of God, that he was resurrected from the dead. I don't believe that his death was necessary to win us God's forgiveness and compassion . . . I don't believe . . . I can't help it!' " (192). Reinhard immediately calls off the engagement and soon marries a more tractable bride. Jenny returns to her family and eventually develops into an independent, mature woman who spends her time with intellectual and artistic pursuits and devotes herself with Eduard to the future emancipation of the Jews.

As this brief outline suggests, Fanny Lewald's *Jenny* calls for both an end to religious intolerance and a feminist alternative to domestic virtue. Equally progressive in its advocacy of Jewish emancipation and women's rights, it remains one of the few nineteenth-century German novels by a woman in print today. *Jenny* nevertheless contains certain elements of compromise and contradiction that qualify its unquestionably liberal thrust. For example, Irene Stocksieker Di Maio has focused on the tension that arises between Lewald's call for the recognition of the ethnic difference of the Jews and her desire that they be integrated into the mainstream of German political life.[38] Eduard is loyal to his Jewish identity and also a liberal German patriot; he works toward a society in which the two demands would not be mutually exclusive. Lewald makes both Jenny and Eduard into appealing, non-threatening characters who merit inclusion into German society.[39] In developing positive Jewish role-models, however, Lewald distances her protagonists from negative Jewish stereotypes. Only from this perspective do the otherwise puzzling anti-Semitic caricatures in *Jenny* make sense. When the Meier family is doing its best to welcome Clara Horn into their midst as a potential daughter-in-law, they receive an annoying visit from a Frau Steinheim who gossips in a loud voice with a Jewish accent, gesticulates vigorously, and embarrasses the Meiers by accentuating the ethnic differences that they are trying to minimize. As Eduard later explains, " 'Steinheim's bad habit is partially national. The old Oriental elements still prevail in the Jews; and still today, for example, the uneducated Jew enjoys little stories, like the Oriental' " (78). This split between an acculturated, secular German Jew and the crass mannerisms of the *Ostjuden* provides a good example of what Sander Gilman has analyzed as Jewish self-hatred.[40] Eduard envisions a liberal constitution that allows for ethnic diversity, yet the process of assimilation threatens not only to efface Jewish identity, but also to turn assimilated Jews into their own worst enemies, as they adopt the Christian-German prejudice against certain unpleasant "national" characteristics of the "Oriental" Jews.

A different sort of ambivalence surrounds Jenny's decision to remain unmarried. In many ways Reinhard's rejection is the best thing that could have happened to her, as she gets to keep her family, her money, and her independence. The price, however, is that she remain celibate. When her mother dies of a sudden illness, Jenny steps into her place: "Now Jenny stood alone at the head of the household; her father was dependent on her. This realization raised her self-esteem and removed every desire from her heart but one: to live for her father and to brighten his old age" (204). Eight years later a potential suitor named Count Walter observes Jenny from a distance, "who hung chatting on her father's arm and was concerned only with him" (208). This image could almost have been taken from the conclusion to *Julchen Grünthal*, except that Jenny's return to her father enables the continuation rather than the end of her intellectual development. It was Jenny's family that had molded her into an impetuous, irreverent, and frequently sarcastic young woman; eight additional years at home have allowed Jenny to grow in ways that would have been denied her as Reinhard's wife. Julchen Grünthal's regression to pseudo-virginity becomes the precondition for Jenny Meier's ongoing personal maturation.

For this reason Jenny resists Count Walter's advances: " 'I have grown used to a certain freedom that I can no longer do without and which I would, after all, have to give up in marriage'" (227). There are indications, however, that Jenny is not completely happy with her decision to remain single. She realizes that her reluctance to marry is based in part on her unwillingness to admit to others and herself that she is capable of loving another man. Having lost her first love, Jenny makes what the narrator terms the irrational decision [*Schwärmerei*] to remain single. In addition, Jenny harbors what turn out to be justified doubts concerning the social acceptability of a marriage between an aristocratic man and a Jewish woman. When she finally does agree to marry Graf Walter – with her father's permission – her happiness is short-lived. Walter soon dies from wounds received in a duel against an anti-Semitic nobleman, and Jenny promptly dies of grief.

Lewald's otherwise realistic narrative takes a sudden melodramatic turn in its conclusion, which one critic has termed "overwrought, unmotivated, and sentimentalized."[41] That the otherwise robust Jenny should drop dead of grief certainly strains credulity, but Lewald uses this death to make a point: German society was not ready to accept such a union across class and religious lines, and any attempt to allow her Jewish heroine to walk off into the sunset with a Christian aristocrat would have been even more unrealistic.[42] But why could Jenny not return to her largely satisfying life as an unmarried woman living with her father and brother? It would seem that the engagement has forced Jenny to confront the inherent contradictions of her position as an emancipated woman living at home. Through Walter she realizes that she has gained intellectual freedom only by remaining loyal to the man who rudely rejected her, and by believing foolishly that it is now her duty to remain single while she cares for her father. Walter offers Jenny the chance to realize her marital ideal, in which the woman is no longer a supplement to the stronger man, but an equal partner – she likes the image of two trees with intertwined branches. When social prejudice cuts short this marriage, Jenny finds it equally impossible to return to a life of self-deception with her family. Stated positively, Lewald sketches both a political utopia, where German Christians and Jews could participate equally in an enlightened, constitutional state, and a private utopia, which would enable men and women of different religious and social backgrounds to enter marriage as equal partners. Jenny's death makes clear that neither goal will be realized soon.

Having portrayed an unhappily married woman in her first novel and an unhappy unmarried woman in her second, Lewald turned next to defend the morality of divorce. "'Don't you believe,'" cries the protagonist of *Eine Lebensfrage* [A Vital Question] (1845), "'that in a thousand cases the separation of a marriage can be a highly moral act, indeed, that in such cases it can become a holy duty?'"[43] As was the case in *Clementine*, Lewald's characters are not opposed to the institution of marriage itself; on the contrary: "Marriage and family life are the basis of the state, and it is its duty, therefore, to protect them" (225). The problem, according to the figures in this novel, is that the state has its priorities backwards: it brands those seeking escape from intolerable marriages as criminals while turning a blind eye toward the fate of young women forced to marry against their will. "Its goal should be to make happy marriages possible, not to hold unhappy marriages together" (227). Lewald links the personal freedom to divorce to the public welfare of the state, enlisting the conservative belief in the sanctity of marriage and the family in the defense of liberal divorce laws.

The novel focuses on the unhappy marriage between Alfred von Reichenbach, a wealthy aristocrat and respected writer, and his wife Caroline. Engaged to Caroline as a nineteen-year-old soldier, Alfred was forbidden by a codicil in his uncle's will to marry before he turned twenty-four. By that time he had developed strong reservations about his compatibility with Caroline, but felt obliged to keep his promise. The novel opens when Alfred, now in his mid-thirties with a ten-year-old son Felix, separates from his wife after a bitter quarrel. Leaving her and the boy on his estate, Alfred moves to Berlin. On the way he encounters Therese von Brand, a woman who had once loved him and whose brother Julian had facilitated the publication of Alfred's first book of poetry. Alfred and Therese rediscover their love for one another, and after a series of delays Alfred finally does divorce his wife and marry Therese.

In an effort to maintain sympathy for her protagonists and hence her controversial thesis, Lewald makes it clear that Alfred only chooses divorce as a last option after having considered the consequences from all possible angles. Julian advises Alfred against divorce, pointing out that he risks alienating his loyal readers; besides, he continues, there is no need for a formal divorce when Alfred can do as he pleases while living alone in Berlin. Less self-serving arguments than Julian's against divorce present themselves when Alfred returns briefly to his estate. His subjects love and respect him, for Alfred has been an efficient manager and a just ruler. In his absence, however, things have quickly fallen apart: the peasants are unhappy and the estate poorly maintained. While home Alfred discovers that in the case of divorce the Catholic Church will take control of his lands, and that Caroline will gain custody of Felix. For the sake of his son and his subjects, Alfred renounces his desire for Therese and resolves to live with unhappiness. Still later a scheming chaplain tries to pressure Alfred into divorce by publishing a notice in the paper to the effect that Alfred will soon leave his wife to continue an affair with Therese. The only effective counter to the slanderous message is to remain married, and for the second time Alfred grits his teeth and tries to reconcile his differences with his wife. Therese's own respect for the sanctity of marriage and mother-hood make her extremely reluctant to press for divorce. Like Jenny, however, Therese finally concludes that renunciation is wrong, while Alfred concedes that reconciliation with Caroline is impossible. Only then does he plan divorce and remarriage.

The high moral standards of Alfred and Therese stand in sharp contrast to Julian's behavior. He enters the novel as an aging rake involved with the actress Sophie Harcourt. Although Sophie has a past, she swears that Julian is the first man she has really loved. Julian nevertheless remains indifferent to her pleas and abandons her. Broken-hearted, Sophie quits the theatre and considers retiring to a convent, before eventually becoming a nurse in her native Paris. Meanwhile Julian toys with the idea of seducing a sixteen-year-old girl. His conscience gets the better of him on Christmas Eve, however, and he rushes out into the cold to send Sophie a bouquet. With less-than-subtle poetic justice, Lewald has Julian catch cold and nearly die from his belated attempt to make amends. The entire episode exposes the Young German call for the "emancipation of the flesh" as an exercise in male self-indulgence, and challenges public opinion by insisting that the "fallen" woman acts in accord-ance with higher moral principles than her lover.

The choice of a land-owning aristocrat as protagonist enables Lewald to introduce political concerns into a novel about the seemingly personal question of divorce. As mentioned, Alfred faces a dilemma: he can either remain in his role as an effective manager of his estate and just ruler of his subjects, or he can retreat from his public role to find happiness in marriage. He can find private bliss, that is, only if he abrogates his public responsibilities. That Alfred is fully aware of the consequences of his choice becomes clear in the long letter he writes to Therese near the end of the novel, in which he acknowledges that he will lose control of his estate. As if trying to convince himself, he argues that what he did for his former subjects will have to be enough, but past experience has shown that the order of his old estate quickly disintegrated in his absence and there is no reason to expect that things will change when it reverts to the Catholic Church, which Lewald portrays as an insatiable institution fueled by hypocrisy and greed. When married to Therese, Alfred plans to do good within a limited sphere of influence that sounds very much like a Biedermeier idyll: "'Free and with you! I will feel like a happy lord under the modest roof of a simple country home, and peace and love will reign above us and in us – and will enliven and protect us'" (348).

Alfred's choice between domestic bliss and benevolent patriarchy stands in an awkward relation to the political discussions he hears in the Berlin salons. If Julian exhibits the licentiousness that Lewald condemns in the Young Germans, he also voices liberal political viewpoints with which Lewald would have been more sympathetic. Julian, who works as a civil servant in the Prussian state bureaucracy, denies that he wants to do away with the nobility: "No one in our country is demanding the abolition of the aristocracy, or the limitation of property-owners' rights; everyone just wants space to develop freely, to be recognized for what he is, and to achieve that for which reason gives him inclination and ability" (276). He dates the resurgence of German liberalism to the influence of the 1830 July Revolution, but even then the country was slow to awaken from its fifteen-year sleep since the Wars of Liberation: "our dear fatherland . . . rubbed its eyes for ten years, while our neighbors on the other side of the Rhine . . . made great progress. Now our day has dawned" (275). By the end of the novel, however, Julian has barely recovered from a near-fatal illness, while Albert is about to retire from public life. If Germany's day has indeed dawned, neither man seems likely to lead the country into a brighter future.

Therese, at least, has finally found happiness, having renounced renunciation and accepted Albert's proposal. But where does this leave Caroline? For the most part, Lewald seems anxious to paint an unforgiving portrait of her that justifies Alfred's decision to seek divorce. Hence Caroline detests Alfred's poetry, scolds her child harshly, befriends an unctuous Catholic priest, and spies on her husband. On rare occasions, however, Lewald reminds us of what Caroline stands to lose in a divorce. While her husband enjoys the company of a supportive group of friends in Berlin, she must remain alone on her rural estate. Alfred returns briefly, but only to leave again for Berlin, this time taking their only child with him: "A scream of pain that made Alfred tremble tore itself out of [Caroline's] breast; it was one of those sounds of nature that the primitive has in common with the most civilized human being" (152). Although Lewald usually goes out of her way to suggest that Caroline gets what she deserves, this scene, placed strategically at the end of the first volume, serves as a poignant reminder of the pain that she will suffer in divorce. By including this passage, Lewald adds further nuance to her *roman à thèse*: divorce may indeed be a "highly moral deed" in certain circumstances, but in this particular case, at least, the justifiable divorce leaves lasting scars on the divorcée and forces Albert to turn his back on his public responsibilities.

One year after this problematic look at divorce among the aristocracy, Lewald published a simpler study of middle-class romance. *Der dritte Stand* [The Third Estate] (1846), which at 201 pages stands somewhere between a long novella and a short novel, reflects Lewald's continued move toward engagement with contemporary social issues in her fiction. The work begins as the factory owner Wallbach plans to celebrate the twenty-fifth anniversary of his cotton mill in Berlin. Wallbach plans to commemorate the occasion by building a hospital for his employees, and the loyal workers respond with a hearty cheer. "It was an uplifting moment full of high, inward reverence, full of warm thanks for a happy fate, which the family realized that they owed to the beloved father."[44] Alfred's paternalistic concern for his rural subjects recurs in the capitalist's care for his urban factory workers. As Wallbach's son Franz later explains, this seeming largesse is actually a shrewd business policy: "Humanitarianism and self-interest can go hand in hand here [in the factory], and many an egotist would become merciful if he realized what profit it would bring him" (146). Whether motivated by greed, generosity, or both, Wallbach's management policies produce contented workers.

Two romances carry the plot of this short novel. Franz Wallbach loves General von Dohnen's daughter Anna, but her family prefers that she marry Baron Soldern. In the end love breaks down class barriers, as Anna rejects the idle aristocrat in favor of the hard-working businessman. Meanwhile Franz's younger sister Luise has become infatuated with her extravagant music teacher, while resisting the advances of a worthy young man. She discovers just in time that the musician only wants her money, however, and we last see her poised to choose the more respectable husband. In both cases, middle-class virtue triumphs: over aristocratic pride in the first marriage, and over artistic pretensions in the second.

The break between the aristocracy and the bourgeoisie is not absolute, however. As it turns out, it was General von Dohnen who had loaned Wallbach the money to begin the business from which he and his family are currently reaping the profits. In this case it was an alliance between aristocratic capital and bourgeois labor that worked for the benefit of all involved. The main difference between the social classes is less wealth than taste. The general's wife finds the Wallbach's bourgeois companions coarse, and Wallbach himself condemns all art as a frivolous pursuit in times of social misery. He fails to distinguish between the sort of romantic *Schwärmerei* and aristocratic self-indulgence Lewald would also condemn, and her own socially engaged novels. As von Dohnen points out to his wife, moreover, a better-educated second generation of capitalist entrepreneurs will soon acquire the social graces their parents lack. Education has taken the place of birth in determining social class: "Now there are only two classes, the educated and the uneducated, and all educated people can and must be placed equally in society, just as all people are supposed to be equal before the law" (126).

With this statement Lewald anticipates the aspirations of the *Bildungsbürgertum* of the later nineteenth century. As a liberal member of the "third estate," Lewald takes aim at aristocratic abuses while stopping far short of Karl Marx's demand that the workers of the world unite to throw off the chains of capitalist exploitation. In the place of inevitable class struggle, Lewald offers a rosier scenario in which workers love their fatherly factory owners, and aristocrats not only admire middle-class diligence, but even allow their daughters to marry beneath their station for love.[45] Altruism prevails in this slight novel, but as in the case of Wallbach's kindly attitude toward his workers, Lewald makes it clear that aristocratic self-interest lies in acquiescence to the demands of the rising middle class.

Just two years later fighting would break out on the streets of Berlin, and for a brief period it seemed as though the Restoration was finally coming to an end. In the months leading up to and immediately after the March Revolution Lewald was at work on a new novel, *Prinz Louis Ferdinand* (1849).[46] While her first three novels had addressed a variety of social issues in her contemporary Germany – arranged marriages, Jewish emancipation, divorce – the new novel would be set in the past. *Prinz Louis Ferdinand* begins in 1799 on New Year's Eve in Berlin and follows its hero until his death on the eve of the battle of Jena in October, 1806. Thus Lewald selects one of the least glorious periods of Prussian history: the years leading up to the defeat that began the period of Napoleonic occupation. Lewald condemns King Friedrich Wilhelm III's policy of appeasement toward France that led to the humiliating setback, but she also uses her historical fiction to criticize the Prussian government of the *Vormärz*.

Lewald's analysis of the conflict between Prussia and Napoleonic France in *Prinz Louis Ferdinand* stresses the contrasting motivations for the two armies. The French fight for freedom, while the Prussians merely obey orders. Instead of uplifting its citizens in pursuit of common ideals, the Prussian state literally beats its subjects into submission, and Lewald includes graphic descriptions of the Prussian penchant for corporal punishment in her novel. As the battle of Jena will demonstrate, an absolutist monarchy based on military principles of subordination cannot compete with a republic that draws its strength from nationalist enthusiasm. By identifying the Prussian weakness of 1806 in its outmoded absolutism, Lewald offers a barely veiled critique of the Restoration principle of legitimacy that works to undermine nationalist aspirations in the *Vormärz*. The German princes prevent the development of representative government in a united nation in a way that, in Lewald's opinion, can only be detrimental to the common good.

Despite her criticism of the Prussian aristocracy, Lewald introduces her noble protagonist in the effusive tones of popular fiction: "He was Prince Louis Ferdinand, the nephew of Frederick the Great and the cousin of the reigning king; a youthful heroic figure, in the fullness of beauty and majesty."[47] Women adore him, his subjects look up to him, and the troops want him in command. When the prince turns on the charm, even his enemies find him irresistible. He is also a shrewd judge of the Prussian military situation, recognizing the danger posed by Napoleon's troops and the folly of the king's attempts to keep the peace, yet his loyalty to the throne prohibits him from openly challenging royal policy. As a result, Prince Louis

Ferdinand spends the years leading up to the Prussian defeat in a kind of limbo, as circumstances prevent him from assuming the role of the Prussian hero he seems destined to play.

What is an under-employed prince to do? In his better moments Louis Ferdinand tries to work in small ways for the Prussian people, but he only succeeds in provoking the king's wrath. The frustrated prince responds by going into voluntary exile on his country estate in Schricke, where he longs to escape the "golden chain" that binds him to the throne: "Then give me the freedom to be a middle-class citizen; give me the freedom that is rooted in the equality of mankind!" (171; 1:81). In his brief idyll in Schricke Ferdinand learns to appreciate values that Lewald herself held dear. Chief among these is his recognition of the family as the basis of the social order. Ferdinand moves into a simple rustic home with his mistress Henriette and their child, and although class difference prevents an official union, he settles into a quiet domesticity identical in other respects to a bourgeois marriage. He becomes so absorbed in his new role that he even begins to entertain hopes for a constitutional government: "He felt that in a state in which the citizen had a share in the government, every landowner was himself a monarch who ruled his free land according to the general principles of a monarchial system of government. Longing for power, he had wished for a free constitution because he was not a monarch but only a subject" (187; 1:100–01).

Just as Ferdinand's position as powerless prince makes it impossible for him to rule as an effective monarch, the same position makes it equally impossible for him to maintain the illusion he is a rural *pater familias*. Pressing state business soon tears him out of the idyll and forces a reconciliation with the king, and before long the prince has gone back to his old bad habits. Bored with the simple peasant girl he has taken as his mistress, he begins to pursue the wife of a disloyal subject. The prince recognizes that he is abusing his power in the old seigniorial style, particularly when he invites himself into her home in the company of a French officer: "He, the zealous advocate of personal freedom, of German national consciousness, trampled both in the presence of a Frenchman" (243; 1:168). Ferdinand nevertheless seduces the man's wife and continues a torrid affair that ends only when he is called back to Berlin and her husband flees the country. Months later Prince Ferdinand learns that the woman died shortly afterward, but by this time he is involved with yet another married woman. Disgusted with himself and a life that brings him no happiness, the prince is only too glad to seek death in the struggle against Napoleon.

Prince Louis Ferdinand alternates between a variety of roles: he is by destiny a noble prince, by inclination a quiet *Bürger*, and only by default a bad aristocrat. His dilemma recalls the situation in *Eine Lebensfrage*, where Alfred von Reichenbach faces a similar choice between his public responsibilities and his desire for private happiness in marriage. Alfred must choose one or the other, but Prince Louis Ferdinand can have neither: as long as his cousin remains on the throne, he cannot act as prince, and he is far too prominent a figure to vanish into the backwaters of a rural Prussian estate. By selecting the prince as protagonist for her historical novel, Lewald may well have been making an indirect comment on the status of the Prussian aristocracy in 1848: as an individual, Louis Ferdinand is not intrinsically evil, but he is a member of a social class that is becoming increasingly anachronistic, as economic and political power shifts to the Third Estate. Lewald complicates this parable of aristocratic decline by stressing both the positive personal traits of the prince and his enlightened opposition to the mindless extremes of Prussian discipline. If the aristocracy is in decline, in other words, it is at least in part because it remains hostile to progressive reforms that could have retained its vitality.

The bourgeois family stands as the positive alternative to the troubled aristocracy. Land ownership and the ability to participate in the government will create the sort of enthusiastic citizens present in England and France, Lewald suggests, but denied in the Prussian state. One more ingredient is necessary before the family can become the basis of the state, however: husband and wife must be equal partners. For this reason alone, Prince Louis Ferdinand cannot find lasting happiness with his rural mistress; he has "fallen into the error of all men who choose a childish, weak woman's nature for their mate, so that they may have a creature who looks up to her protector with moving humility" (189; 1:103). The prince's only intellectual equal is his good friend Rahel von Varnhagen, but he fails to recognize her love and in any case could hardly marry a Jewish woman. Through the historical figure of Rahel von Varnhagen, Lewald voices many of the same protests against Prussian anti-Semitism she included earlier in *Jenny*, and she once again links the demand for women's emancipation to Jewish emancipation.[48]

Like the prince, Rahel recognizes the extent of the French threat, and in this awareness, coupled with her love for the prince, lies the source of a true German patriotism: "With the passionate love of a woman had united in her soul, a love of the fatherland and an enthusiasm for national independence, which produced a spirit with strength and eminence, and therefore, with a capacity to suffer only rarely equaled" (273; 2:18). Rahel's capacity for suffering would have been sorely tried in Lewald's Germany, for by the time *Prinz Louis Ferdinand* was published, it was already clear that national unification under a constitutional government would have to wait. The novel captures a sense of lost opportunities, both in the Prussia of 1806, and in that of 1849.

During the same year in which Fanny Lewald was completing work on her historical novel, she was also recording her impressions of contemporary political developments in letters she would later publish as *Erinnerungen aus dem Jahre 1848* (1850). The narrative begins as Lewald leaves Oldenburg for Paris on February 28, 1848; one month later she returned to Berlin, and after traveling to Hamburg and Helgoland over the summer, she ended the year observing the new German parliament in Frankfurt.[49] In the letters she makes no secret of her sympathy for the Revolution: "I believe in humanity, in the future, in the survival of the Republic."[50] Lewald is thrilled to be in Paris just weeks after Louis Philippe was forced to flee, and cites with pride numerous episodes from the uprising that demonstrate the heroism and restraint of the French people. The events in Paris raise Lewald's hopes for similar progress in Germany, but even when news from Berlin sends her hurrying back to the Prussian capital, she remains skeptical about the German's readiness for reform. "How gladly one would even now like to believe in this possibility, in the republican constitution in Germany, if only one could!" (1:214–15). The Prussian faith in blind obedience to authority that had led to their defeat at the time of Prince Louis Ferdinand had not changed, and Prussia can expect only misery if it continues to train its youth to become "obedient Christians, rather than thinking human beings – subjects of the authorities in power, rather than citizens of the state" (3:328). By the end of the year Lewald already suspects that her fears were justified, and by the next summer the Revolution was indeed effectively over.

Lewald looks back at the Revolution in the novella *Auf rother Erde* [On Red Earth] (1850), which takes place between the summer of

1848 and the spring of 1849. Twenty-year-old Anton Werder travels with his father from Berlin to the "red soil" of the Westphalian countryside. The father is a member of the National Assembly whose sympathies lie with his own social class, the wealthy property owners and entrepreneurs of the Third Estate. His son, in contrast, has begun to think that the desires on the part of the lower classes for broader democratic reforms may not be unjustified. While in the country Anton falls in love with Marie Schmidt, daughter of a wealthy Westphalian farmer. Both sets of parents object to the match, as each has plans to marry their child to a partner of a more similar social background. The conflict between father and son intensifies when Anton Werder becomes increasingly sympathetic with radical democrats. When the radicals begin to clash with the police in the spring of 1849, Anton rushes to the barricades: "he did not believe in victory at this moment, but it seemed his duty to risk all, even his life, in order to demonstrate his recognition that loyalty to the united fatherland, adherence to the constitution given by the elected representatives of the German people, was the highest and most holy [task]."[51] Anton is badly wounded in the fighting, but his loyalty to the people wins the sympathy of his future father-in-law. His own father, who is primarily concerned that his son's subversive activity does not tarnish his own career, also reluctantly offers his blessings. The novella ends with a flash-forward: one year has passed, and Anton and Marie are happily married and living on a farm – on the Mississippi! Democratic reform did not come to Germany after all, and Anton, like many of the most committed German patriots of the 1848 Revolution, must leave the country.

In this novella Lewald places particular stress on the link between patriotic enthusiasm for a constitutional government in a united German state and republican virtue in the home. The romance between Anton and Marie, which at first glance might seem only a concession to popular taste in a novella freighted with political discussions, actually underscores one of Lewald's central convictions: democratic reform and the bourgeois family go hand in hand. " 'Do you think that Anton, who retained sworn loyalty to the German Reich, would desert the bride to whom he had plighted his troth?' " questions Marie's elderly aunt (168). The couple united in love would also be true to the fatherland, but republican virtue has no place in the post-revolutionary Germany that forces the idyll into exile. By tying the fate of the family so closely to her political agenda, Lewald encounters the familiar contradictions of an ideology that restricts women's freedom even as it advances the cause of democratic reform. Indeed, as Lewald expresses her political ideals more openly in this novella, she retreats from the outspoken feminism of earlier fiction. In the place of the mature, independent, intellectual Jenny, we have the suitably named Marie, who combines virginal innocence with maternal warmth.[52] She loves children and Anton loves her: "She appeared to him as a Madonna, who, surrounded by the soft air of virginal motherhood, is adored by the child she has born" (74–75). Like Pygmalion, Anton looks forward to the time when he can mold his innocent bride into a pleasing helpmeet: "she was to be his creation, herself and her happiness" (114). Although we learn on the final page that it is Marie who is teaching her husband how to run a farm, he instructs her "in all other matters" (171). Lewald's liberal paternalism survives on the banks of the Mississippi, while Anton's mother "hopes for a peaceful solution to party strife in Germany that will bring her son and daughter-in-law back to her and to the fatherland" (171).

LOUISE ASTON: "AMAZONS," ARISTOCRATS, AND OTHER REVOLUTIONARIES

In her life and works Louise Aston (1814–71) easily qualifies as the most radical German feminist of the *Vormärz*.[53] Before she had published a word the cigar-smoking, beer-drinking, cross-dressing divorcée had already gained considerable notoriety with the Berlin public and also the police. Born in Halberstadt as the daughter of a Lutheran minister and a disinherited duchess, Louise Hoche was coerced into marriage with a British industrialist living in Magdeburg when she was only seventeen. The couple was divorced in 1838, reconciled at their daughter's sickbed and remarried in 1841, only to divorce again in April, 1844. Within a few months Aston had moved to Berlin, where she began to associate with a group of young intellectuals given to all-night revelry. Remembered fondly by one of her companions as "an irrepressible bar-room genius" [*Kneipgenie*], Aston usually dressed as a handsome young man and would fly into a rage if she were addressed as "Louise" rather than "Louis."[54] Perhaps predictably, the general public took offense at her unconventional behavior. One anonymous tipster felt compelled out of a sense of patriotic duty to report her to the police as an evil seductress who "together with many men – *poets, artists, officers, Jews,* etc. – had entered into a plot against the state, the king, and religion."[55]

Reports of Aston's licentiousness were greatly exaggerated, according to one of her former lovers,[56] but she did hold views extreme enough to provoke the wrath of the Prussian authorities. When tricked into a confession of atheism by the police, Aston did not deny the charge; she only insisted that her personal views were her own business.[57] More shocking still was her open repudiation of marriage as an immoral institution that gave license to injustice under a veneer of respectability.[58] The police had heard enough, and on March 21, 1846, they ordered her to leave Berlin within eight days.[59] Aston retreated under protest to nearby Köpenick, where she began to develop ties to some of Germany's most liberal democrats. It is possible that she fought on the barricades during the March Revolution, and certain that she accompanied German nationalist troops in the campaign against the Danish later that spring. Here she tended the wounded on the battlefields and was herself grazed by a passing bullet – a badge of honor she allegedly displayed with pride.[60] Back in Berlin that summer she engaged actively in political debates, and could be seen sitting behind the most extreme left wing of the Prussian National Assembly. As the Revolution turned sour, Aston's fortunes also took a turn for the worse. Expelled from Berlin for the second time in November, 1848, she was later barred from Leipzig, Breslau, Munich, and Zurich.[61] Aston eventually remarried and spent her remaining years in restless exile. The once-famous figure died in obscurity in a small Austrian town.

For the sake of her life alone, Louise Aston would merit inclusion as a fascinating footnote to the social and political upheavals that culminated in the 1848 Revolution. Of greater significance are the literary works that she produced between the years 1846 and 1849. Aston entered the world of letters indirectly as the addressee of two blasphemous poems by Rudolf Gottschall in praise of "free love":

> Die freie Liebe wird die Welt befrein.
> Ihr sollt dem alten Schreckgespenst der Schande
> Nicht länger der Entsagung Tränen weihn.
> Die Kinder dieser Welt, nicht spröde Nonnen,
> Sind unsre neuen, heiligen Madonnen.[62]

Aston's own literary debut with a collection of poems entitled *Wilde Rosen* [Wild Roses] (1846) was hardly less provocative: she described marriage as a curse and celebrated "the *liberated woman*" ["das *freie Weib*"] in a paean to her idol George Sand.[63] Aston went public again with a strongly worded self-defense after the police banned her from Berlin. *Meine Emancipation, Verweisung und Rechtfertigung* [My Emancipation, Expulsion, and Self-Justification] (1846) contains a damning exposé of heavy-handed police tactics and an uncompromising demand for the emancipation of women, defined as the need "to restore the right and the dignity of women to freer relations, to a nobler cult of love."[64] More poetry followed, and for a brief period in late 1848 Aston edited the literary journal *Der Freischärler* [The Volunteer]. Louise Aston's most significant literary works were the three novels she published in her brief, but prolific, literary career: *Aus dem Leben einer Frau* [From a Woman's Life] (1847), *Lydia* (1848), and *Revolution und Contrerevolution* (1849). These works combine personal experience, political engagement, and literary sophistication in a way that makes them unique contributions to the history of the German novel at a time of revolutionary upheaval.

Given the rather sparse information available on Aston's youth, it is often difficult to tell where autobiography ends and fiction begins. *Aus dem Leben einer Frau* – the story of a young woman forced into an unhappy marriage with a rich industrialist – contains such obvious allusions to Aston's own life that it has been used as source material when reconstructing her biography.[65] In the preface to the novel Aston herself underscores the proximity of her work to lived experience: "We write fleeting lines, but we write them in our heart's blood!"[66] At the same time, however, Aston elevates her personal remarks into a paradigm for modern experience and modern art in general.[67] She begins her preface with a bow to the precepts of autonomy aesthetics: "Life is fragmentary; art should create a whole!" (v). Adopting the false modesty of the practiced rhetorician, Aston concedes that the following pages will be aesthetically worthless but historically relevant. A future genius may well achieve immortality by transforming the current chaos into a lasting work of art, Aston continues, but she declares herself incapable of this task. While paying lip-service to the aesthetics of Germany's classicist past, Aston provides an indirect defense of her own work's modernity. She guarantees her confession's authenticity by insisting on its anti-aesthetic character: what follows is true because it is not art.[68]

The novel itself begins with an ironic citation of the literary genre of the idyll. Evoking the familiar images of bucolic bliss made fashionable by Voss's *Luise* (1783–84) – the shady tree, a walk through the fields, afternoon coffee, "and if you're lucky, a wedding bed" (1) – Aston savagely denounces the genre as "the utopia of a Philistine imagination (2). Her anti-idyll begins with seventeen-year-old Johanna on her knees before her aging father, begging that she not be compelled to marry a grotesquely fat, tasteless, but rich factory owner. Johanna dares to defy her father until the "old man with dark, sinister features" (3) shakes his daughter wildly by the hair, kicks her to the floor, and curses her, whereupon he promptly suffers a massive stroke. Understandably nonplussed, Johanna agrees to the marriage after all in the hope of placating her father, but he can no longer speak and she must enter married life with his curse unrevoked.

Whether or not Louise Hoche's own marriage to the British steam-engine manufacturer Samuel Aston took place under such melodramatic circumstances is impossible to determine; more important is the way in which Aston uses what had become a hackneyed literary convention to reveal the brutal reality of many women's experience. The depiction of paternal abuse in domestic fiction is of course not without precedent: for every pastoral idyll of the sort that shelters Agnes von Lilien and her stepfather we have a Clarissa Harlowe imprisoned in the home by a cruel despot. What is different in Aston's work is the way in which her protagonist reacts to her father's curse. Clarissa Harlowe starved herself to death in hope of heavenly compensation, but Johanna quickly jettisons her youthful idealism and resolves to make the best of a bad situation on earth: "'I only want to live for the world . . . money was my undoing – and it shall remain the fate that I willingly follow, against which I will no longer struggle foolishly! I . . . break with the pious dreams and the holy vows of my youth'" (27).

Four years later we find Johanna Oburn among high society in Carlsbad. As expected, she is unhappy in her marriage, but unlike Schopenhauer's Gabriele, she has long since stopped pining for her first boyfriend. Johanna dismisses her adolescent romance as a foolish infatuation, but she also resists her new admirer's sexual advances. As she explains, her resistance has nothing to do with the perverse self-denial "of those Christian housewives who repress the burning desires of their heart for fear of moral censure or eternal punishment, and who find ample compensation for sacrificed happiness in their sense of virtue" (37). Pride alone holds her back from a pleasure she could only enjoy in secret. No such scruples trouble the evil Prince C., a typically rapacious aristocrat who plans to add Johanna to a long list of conquests. With the aid of an overtly pious but essentially corrupt landlady, the prince manages to rent a room in the converted farmhouse where Johanna is staying just outside town. Just as he is about to rape the sleeping woman another man comes to the rescue through the window. It is the Baron von Stein, a truly noble noble who is also captivated by Johanna's charms. He chases away the prince and cleverly preserves Johanna's reputation by making the incident look like a robbery. On the following morning Johanna leaves town with her recently returned husband, only to learn that Baron von Stein has fallen in a duel with the prince.

As this brief outline indicates, Aston draws on sensational motifs taken from the stockpile of popular fiction, although this sort of thing did happen with depressing regularity in a country where dueling for the sake of a woman's honor was commonplace among the nobility.[69] Aston uses the episode primarily as a means of criticizing the German aristocracy of the *Vormärz*. The critique of lecherous aristocrats is itself not new, but while such earlier authors as LaRoche and Wolzogen distinguished between the decadent Rococo nobility and progressive figures worthy of the titles they hold, Aston rejects "aristocrats of every sort, who had to safeguard their old rights against the demands of a new era" (31). Carlsbad gathers together the reactionary forces who suppressed the liberal nationalist movement in favor of "holy legitimacy" (31). Only Baron von Stein offers a positive image of the German nobility, but as excerpts from his diary reveal, he was a *Burschenschaftler* in his youth and has remained loyal to his liberal nationalist beliefs. In this context, Prince C.'s attempted rape of Johanna suggests that sexual violence is symptomatic of political violence, as Baron von Stein makes clear: "'Isn't it enough for you and all your ilk to feed yourselves from the sweat and blood of the enslaved people? Do you also have to grasp deep into the holiest of hearts and poison souls, souls whose inmost life is a divine service to all great and noble thoughts?'" (70–71).

Aston's novel also differs from earlier domestic fiction by extending the critique of Carlsbad society back into the secluded parsonage of Johanna's father. LaRoche's *Sternheim* again sets the familiar pattern: the innocent maiden, raised in a protective home environment, becomes exposed to aristocratic vice at court, but retreats successfully to recreate her childhood in her own married life. As Aston's opening scene makes clear, Johanna has no such refuge from the world in her father's house: "the *Zeitgeist* presses its way into even the most secluded parsonage" (2). The prince's abuse of his patriarchal authority over his subjects only reproduces on a larger scale the violence already present in Johanna's home.

In the final segment of the novel we find Johanna and Oburn dining sumptuously while the starving workers in his factory threaten to strike. While Oburn insists that his workers respond best to harsh treatment, Johanna pities the plight of those whom she had hitherto ignored. In a noble gesture reminiscent of Schiller's Lady Milford, Johanna sells her jewelry to grant at least temporary relief to the workers' suffering. That such gestures are pathetically inadequate in an era of capitalist expansion becomes apparent when the bank that has been financing Oburn's factory through speculative investment goes under. Meanwhile the prince shows up again, still lusting after Johanna. Grasping at his only chance to stave off creditors, Oburn accepts the prince's indecent proposal: he offers his wife to the prince for one night in return for a loan of 10,000 thaler. "'It wasn't easy for me,'" Oburn explains to his incredulous wife, "'because I love you! You have to —!'" (150). Johanna does not agree, and flees secretly that night, leaving her husband to his fate.

Aston's first novel ends here, with her protagonist about to begin a new phase of her life. Interestingly enough, Aston does not condemn the institution of marriage as she did in *Meine Emancipation*. Instead, her protagonist defends her decision to leave her husband in terms similar to those used by Lewald to justify divorce in *Eine Lebensfrage*: "*She saved the sanctity of marriage by tearing it apart!*" (154). Given the pervasive corruption Aston describes in *Vormärz* society, however, it is difficult to imagine that her protagonist will soon settle into a happy marriage. Despite Aston's initial disclaimers about the desultory character of her work, the novel is actually tightly organized in three sections: the first exposes patriarchal abuse in the home, the second reveals aristocratic abuse in the state, and the third uncovers the unholy alliance between the industrialists and the aristocracy in an era of capitalist expansion and financial speculation. *Aus dem Leben einer Frau* thus exposes a common pattern of exploitation and abuse that cuts across disparate spheres of *Vormärz* society, from the family to the factory to the state. Aston also links political power with sexual violence. In each section the woman serves as the medium of exchange through which men cement their power relationships: Johanna is the pawn in her father's marital schemes, the object of a near-rape as the prince's latest conquest, and the bargaining chip in her husband's financial deal.

Louise Aston's second novel, *Lydia*, contains its share of sensational adventure, but here again Aston uses conventional means to achieve highly unconventional ends. Baron Richard von Landsfeld – "tall, slender, manly"[70] – arrives at the elegant resort of Bad Pr. . .t in search of a woman who will restore his faith in "pure femininity" (71). While strolling with the aging beauty Cornelia von Hohenhausen he encounters the woman responsible for his current malaise, Alice von Rosen, in the arms of another man. Like her creator, Alice sports the outer signs of emancipation: she smokes cigars, carries a dagger, and occasionally dresses in men's clothing. She even challenges Cornelia to a duel, and Landsfeld stops "the modern Amazons" (92) only after Alice has slashed open her rival's padded dress with her rapier. She insists that she has nothing against her former lover Landsfeld, and will in fact assert later on that he was the only man she ever loved. Yet she also makes no secret of her "views concerning the autonomy of love" (59), which make her unwilling to restrict herself to one man: "*it is against my nature to grant absolute power to any man*" (189). At an evening salon Alice expands on her view of the emancipated woman in an argument that comes down to a simple principle: "'A woman's happiness lies in love. But the joy of love is freedom!'" (172). As in the case of Sophie Mereau's Ninon Lenclos, Alice's equation of women's happiness with love remains traditional; she does not seek professional or political activity. Yet Alice's demand for "individual freedom" that will lead to the triumph of "that which is truly human" (173) is as bold as her accusation that "male capriciousness and compulsion to dominate" (174) are to blame for women's current subjugation. In response to a man's indignant insistence that she oversteps the "natural" limitations of her sex, Alice insists that there is nothing natural about a belief-system that relegates women to second-class citizens, and signals her readiness to breach the artificial walls of custom.

It is against the standard of Alice's outspoken feminism that we need to measure the novel's plot, which features a bizarre variation on the old theme of seduced innocence. Just before his unpleasant encounter with his former lover, Baron Landsfeld had been entranced by the beautiful bourgeois maiden Lydia. She is actually engaged to a young composer named Arthur Berger, although it is none other than Berger who has been secretly seeing Alice! Moments after the two "Amazons" lay down their rapiers, the men take up their pistols for a duel of their own. Landsfeld deliberately misses his opponent, but Berger returns fire and wounds his rival in the arm. Berger proves the real loser, however, for his fiancée rejects him when she learns of his infidelity, and before long we find Lydia engaged to Landsfeld in Berlin.

Until this point the seduction plot follows the familiar pattern: the jaded aristocrat sights his bourgeois prey and maneuvers her into his bedroom. Here the parallel begins to break down: unlike Faust or Lovelace, Landsfeld actually does marry his virginal bride, and the marriage ceremony is genuine, if private, unlike Lord Derby's sham wedding with Sophie von Sternheim. Instead of seducing and abandoning the unmarried bourgeoise, Landsfeld marries Lydia and then decides *not* to consummate the marriage. Lydia, as it turns out, hasn't the slightest idea what to expect on the wedding night: "Her sensuality was a completely closed bud that as yet remained untouched by an enlivening ray of the sun" (132–33). In a protracted bedroom scene that hovers between the titillating and the absurd, Landsfeld slowly undresses his bride, kisses a droplet of blood from her breast, and – leaves the room. She thinks this is normal: "Lydia's imagination was in fact completely pure and spotless" (200). Delighted to have discovered a woman who corresponds to his ideal of feminine virtue, Landsfeld avoids such tempting situations in the future. He wants more than a virgin bride – he also wants a virgin wife.

Of course such a ridiculous situation can't last. Landsfeld slakes his sexual thirst with other women while Lydia stays at home. Meanwhile her jilted fiancé Berger plots revenge together with Cornelia, who mistakenly believes that Landsfeld once thwarted her rendezvous with a lover in Italy. The two succeed in luring Lydia away from her sick mother in Landsfeld's absence, and Berger is about to rape Lydia when Alice fends him off with her dagger. Landsfeld arrives in time for the rescue, but the shock of these events, coupled with her mother's death, leaves Lydia in a state of near-madness. Months later Lydia receives a visit from her pregnant friend Therese, who is astonished to realize that Lydia is still ignorant of the facts of life. Therese helpfully launches into a course of sexual education, but the horrified Lydia soon begs her to stop. Later that evening she shyly puts a question to her husband: "'Richard, am I your spouse, your wife in the fullest sense of the word?'" (266). Another passionate scene follows in which Landsfeld can no longer restrain himself. This time Lydia really does become insane.

But why? She is already in a state of fragile physical and mental health. Landsfeld then provokes a crisis by confessing that his original motivation for the marriage had been to test the extent of his bride's virtue. Already astonished that she has been the unwitting object of her husband's grotesque experiment, Lydia undergoes further trauma when he begins to have his way with her, for the sexual act awakens the repressed horror of Berger's near-rape. By the time Landsfeld drifts off into a sated slumber, Lydia feels violated and humiliated: "It was a terrible moment. – A quadruple murder: – of her *innocence* – her *love* – her *pride* – her *reason*" (272). Even under the best of circumstances it would have been difficult for a woman as ignorant as Lydia to make the transition from virgin bride to Landsfeld's wife "in the fullest sense of the word," for her over-protected youth has set her up for disaster. Lydia would never have allowed the sham marriage to continue for so long had she not been sheltered by her mother from all knowledge of sexuality, and Landsfeld would not have found her so attractive if she did not represent in exaggerated form the model of virginal innocence set up by society as the feminine ideal. Aston's critique cuts two ways: against the sort of arrogant aristocrat who sacrifices virgins in pursuit of his own lost idealism, and against the sort of mother who cultivates rare lilies destined to die on the altar of lust.

We are left, then, with Alice von Rosen as the only viable alternative in a novel full of decadence and equally untenable innocence. Once again, Aston offers a new twist on an old paradigm: for all her sympathy for Lydia's plight, her primary concern is to set up Alice as a new type of feminist heroine. *Lydia* is not primarily about innocence lost (*Clarissa*), and not at all about innocence regained (*Sternheim*), but about maturity preserved. It is Alice who warns Landsfeld in time to stop Berger's rape, and she who comes to Lydia's rescue in the end. "'You are different than I thought'" (239) confesses a chagrinned Landsfeld as he rushes off to save his wife. It is too late to save Landsfeld from his failure to recognize Alice's good qualities. Two years later Landsfeld visits Alice in Dresden, looking rather worse for wear. She shows him the child that resulted from his disastrous "wedding night," but when he bends to the crib he realizes it is dead. "'What would you do in my place, Alice?' 'Die,' she said calmly" (281). Without further ado, Landsfeld kisses Alice goodbye and blows out his brains. His body slumps over the crib. Alice retrieves Lydia from her insane asylum to show her Landsfeld's corpse, which seems to shock her back to sanity. The novel ends with the two women in mourning as they drive off to Italy.

Alice and Lydia return in Louise Aston's last novel, *Revolution und Contrerevolution*. Evidently written and published in haste – Aston spells the name of one of her main characters three different ways – the novel nevertheless offers a fascinating account of the revolutionary year 1848.[71] The novel begins in Vienna in early March on the eve of the Revolution, moves to the streets of Berlin later that month, and ends in September in Frankfurt after an interlude on the German–Danish border. In its timing and setting, therefore, *Revolution und Contrerevolution* corresponds roughly to Fanny Lewald's *Erinnerungen aus dem Jahre 1848*, but while Lewald's reflections took the form of an autobiographical travelog, Aston wrote an unconventional novel. In the preface Aston defends her attempt at historical realism in terms that recall her opening remarks in *Aus dem Leben einer Frau*: instead of abstracting her work from the mundane details of everyday life in the effort to achieve transcendent beauty and eternal truth, she employs historical events as the organizing force of her aesthetic construct. As she explains, it is easy to write novels in boring times, but in times of crisis, history itself becomes a compelling spectacle that needs no further invention on the part of the artist.

As the title suggests, Aston depicts a revolution that *almost* succeeded, but that quickly succumbed to counter-revolutionary forces: "*Almost* – this 'almost' is the curse of our time, the hair by which the devil of the reaction holds fast to the deceived people, so that he can soon grab it by the hair and harness it to the old yoke of servitude."[72] At stake in the streets of Berlin is nothing less than the birth of a nation: "The 18th of March is truly a memorable day in *Prussian* – I meant to say: *German* history" (2:1). By the fall of 1848 the people who had come together with great hope found themselves disappointed: "It was once again only a delusion that drove us here to enter battle and death for German greatness, unity, and freedom"

(2:205). Efforts to gain popular sovereignty fail, and Germany is once again under aristocratic control: "O poor, deceived fatherland, that these miserable people dare to debase you to a plaything of princely moods!" (2:242). Aston concludes the second book of the novel with an italicized statement that seems to sum up her attitude toward the Revolution and its aftermath: "*Only the completed counter-revolution can become the mother of a completed revolution*" (2:186). This cryptic remark would seem to suggest that the triumph of the reaction will eventually provoke renewed and successful revolution, although it may be a cynical comment on the inevitable failure of German attempts at revolutionary change.[73]

The novel contains vivid accounts of popular demonstrations and street fighting in Berlin, but most of *Revolution und Contrerevolution* centers on murky intrigues among different aristocratic factions. Alice, now a baroness, supports the revolution, while Father Angelikus, confessor to Metternich's wife, works to uphold the status quo. Between these poles lie two figures whose sympathies are not immediately clear. Chevalier Arthur von Saint-Just seems to sympathize with disgruntled workers in Berlin, but eventually betrays the revolutionary cause, while Prince Lichninsky supports the Revolution in Vienna, but turns against it in Berlin. At the opposite end of the social spectrum is a poor worker's family in the Voigtland district of Berlin, which includes the daughter Anna, a penniless factory-worker, and her brother Ralph, a disgruntled machinist and member of a revolutionary organization. These exploited members of the proletariat have no sense of belonging to the rest of the city, as Anna explains, but only a sad awareness of their collective misery: "Indeed, whoever is born and raised in the Berlin Voigtland has no paternal city [*Vaterstadt*], but only a fatherland: the fatherland of deprivation, of human bondage, of the violation of the soul . . . They form a nation of their own, a nation of degradation in the lap of the shining capital of the mighty, pious, intelligent Prussia" (1:127–28). In Alice's view, the events of early 1848 hinge on the resolution of a simple question: "Who will enjoy the fruits: the *aristocracy* or the *proletariat?* Where do you stand . . . *revolution or counter-revolution, democracy or absolutism?*" (1:192).

Alice functions as a connecting link between the opposing social spheres. As a baroness she can circulate among the highest circles of the Austrian and Prussian aristocracy. In her actions and beliefs she also distances herself from any notion of bourgeois virtue: she is a self-proclaimed atheist, romantically involved with more than one man, and not above using her physical charms to extract confessions of political faith from her fellow aristocrats. Alice herself concedes to Prince Lichninsky that she has been considered "an aristocrat incarnate" (1:226). Somewhat implausibly, Alice is not only an outspoken supporter of democratic revolution, but also a founding member and current president of the proletarian workers' organization in Berlin. She communicates secretly with them about the events in Vienna, and when the revolution breaks out in Berlin, Alice joins them on the barricades.

Aston's choice of an aristocratic heroine with proletarian sympathies becomes understandable in light of her analysis of why the Revolution failed. The first reason is that reactionary forces among the nobility won out over the liberals, quickly crushing the movement toward democratic reform. As Karlheinz Fingerhut observes, Aston's hope that enlightened aristocrats could spearhead social reform shows a surprising similarity to the beliefs of the arch-conservative Eichendorff,[74] although he was hardly a proponent of political insurrection. The second reason for the failed revolution lay in the treachery of the bourgeoisie, whose members betrayed the revolutionary workers and rallied to support the throne: "But the people who had struggled and bled and won let themselves be deceived by the Philistines whom they had viewed as brothers" (2:140). The result is an analysis of the failed revolution that differs fundamentally from that of Fanny Lewald. Lewald remains firmly committed to the middle-class respect for family as the basis of a nation-state, while Aston accuses the bourgeoisie of collaboration with the nation's aristocratic enemies. Aston portrays Prince Lichninsky as a fence-sitter who vacillates between sympathy for the people and the aristocracy; he assures Alice that they can at least agree on one thing: "hatred and contempt for the bourgeoisie and all of the wretchedness that hangs from the Philistine's pigtail" (1:193). Alice fights on two fronts: she tries to encourage wavering aristocrats to side with the people, and she fights with the workers in their struggle against the state. In other words, she tries to bring about a revolution from above and a revolution from below; what she abhors is the middle ground of "the cowardly wheat-beer bourgeois" ["die feigen Weißbierbourgeois"] (2:139).[75]

For this reason, Aston styles her heroine into the antithesis of bourgeois virtue. While Lydia has become a "veiled, introverted [figure] of almost melancholy modesty," Alice appears "radiant, intelligent, looking around with almost knightly pride: the character of a woman who is aware of her value and is strong in this awareness" (1:9). No wilting violet in search of a protective man, Alice impresses others by her strength of intellect and will. As in *Lydia*, Alice still enjoys dressing as a man, particularly in moments that require her to act decisively. When the Revolution breaks out in Berlin, "Alice hurried home to throw herself into her men's clothing . . . 'Don't you hear the cannons roar?'" she exclaims to Lydia, "'Ha! the dance has already begun, and I am still not in my formal dress'" (2:77–78). Alice views the Revolution as theatre, as a costume ball in which the aristocratic woman plays the role of a proletarian man. In her "masculine" assertiveness Alice recalls the figure of Sophie Mereau's Ninon Lenclos, another aristocratic libertine whose activities break free from the constraints of domestic virtue. In *Revolution und Contrerevolution* Aston presses this pre-revolutionary model of female emancipation into service for a pro-revolutionary political radicalism. The aristocratic feminist becomes a proletarian revolutionary.

Aston's novel contains a lurid subplot, in which the Spanish noblewoman Ines raises her son Salvador to revenge the man who betrayed her – his father. The man is none other than Prince Lichninski, the noble who eventually moves from revolutionary sympathizer to reactionary traitor. The novel's final scene depicts a popular uprising in Frankfurt in which a mob attacks and kills Lichninski. Salvador leads the charge, and we discover on the novel's final page that he killed the prince – his father – before burying the same dagger in his own heart. One of the revolutionaries emerges from the house with a sign whose message is the last sentence in the novel: "'*Thus dies a traitor to the fatherland!*'" (2:275). The novel ends with vengeance against public and private treachery: the people kill the prince, and the son murders his father. The mob wins a Pyrrhic victory, however, for Aston has long since made it clear that the counter-revolutionary forces will triumph, at least in the foreseeable future. No democratic band of brothers will replace the fallen leader. Private revenge fares no better, as Salvador's deed leads only to suicide. Although the reactionary forces would not cement their victory until the following year, Aston makes it clear that the Revolution of 1848 was already all but over.

CHAPTER 6

Eugenie Marlitt: the art of liberal compromise

In January, 1853, a new journal appeared as a *Beiblatt zum Illustrirten Dorfbarbier* [Supplement to the Illustrated Village Barber] entitled *Die Gartenlaube* [The Garden Bower]. Its editor, Ernst Keil (1816–78), was no newcomer to the publishing industry. Keil had begun his career as an apprentice bookseller in Weimar, where he soon came into contact with the writings of the Young Germans. He became a sharp critic of the reactionary *Vormärz* government, and an ardent supporter of liberal reform in a unified Germany. In 1845 Keil began publishing his first literary journal, *Der Leuchtturm* [The Lighthouse], which soon attracted the attention of the German censors. For three years he was on the run, as his liberal journal was forbidden in one German province after the next. His fortunes seemed to take a turn for the better when freedom of the press was granted throughout Germany in March, 1848, but the Prussian government soon clamped down with even tighter censorship laws when King Friedrich Wilhelm IV refused to accept the constitution of the Frankfurt National Assembly. The government revived its case against Keil's *Leuchtturm*, and by 1852 Keil found himself serving a nine-month prison sentence for his allegedly seditious journal.[1]

It was here that Keil first conceived *Die Gartenlaube*, and by the end of the year the journal was underway. From the opening page of the first edition it becomes clear that Keil's new publication no longer targeted left-wing intellectuals of the *Vormärz*. The masthead includes an illustration of a family gathered together around a table under a garden bower, where a grandfatherly figure reads aloud to mother, father, and young children.[2] A servant-girl cocks an attentive ear in the background. Keil's prefacing note promises an instructive and entertaining journal "for the home and for the family" that will create a mood of "good German coziness" [*gut-deutsche Gemüthlichkeit*] for its readers. The most striking indication that Keil has changed his ways lies in his stress on the apolitical character of the new publication: "Far from all calculating politics and all differences of opinion in religious and other matters, we intend to introduce you to the history of the human heart and of [different] peoples, to the struggles of human passions and earlier times in truly good stories." Keil's transformation from political activist to apolitical editor of a family magazine typifies the move from the radical 1840s to the conservative 1850s. Reactionary forces had triumphed again, just as they had done in the wake of the Napoleonic Wars, and German liberals were forced either to adapt to the new regime or to face imprisonment or exile.

Die Gartenlaube appeared as an independent publication already in its second edition, and circulation increased rapidly from 35,000 readers in 1855 to 170,000 in 1866.[3] In September, 1865, Keil published a short story in four installments entitled *Die zwölf Apostel* [The Twelve Apostles] by a certain E. Marlitt. The author was actually Eugenie John (1825–87) of Thuringia, an unmarried, thirty-nine-year-old woman who had spent a decade as companion to a local aristocratic woman after failing in her effort to become a professional singer.[4] After Keil accepted her story, Marlitt sent him the complete manuscript of her first novel, *Goldelse* [Gold(en-haired) Elisa(beth)] (1867).[5] Keil liked it so much that he decided to break with his policy of printing only short stories, and began serializing it in January, 1866. Keil's editorial decision was a wise one, for *Goldelse* proved extremely popular with the *Gartenlaube* readers. By the time of Keil's death in 1878, Marlitt had published six novels in the *Gartenlaube*, and circulation of the journal had climbed to 375,000.[6] With steadily increasing literacy rates and continued technological innovations in the publishing industry, Germany had for the first time something approaching a mass readership, and the new genre of the family journal (*Familienblatt*) was in a position to reap the profits.[7] The practice of serial publication also inspired a new intimacy between authors and their readers, who watched a novel unfold over a period of weeks and months and who began to anticipate the arrival of each new chapter with feverish excitement.[8] Marlitt proved exceptionally skillful at holding her readers' attention; with her help *Die Gartenlaube* soon became the most widely read German journal, and she one of the best known – and most highly paid – German authors.

It was more than mutual financial success that kept Keil and

Marlitt together, however, for they also had a common commitment to liberal politics. In Marlitt, Keil found a sympathetic colleague who shared his distrust of aristocratic privilege, his impatience with religious intolerance, and above all, his belief in the bourgeois family as the bedrock of the newly unified nation-state. In keeping with the stated policy of *Die Gartenlaube*, Marlitt's novels do not foreground contemporary historical events in the manner of a Caroline de la Motte Fouqué or a Louise Aston. The novels are nevertheless just as much *Tendenzliteratur* as the works of the previous generation of *Vormärz* authors, in that they address issues of central public concern in the years immediately preceding and following German unification.[9]

Two different but related topics recur throughout Marlitt's fiction: the conflict between the aristocracy and the bourgeoisie in the era of rapid economic and industrial expansion known as the *Gründerzeit*; and the role of the family in the new nation at a time when the German women's movement was beginning to organize itself for the first time.[10] In many ways Marlitt's novels continue the work of the *Vormärz* generation. She extols middle-class virtue against aristocratic excess, champions free-thinkers while condemning religious zealots, and creates intelligent heroines who meet adversity with a strong will and an independent mind. In each case, however, Marlitt mutes radical protest into the art of liberal compromise: novels that begin with a sharp rejection of the status quo end with qualified support for existing social hierarchies, and each heroine eventually finds her man and fulfills her destiny in the home. Marlitt's novels are thus neither radical nor reactionary, or rather, they are both: radical in their initial impulse, and reactionary in their resolution.[11] The result of this careful balancing act was a series of novels that attained unprecedented popular and commercial success. Marlitt's fiction reached both women and men, servants and masters, the bourgeoisie and the aristocracy, encouraging the hopes and flattering the desires of the subjugated, while remaining unthreatening to those in control.

Marlitt's first novel gives a good example of her ambivalent attitude toward aristocratic privilege. *Goldelse* begins by setting up a clear moral opposition between the sinful Gnadewitz family, a degenerating aristocratic clan with roots back to the seventeenth century, and the virtuous, middle-class Ferbers. The Gnadewitz lineage faces extinction because a peasant has murdered the current patriarch's only son. The aging aristocrat, Wolf von Gnadewitz, retires to Silesia under the care of a distant relative, a beautiful young woman named Anna Marie. Gnadewitz soon tries to marry his young nurse, but she rejects him and her own noble lineage in favor of the young, middle-class Adolf Ferber. The young officer lives happily for ten years with his wife, but in the eleventh – 1848 – he faces a difficult choice between conflicting duties. "The one, which his father had sung to him already in his cradle, was: 'You should love your neighbor as yourself, but above all, your German brothers.' The other, which he had imposed upon himself much later, commanded him to lift his sword in the interest of his lord."[12] Ferber chooses loyalty to the German nation over allegiance to his feudal lord, but loses his position in the army as a result. He later begins work as a bookkeeper, but he loses this job too when he openly disagrees with his employer's Pietist beliefs. Ferber is left to eke out a pitiful existence as a copyist; his brother, a forester on the old Gnadewitz estate, supplements his meager income, as does Ferber's daughter Elisabeth, by giving piano lessons in the city.

Thus *Goldelse* captures the sense of disappointment among many post-1848 liberals: Ferber is a double victim of political reaction and religious intolerance, while Anna Marie's decision to marry for love alienates her from her family and social class. Wolf von Gnadewitz wills most of his property and fortune to another distant relative, Rudolf von Walde, but surprises Anna Marie by granting her a ruined castle on the old Thuringian estate. The division of the property sets up a clear moral topography within the novel. The happy Ferber family, now reunited with the forester-uncle, moves into the few habitable rooms of the old castle on the mountain and begins a busy program of home improvement. Down in the valley an unsavory group of aristocrats sets up camp in the Italianate palace built by more recent generations of the Gnadewitz clan. Contact between the two spheres begins when Elisabeth Ferber gives piano lessons to the sickly Helene von Walde, while Helene's brother Rudolf travels in pursuit of his archaeological research. The plot then develops along familiar lines established in such works as LaRoche's *Sternheim* and Wolzogen's *Agnes von Lilien*: the innocent outsider soon becomes the target of aristocratic prejudice, religious hypocrisy, and the lecherous desires of Emil von Hollfeld, Rudolf's cousin. Fortunately the real heir to the Gnadewitz fortune shares none of the aristocratic vices of his family. He returns home to punish his evil relatives, restore justice to his suffering subjects, and marry the middle-class Elisabeth Ferber.

The happy ending to this romance complicates the seemingly clear moral opposition between the middle class and the aristocracy established early on in the novel. Marlitt allows love and virtue to win out over class prejudice, but at the same time writes an old-fashioned fairy tale, in which the poor servant-girl marries the lord of the manor. As it turns out, Elisabeth is not really from the lower classes at all. We know from the outset that her mother is a distant relation to the Gnadewitz family and thus of noble blood. Through a chance discovery while renovating the ruined castle the male Ferbers discover that their own family line can be traced back to a foundling who was actually the illegitimate child of a seventeenth-century Gnadewitz lord. Thus Elisabeth not only marries the current master of the Gnadewitz estate, but is herself descended on both maternal and paternal sides from the old aristocratic family. Elisabeth, however, will have nothing to do with the Gnadewitz name. As far as she is concerned, the old Ferber who adopted the rejected Gnadewitz baby acted with true nobility, and she is proud of her family and her social status: "'I am a middle-class woman'" ["'ich bin eine Bürgerliche'"] (299). Upon her insistence, Rudolf von Walde marries her not as Elisabeth von Gnadewitz, but as Elisabeth Ferber. On the one hand, then, Marlitt allows middle-class values, based on hard work, reverence for the family, and loyalty to the nation, to triumph over aristocratic birthrights. On the other hand, however, Marlitt holds on to the concept of nobility as verification of inner worth: Elisabeth Ferber proves her genuinely noble character by rejecting the privileges associated with nobility by birth. As in LaRoche's *Sternheim*, the final opposition is not simply between the bourgeoisie and the aristocracy, but between two types of aristocrats: those who rely exclusively on class privilege, and those who act with true nobility. The novel portrays the ennoblement of middle-class virtue: the best aristocrat acts like a bourgeois, and the bourgeois heroine discovers she is really an aristocrat. The combination allows Marlitt to affirm the moral superiority of the bourgeoisie without altering fundamentally the social hierarchies that continue to privilege the aristocracy.

Reichsgräfin Gisela [Countess Gisela] (1870) begins with an extensive prelude that again seems to establish an absolute distinction between bourgeois virtue and aristocratic vice. The nobles deceive one another, are obsessed with holding on to power for its own sake, and remain indifferent to the plight of the poor. The Baron Fleury sums up this attitude in particularly crass language: "'I am by no means a servant of the people . . . rather [I am] nothing more than a protector and extender of the dynastic splendor – that is my desire; I know no other!'"[13] In an old tradition that gains new topicality on the eve of the Franco-Prussian War, Marlitt makes this unscrupulous aristocrat French by birth. Fleury vacations in Paris and his wife runs up exorbitant bills on French fashion. As an old widow bitterly observes, it was just this sort of noble "'who, by means of aristocratic kicks and whiplashes, gradually drove the French people to Revolution'" (53). The present generation of nobles proves equally unscrupulous. Marlitt's prelude recounts the story of how Theobald Ehrhard breaks off his engagement to Jutta von Zweiflingen when he discovers that his noble bride suppressed news of her middle-class fiancé in order to obtain a position at court. "'I *do not want* a woman who has breathed court air!' he exclaims. 'I want an unspoiled, untouched soul beside me'" (126). He storms out of the palace with his younger brother Bertold, but on the way home both fall into a raging torrent. Theobald manages to rescue his brother, only to be swept away to a death he seems to welcome. Soon only driftwood floats "where so much youth and beauty and a brave German heart had gone under" (135).

The primary events of the novel take place some eleven years later and focus on the budding romance between the Countess Gisela and Bertold Ehrhard. Raised in strict isolation, Gisela has been taught to venerate the memory of her aristocratic grandmother, and to consider herself superior to those of common birth. Bertold has made his fortune in Brazil and returns to Germany disguised as a Portuguese nobleman who owns the local iron and steel works. His real purpose is to expose a dark secret: years ago Gisela's grandmother had been the mistress of reigning Prince Heinrich. The prince had originally intended to leave his fortune to his lover, but disinherited her with a new will on his deathbed. With Baron Fleury's help, the grandmother suppressed the revised will and kept the money for her own family. In the course of the novel Gisela discovers to her horror that her wealth is based on theft from the legitimate rulers of the province, but the current prince forgives her as an unwitting accomplice to an old crime. Fleury commits suicide, while Gisela marries Bertold Ehrhard, who has shed his Portuguese disguise: "'Before you stands the plain German with a simple name, which he will never give up again'" (380). The prince offers to grant "'the foremost industrialist' of his land" (398) a patent of nobility to match his blueblooded bride, but Ehrhard proudly retains his bourgeois name and rank.

Reichsgräfin Gisela thus seems to be a simple parable about imported aristocratic vice eradicated by indigenous German virtue. The enterprising bourgeois gains a fortune that soon surpasses that of the local prince. In his role as factory owner, however, Ehrhard complicates the relation between the two classes.[14] He goes out of his way to care for his factory workers, paying them high wages and demonstrating his constant concern for their well-being. The workers reward Ehrhard with good labor, and within a brief period he transforms the sleepy old factory into a model of efficient productivity. Although proud of his bourgeois name, the factory owner functions in a manner that is directly analogous to previous models of benevolent aristocratic rule. Significantly, Ehrhard's Portuguese title of nobility is genuine; he owns a Brazilian estate and is known there as Lord Oliveira. Neither he nor his older brother ever want to do away with the nobility altogether. "'Every civil servant, high and low, is a servant of the Prince and the people at the same time, a connecting link between both,'" argues Theobald Ehrhard, "'and it is to a large extent his responsibility to strengthen the love of the people for the ruling dynasty'" (112). In keeping with Marlitt's liberal, but not radical, beliefs, the brothers recognize the the local prince's legitimacy, even though financial and moral leadership have moved from the old aristocracy to the new captains of industry. Marlitt objects not to the aristocracy per se, but to a certain type of aristocratic behavior that is not necessarily restricted to those with impeccable blood lines.

Thus in several novels Marlitt updates her critique of the old aristocracy by birth to include the new aristocracy of wealth that emerged during the *Gründerzeit. Das Geheimnis der alten Mamsell* [The Old Mamsell's Secret] (1868), for example, portrays the contrasting fortunes of two families: while the von Hirschsprung clan has been in gradual decline for the past two centuries, the bourgeois Hellwig family has enjoyed a corresponding increase in power and wealth to the point that they have purchased the seventeenth-century mansion built by the Ritter von Hirschsprung. The novel begins with the accidental death of Madame Orlowsky, wife and partner of a

traveling Polish magician. Cursing his disreputable profession, Orlowsky flees the city, leaving behind a three-year-old daughter
named Felicitas in the care of the Hellwig family. Felicitas encounters
open hostility from all family members except the father, but he soon
dies, and her own father never returns. Felicitas's only friend is
Cordula Hellwig, the "old Mamsell," an elderly member of the
Hellwig family who has been banished to her apartment for
unspecified crimes and allegedly blasphemous behavior, which includes playing secular music on the Sabbath. When Felicitas finds a
copy of *Die Gartenlaube* on her coffee table, however, the reader knows
that Cordula can be trusted. Johannes Hellwig, the oldest son and
legal guardian of Felicitas after his father's death, gradually begins to
fall in love with his stepsister, but must first overcome his prejudice
against the orphaned child of a traveling entertainer. As it turns out,
Felicitas's mother was none other than Meta von Hirschsprung,
descended from the last remaining branch of the old aristocratic
family. Meta's father disowned her when she married Orlowsky.
Johannes, for his part, discovers the old Mamsell's humiliating
secret: while renovating the old estate, the Hellwig family had
unearthed buried treasure belonging to the Hirschsprungs and kept
it for themselves. Johannes repays Lutz von Hirschsprung, Meta's
brother, who accepts the money but tells Felicitas that his father will
never accept her back into the family. Felicitas has no interest in
claiming her aristocratic birthright, however, and marries Johannes
Hellwig instead.

Marlitt develops a two-pronged critique of aristocratic behavior in
Das Geheimnis der alten Mamsell: by disowning both daughter and
granddaughter, the Hirschsprung patriarch acts with the stubborn
pride of an old aristocrat. The Hellwig family proves no better,
however, for they too assume their superiority over the daughter of a
Polish magician. The upwardly mobile bourgeois family has not only
captured the home and fortune of the old nobility, but has adopted
its arrogance as well. *Im Hause des Kommerzienrates* [In the Councillor's
House] (1877) features a similarly corrupt group of parvenus. Moritz
Römer, the son of an artisan, marries the daughter of a rich banker
and his aristocratic wife. Römer grows fabulously wealthy by
speculating on the stock market and is granted a patent of nobility,
but he forgets his humble origins and ignores the needs of the local
workers. His punishment comes in the stock crash of 1873, which
bankrupts his family and sends him into American exile. In *Das*

Geheimnis der alten Mamsell, Johannes Hellwig must learn to overcome his class prejudice against the orphaned servant-girl and to recognize her equal worth as a human being. Like Elisabeth Ferber, Felicitas Orlowsky proves that she is of noble character by rejecting her aristocratic birthright, and yet, Felicitas [von Hirschsprung] marries into money and moves back into her ancestral home.

Chief among the sins of the aristocracy is a willingness to allow considerations of rank and wealth to determine the choice of a marriage partner. Marlitt's heroines fall in love with their future husbands; for them differences in social status are only obstacles to be overcome on the path to marriage. In this regard Marlitt continues the tradition of German domestic fiction that links respect for ability over birth to personal choice in marriage, and that combines a belief in the family as the central unit in society with loyalty to the nation over local nobility. In adopting these beliefs, however, Marlitt also inherits a problem: how can she reconcile the enlightened call for human equality with a gender politics that excludes women from the public sphere? As in the case of her attitude toward aristocratic privilege, Marlitt draws on the progressive legacy of the *Vormärz*, but moderates radical feminism into something more palatable to the mainstream readers of *Die Gartenlaube*.

Outspoken feminists in the mold of Louise Aston's Alice find a decidedly unsympathetic reception in Marlitt's fiction.[15] Charlotte Mericourt of *Das Heideprinzeßchen* [The Little Moorland Princess] (1872) smokes cigars, drives fast horses, and has delusions of grandeur: "'Charlotte is beautiful, isn't she?'" questions the innocent heroine Lenore von Sassen. "'For my taste a little too colossal, too emancipated and assertive,'" answers the local princess.[16] The adopted Charlotte convinces herself that she must be of noble blood, but is in fact the result of a liaison between a lascivious thief and a French officer – again suggesting a link between immorality, the aristocracy, and France that contrasts with "the strict spirit of the genuine German middle class" ["Der strenge Geist echt deutschen Bürgertums"] (268). Marlitt develops a particularly savage caricature of the emancipated woman in *Im Hause des Kommerzienrates*. Flora Mangold is another smoker who likes expensive clothes and rides fast horses. Even worse: Flora is a pseudo-intellectual who fancies herself an inspired writer. She has published articles on the working class, but she knows nothing of them and they will never read her work. Her magnum opus, *Die Frauen* [Women], spends more time in the mail than on her desk, as one publisher after the next returns the rejected manuscript. To complete the negative picture, Flora is not only an *artiste manquée*, but a morally despicable individual whose character traits include greed, mendacity, vanity, and cowardice.

Against such figures Marlitt's heroines stand out for their genuine strength of character. All have the courage to speak out against injustice and to stand up for their convictions. Felicitas proudly renounces her claim to the Hirschsprung name when confronted by her aristocratic uncle; Liane matches wits with Baron Mainau's corrupt uncle in *Die zweite Frau* [The Second Wife] and fends off the advances of a Jesuit priest; Lenore defies public prejudice in *Das Heideprinzeßchen* when she declares proudly that her grandmother was a Jew. In addition to intellectual fortitude, Marlitt's characters also display considerable physical strength and courage. Elisabeth Ferber saves her future husband's life by disarming a would-be assassin; Felicitas Orlowsky climbs across a treacherous rooftop in a thunderstorm to prevent the old Mamsell's diary from falling into the wrong hands; Käthe Mangold stands up to a rough crew of disgruntled workers and carries her ailing half-sister across the fields to the doctor. While Fanny Lewald was insisting on women's right to better education and meaningful work in her polemical tracts, Marlitt was creating fictional characters who demonstrated an equally fierce determination to learn and to become financially independent. Felicitas complains bitterly at her step-family's decision to deny her higher education. The noble Lenore von Sassen does not find it beneath her dignity to address labels on seed packets to supplement her income. Felicitas, tired of receiving charity from the Hellwig family, plans to celebrate her maturity by becoming a salaried companion to an aristocratic lady. Most ambitious is Käthe Mangold, who takes over her grandfather's mill and runs the business efficiently: "The 'business without a man' [*Das 'herrenlose Geschäft'*] rested in strong, certain hands and was directed with an intelligent eye" (374). Particularly interesting in the light of Marlitt's own successful career as a novelist are the number of women who earn money through art in her fiction. Elisabeth Ferber helps support her family by giving piano lessons; Juliane von Trachtenberg earns money by illustrating her brother's scholarly work on fossil plants (to the horror of her aristocratic mother), and Käthe Mangold has published original music with a prestigious firm.

How do Marlitt's heroines get away with their assertiveness, while the Flora Mangolds of her world come in for strictest censure? For one thing, the good girls are suitably modest, while Flora Mangold and Charlotte Mericourt are not. Liane's brother publishes his book under his own name, but his illustrator remains anonymous. Käthe does not seek fame like her sister; her music teacher contacted the publisher without her knowledge, and her music was also published anonymously. The most important difference between the heroines and their foils, however, is that they never challenge the primacy of marriage and motherhood as women's true calling. It is only with this caveat that Marlitt defends a moderate program of female emancipation. In *Das Geheimnis der alten Mamsell*, for example, Johannes Hellwig's relatively liberal friend Frank chides him for his "medieval" unwillingness to allow women to participate in human progress. "'Encourage women to think seriously, expand the circle that you egotists draw narrowly enough around their souls and call their female vocation, and you will see that vanity and weakness of character disappear!'"[17] The purpose of such education, to be sure, is less to further women's personal development than to prepare them for motherhood: "'The woman [*Das Weib*] has your sons' souls in her hands at a time when they are most receptive'" (114). That "the woman" may also have a daughter's soul in her hands seems of lesser concern. Baron Mainau of *Die zweite Frau* declares his ineradicable hostility to emancipated "bluestockings," but goes on to confess that he now believes that certain women may have an intellectual curiosity that drives them to investigate nature just like men, "'independently, without the apron strings of tradition . . . while nevertheless making allowance for this impulse only *secondarily*, as they say to themselves, that watching over the holy hearth, that holding together 'the house' with soft, gentle, and yet strong arms is the primary task of their life.'"[18] Dr. Bruck of *Im Hause des Kommerzienrates* also takes a relatively liberal position in favor of women's emancipation when he approves Käthe's decision to run the family business. "'I actually encourage this sort of independence for women warmly, and I know too that with your strength and energy you would be on the right track immediately, but that is not your calling, Käthe. You are called to found a happy family.'"[19]

In each case what is granted with one hand is denied with the other: Marlitt's characters argue strongly in favor of women's right to an education, their capacity for intellectual development, business acumen, and artistic creativity, while at the same time insisting that women never lose sight of their primary calling in the home. The novels' conclusions reinforce this mixed message: heroines who have demonstrated their intelligence, independence, and strength of character throughout the novel suddenly turn to putty in the strong, protective arms of their husbands – although it is precisely the women's exceptional talents that have attracted the men's attention in the first place.[20] In several instances Marlitt seems to go out of her way to stress the protagonist's transformation from plucky heroine to submissive bride. Felicitas modestly states that she cannot hope to compensate for the suffering Johannes Hellwig's family has caused him, "'but whatever a humble woman can think of and do to brighten the life of a noble man will certainly be done!'" (301). Juliane von Trachtenberg, who has been ready to divorce Baron Mainau for most of the novel, changes her tune when he shows signs of genuine affection: "She was no longer afraid of him. The tall man, who leaned against the wall with crossed arms next to her chair, protected her" (297). Käthe Mangold, who has proven more than capable of running a profitable business, does not protest when her future husband enters her office, closes her books, and declares: "'The career of the pretty miller [*Müllerin*] is over'" (386).

Thus Marlitt's fiction produces two mutually contradictory images of women: the one self-assertive and capable of emotional and financial independence, the other submissive and eager to retreat to her place in the home. Both character traits spring from the same source: the revolutionary bourgeois ethos that demands personal autonomy for all "men" and simultaneously requires subordination for women. Marlitt exposes this contradiction and leaves it unresolved, or, more precisely, the perfect resolution of each romance in marriage requires an abrupt transformation in the heroine's character – a change she experiences as intensely pleasurable. From today's perspective it is tempting to look for clandestine subversiveness in Marlitt's fiction; the inevitable happy endings could be seen as sops to the censor that deflect attention away from the heroines' less conventional behavior elsewhere in the texts. Käthe Mangold's transformation from successful professional artist and chief executive officer to happy housewife is so sudden and so extreme that Marlitt almost seems to be drawing attention to its implausibility, but one looks in vain for signs of protest on the part of Käthe or any other Marlitt protagonist. Together they reinforce the same "message":

women are quite capable of standing on their own, but given the choice, they would rather be happily married.

In her moderate stance toward women's emancipation, Marlitt embraces the relative conservatism of the German women's movement in contrast with England or America. As Richard Evans observes, the early German feminists "accepted . . . for the most part the stereotype created by official ideology of the 'true German woman,' emotional, subordinate and above all motherly . . . Instead of arguing that this stereotyped view of women was false, they accepted it as valid and tried to ennoble it."[21] While English and American feminists argued for social equality based on equal rights for men and women, the Germans stressed the biological specificity of women that destined them to their calling as mothers.[22] In *Für und wider die Frauen* [For and against Women] (1870), for example, Fanny Lewald argues for better access to higher education for women and the right of unmarried women to meaningful work outside the home, yet goes out of her way to stress that women's primary task is to get married and raise a family.[23] Marlitt shares the optimistic view that the better- educated working woman will be the better wife and mother; that the transition might prove difficult remains unreflected in her fiction.

Of course, not just any man will do. Marlitt's heroines are just as vigorous as their predecessors in resisting the advances of inappropriate lovers, whether they be aristocratic libertines or religious hypocrites. Acceptable heroes tend to be either liberal aristocrats with artistic talents or members of the educated middle class [*Bildungsbürgertum*]; Marlitt is particularly fond of medical doctors and archaeologists. These male leads reflect Marlitt's own liberal political allegiances, and do not differ significantly from previous protagonists in German domestic fiction. Less usual is the way in which the love develops between the hero and the heroine. Again and again lovers who come together in the final pages of the novel are not merely indifferent, but openly hostile to one another throughout much of the text. Earlier writers tended to divide attention between a superficially appealing, but essentially evil seducer (Lovelace, Derby), and an essentially good, if ineffectual or unobtainable lover (Seymour, Hippolit). While Lord Derby charms his unsuspecting prey, Marlitt's heroes spend most of their time persecuting their future wives, and the women find themselves inexplicably drawn to men who mistreat them.

The pattern begins already in *Goldelse*, as Elisabeth Ferber finds herself preoccupied with Rudolf von Walde, but "then she thought, as she walked along quickly, that it was very foolish to waste thoughts and feelings on a man who deliberately showed her the roughest side of his character" (189). By the end of the novel Elisabeth reinterprets this very roughness into a sign of righteous anger that inspires her love and admiration: "'No, Rudolf, it was love that has been living in my heart ever since I – doesn't it sound strange – looked into your angry eyes, since I heard your voice mercilessly condemn human cruelty and violence'" (319). In *Das Geheimnis der alten Mamsell* Johannes Hellwig cruelly cuts off Felicitas's access to further education, and as a result, she regards him with a mixture of resentment, anger, and even hatred for much of her youth. When Hellwig first proposes marriage, Felicitas screams and struggles in vain to escape his clutches, but by the end of the novel she rests sweetly in his strong arms.

Lovers become even more abusive in Marlitt's next novels. Countess Gisela meets Bertold Ehrhard on the day that his brother is rejected by his aristocratic fiancée. Furious at all members of her social class, Ehrhard storms out of the palace to encounter the six-year-old countess, whom he curses and pushes out of the way. Gisela goes into shock and spends the next decade as an invalid who is not expected to reach maturity. She eventually does recover, only to marry the man who was nearly responsible for her death. In *Die zweite Frau*, finally, Baron Mainau marries Juliane von Trachtenberg because he needs a stepmother for his child, because of her impeccable aristocratic pedigree, and, above all, because he wants to insult another woman who had once rejected him. Mainau not only makes it clear that he will not love his wife of convenience, but also goes out of his way to demean her. He ridicules her appearance, belittles her family, and gives her a guided tour of his former lovers' portraits, which still hang on his bedroom walls. Mainau even cracks Juliane across the hand with his bullwhip, if inadvertently, raising an angry welt that she does her best to conceal. Once again, everything turns out for the best, and we close the novel certain that Juliane and Mainau will live happily ever after.

When reduced to this paraphrase, Marlitt's novels appear as prime examples of anti-feminist backlash, as they suggest that women are attracted to men who humiliate and abuse them. It is tempting to read this motif in Marlitt's fiction as a psychological allegory: the heroine, who is without exception an innocent virgin, experiences the awakening of tabooed sexual desire as a threat. In the course of the novel she undergoes a kind of sentimental education, whereby she accepts her own sexuality and learns to reinterpret male aggression as a sign of affection.[24] From a slightly different – if hardly more palatable – perspective, the novels offer training in masochism to their female readers, who learn to enjoy pain.[25] Gisela seems to encourage such an interpretation when responding to Ehrhard's threat to reveal dirty secrets about her family's past: "'Stab away! . . . I have learned to suffer in a few days time – I know all too well what heart pains are! . . . You yourself have accustomed me to dagger thrusts! You shall see: I will smile while you do it!'" (342). The Marquis de Sade would have appreciated this passage, whose sexual innuendo – whether intended or not – is obvious enough to render understandable one critic's charge in a widely discussed article of 1885 that Marlitt's novels were full of "hidden sensuality and lasciviousness."[26] When measured against such earlier fiction as Therese Huber's *Luise* (1796), for example, the disturbing nature of Marlitt's works becomes apparent. Huber portrays in excruciating detail the physical and pyschological sufferings of a woman coerced into an arranged marriage with a brutal husband. Luise tries in vain to reinterpret her husband's torments as signs of his affection, but in the end she is dead and spousal abuse remains spousal abuse. Marlitt, in contrast, offers her readers the doubly dangerous fantasy: either that a man's mistreatment is a sign of his affection misinterpreted by a hysterical female imagination, or that women can learn to derive pleasure from suffering. Huber, together with Schopenhauer, Lewald, and Aston, knew better.

Why, then, was Marlitt so popular? Certainly in part precisely because of the extent to which her fiction gave expression to antifeminist sentiments in the wake of the *Vormärz*. One telling illustration from *Die Gartenlaube* depicts a young woman struggling to escape the clutches of a man who has apparently surprised her from behind. The caption reads: "A little resistance spurs desire" ["Ein wenig Wehren spornt das Begehren"],[27] in other words, a woman's "no" really means "yes." Marlitt's heroines seem to confirm the old cliché, as one after the next succumbs to her lover's gruff charms. The typical male reader could hardly protest works that reenforce the central tenets of patriarchy, but why would a woman want to read such fiction? It was in an effort to answer this question that

Tania Modleski undertook her study of Harlequin romances in the early 1980s. She viewed such fiction as a kind of "inoculation" against the reality many women faced in marriage. The novels take the real fear of masculine abuse and transform it into something harmless: "romantic literature performs a crucial function in assuring us that although some men may actually enjoy inflicting pain on women, there are also 'bullies' whose meanness is nothing more than the overflow of their love or the measure of their resistance to our extraordinary charms."[28] Popular romance remains disturbing to the extent that it encourages women to accept mistreatment in the name of love, but it also offers the woman a covert power fantasy, as she derives vicarious satisfaction from the heroine's ability to transform the violent man into a docile husband.

From this perspective it is possible to develop a more nuanced, and less condemnatory, understanding of Marlitt's appeal. The novels that start out with the humiliation of the heroine end up by humiliating the hero. In *Das Geheimnis der alten Mamsell*, for example, Johannes Hellwig must overcome his own sense of family pride to acknowledge his love for Felicitas, who he believes is the orphaned daughter of disreputable parents. As he explains bitterly, he can only marry her if he ignores all social ties and moves to the desert, or if he can "discover some sort of blemish, an unworthy moment in [his own] family's past!" (266). Felicitas provides the perfect flaw when she reveals the secret of the old Mamsell; ironically, it is only by humbling Hellwig's pride that she wins him as a husband. Bertold Ehrhard goes through similar embarrassment when Gisela tells him of the brute who ruined her childhood with a sudden blow. Although she does not realize that Ehrhard was to blame, he does, and suffers agonies of guilt before winning her acceptance. Baron Mainau undergoes a particularly thorough reeducation in *Die zweite Frau*. At one point the whip-cracking libertine decides to amuse himself by reading his wife's letter to her sister, only to discover that it contains a disturbingly accurate portrait of himself: "without having intended it, she told the man an ugly truth to his face; he had to be ashamed, and she blushed with him" (185). While Juliane longs to escape the arranged marriage, Mainau begins to fall in love with his wife. The climax comes in a confrontation in which Mainau once again feels the extent of his guilt: "Which ever way he turned she cruelly held up a mirror that confronted him with his character portrait in ugly, uncannily precise lines . . . and here, in conflict with an honest female nature, who through his guilt had become severe, the brilliant, sophisticated cavalier suffered a miserable shipwreck" (252). Confessing that he has been a miserable egotist, Mainau begins to woo Juliane "in deep, intimate love" (255). He begins to take an interest in his son's education and removes the lovers' portraits from his bedroom. *Die zweite Frau* is thus about the taming of the libertine, the domestication of the rake into a loving husband and *pater familias*, a project whose success radiates from the parting vignette: "These three beautiful people [Mainau, Juliane, and Mainau's son Leo] formed a group that could not be put together more pleasantly to embody domestic bliss and the sweetest harmony" (272).

Marlitt mastered the art of liberal compromise in creating entertaining works that appealed to otherwise conflicting constituencies. She was committed to middle-class values, but also accepted the legitimacy of the aristocracy and capitalized on its charm. She created emancipated heroines who willingly became submissive wives, and she crafted romantic plots that demonstrate women's power to domesticate men in works that simultaneously suggest that women enjoy being dominated. To either condemn Marlitt's fiction as merely reactionary or to celebrate its emancipatory moments while ignoring its more troubling aspects would be to obscure the careful balancing act that keeps it poised between either extreme. Placed in historical perspective, Marlitt's domestic fiction sums up the internal tensions of a literary tradition that seeks both to disseminate a new middle-class morality, and to protest against the restrictive implications of that morality for women. Looking forward to the twentieth century, we find an equally contested legacy of Marlitt's fiction: she is notorious for having made the mold for a type of popular romance aimed at a more restricted and less discerning audience than the readers of *Die Gartenlaube*. At the same time, Marlitt's career as a successful professional author of politically engaged novels qualifies her as an heir to the *Vormärz* feminists and a forerunner to their twentieth-century descendants.

If it is more difficult today to see the progressive aspects of Marlitt's fiction behind her reputation as the grandmother of pulp fiction, that is because the gap she once straddled between highbrow culture and mass media quickly became an unbridgeable chasm in the twentieth century. Marlitt died in 1887, but her literary reputation was already gravely wounded in the controversy that broke out regarding the alleged immorality of her works in 1885. Several Marlitt fans rushed into print to defend her work, others attacked its quality, but within a few years the entire debate seemed irrelevant.[29] In comparison with the provocative works of the Naturalists, Marlitt's fiction seemed quaint and dated. Paradoxically enough, the perceived quaintness of Marlitt's novels has ensured their survival in the twentieth-century culture industry, where they can be sold as costume dramas evoking a nostalgic image of a simpler past.[30] While most German women writers of the nineteenth century still need all the publicity they can get, Marlitt has received too much of the wrong sort. Viewing her works in historical context can help to defamiliarize the popular icon and reveal the cultural work of Marlitt's fiction.

For the sake of its exemplary ambivalence alone, Marlitt's Janus-faced prose offers a logical point to conclude a study of German domestic fiction. Three further considerations also suggest that with Marlitt, one phase in the history of German domestic fiction comes to a close. First, as mentioned above, Marlitt's emergence as a writer coincides with the first organized women's movements in Germany. After 1865 German feminism entered the public sphere in what we today would call political interest groups that lobbied for the concerns of their constituents. Writers from LaRoche to the early Marlitt worked alone, or with the support of a few friends; their novels belong to the prehistory of German feminist thought. Second, the decade around 1870 also marked a turning point in the history of the German literary institution. Marlitt's popularity was based on a rare combination of individual talent and good timing: she still appealed to the traditional audience of the educated elite, but also attracted new readers of the emerging mass public. Her sudden fall from grace after 1885 had less to do with the intrinsic flaws of her work than changing historical circumstances. By this time the German canon was firmly established in literary histories and the school curriculum, while the modern "culture industry" was beginning to assert its force at the opposite end of the literary spectrum. German women writers between 1771 and 1871, in contrast, worked during a period in which canon-formation was an ongoing process, not a foregone conclusion, and where boundaries between high art and popular fiction remained fluid. Finally, the women writers examined here worked together with their male counterparts to imagine a nation that did not yet exist; after 1871 authors wrote within the reality of Bismarck's Reich, which was united by "blood and iron," not popular democracy. Marlitt's *Goldelse* captures the idealism of a pre-unification nationalism, as the heroine's father defies his feudal lord to fight with his German brothers in the 1848 Revolution. Her depiction of the 1873 stock market crash in *Im Hause des Kommerzienrates*, published just a decade later, projects a sense of post-unification crisis, both financial and moral. It is tempting to draw parallels between the crash of 1873 and the period of economic crisis and moral soul-searching that has followed Germany's second rush to unity. "Germany" exists once more as a unified political state; in what way the Germans will reinvent themselves as a nation in an increasingly transnational era remains a question for the future.

Notes

PREFACE

1 Anderson, *Imagined Communities.*
2 Hobsbawm, *Nations and Nationalism*, 169.
3 Bhabha, *The Location of Culture.*
4 On the German efforts to come to terms with ethnic and cultural diversity in the wake of reunification see Huyssen, "Nation, Race, and Immigration."
5 Armstrong, *Desire and Domestic Fiction.*
6 Gallas/Heuser, "Einleitung," 9.
7 For an overview of efforts to define the "female *Bildungsroman*" see Kontje, *The German Bildungsroman*, 103–09. In raising these objections to the *Frauenroman* or "female *Bildungsroman*" I do not mean to denigrate the work of critics who have chosen to use these terms; I used "female *Bildungsroman*" myself in an earlier article ("Socialization and Alienation"). Some of the best works on German women and the novel include Touaillon, *Der deutsche Frauenroman*; Blackwell, "Bildungsroman mit Dame"; and Meise, "Der Frauenroman."
8 See for example May, "'Wilhelm Meisters Lehrjahre': Ein Bildungsroman?" and Sammons, "The Mystery of the Missing *Bildungsroman*."
9 On these three feminist writers in the age of the French Revolution see Landes, *Women and the Public Sphere.*
10 Goodman/Waldstein, *In the Shadow of Olympus.*
11 Ward, "*Ehe* and *Entsagung.*"
12 Ridderhoff, *Sophie von La Roche.*

1 INTRODUCTION: WOMEN, THE NOVEL, AND THE
GERMAN NATION

1 Becker-Cantarino, *Der lange Weg.*
2 Becker-Cantarino, *Der lange Weg*, 37–45; Lorenz, "Vom Kloster zur Küche"; Klüger, "Zum Außenseitertum der deutschen Dichterinnen."
3 Bovenschen, *Die imaginierte Weiblichkeit*, 80–149; Becker-Cantarino, *Der lange Weg*, 184–89.

4 Sheehan, *German History*, 149. On witchcraft see also Kunze's account of a seventeenth-century trial and execution, *Highroad to the Stake*.

5 Sheehan, *German History*, 24–41.

6 Martens, *Die Botschaft der Tugend*.

7 On the rapid expansion of the German book market and the reading habit among members of the middle class see Engelsing, *Der Bürger als Leser*; Lämmert, ed., *Romantheorie*; S. J. Schmidt, *Die Selbstorganisation des Sozialsystems Literatur*; Ward, *Book Production*.

8 As "privatized individuals coming together to form a public" novel-readers were a central component of the "bourgeois public sphere" (Habermas, *Structural Transformation*, 51).

9 Sheehan introduces the somewhat awkward term "non-noble élites" to distinguish more precisely the social status of this new group of bureaucrats and intellectuals (*German History*, 132). For the sake of convenience, and at the risk of imprecision, I will refer to the values of this group as "middle class" or "bourgeois."

10 On print culture's role in engendering nationalist sentiments see Anderson, *Imagined Communities*.

11 Hausen, "Family and Role-Division."

12 Laqueur shows how changing social attitudes toward women affected seemingly objective scientific research on sexual difference. Biologists reinforced cultural beliefs about the subordinate and passive nature of women (*Making Sex*).

13 On the transformation of eighteenth-century family life see Schwab, "Familie"; Stone, *The Family, Sex and Marriage*; Weber-Kellermann, *Die deutsche Familie*.

14 Ariès, *Centuries of Childhood*.

15 Mosse, *Nationalism and Sexuality*, 18. See also Armstrong, *Desire and Domestic Fiction*.

16 Habermas, *Structural Transformation*; see also Hohendahl, *The Institution of Criticism*, 52.

17 Landes, *Women and the Public Sphere*, 158. See also Hunt, *The Family Romance*, on how women were excluded from the fraternal order of the republican state.

18 Campe, *Väterlicher Rath*.

19 Landes, *Women and the Public Sphere*, 12.

20 Parker et al., "Introduction," 6. See also Anderson, *Imagined Communities*, 7; Mosse, *Nationalism and Sexuality*, 67; and Theweleit, *Male Fantasies*, 2:77–94.

21 "But we are all *brothers*, / And that inspires our courage. / We are united by the holy bonds of language, / *One* God, *one* Fatherland, / *One* true German blood." Körner, *Leier und Schwert*, 92; hereafter cited in the text.

22 "And women's innocence, women's love / Still stand as our most valued possession, / Where the custom of German forefathers remained / And the courage of German youth."

23 On Körner's preoccupation with death and his traditional view of women see Schulz, *Die deutsche Literatur*, 69–76.

24 "What are you crying about, girls, why do you complain, women, / You for whom the Lord did not forge swords, / When we cast our youthful bodies with rapture / Into the hordes of your predators, / That you lack the bold passion of battle? // You can step up happily to God's altar, after all! / For wounds he gave tender care, / He gave you in your heartfelt prayers / The beautiful, pure victory of piety!"

25 "Yes, good sword, I am free / And love you dearly, / As if you were engaged to me / As a beloved bride! / Hurray!"

26 "Therefore press the love-hot / Bridely mouth of iron / Tightly to your lips! / Curse! to him who abandons the bride! / Hurray!"

27 See Sedgwick, *Between Men,* for a seminal discussion of male homosocial desire in English literature. Kuzniar, ed., *Outing Goethe and His Age* contains a series of provocative studies of same-sex desire in German literature around 1800.

28 Theweleit, *Male Fantasies*, 2:80–81.

29 Koonz, *Mothers in the Fatherland*. Mosse, "Fascism and Sexuality," in *Nationalism and Sexuality*, 153–80.

30 Rousseau, *Emile*, 372.

31 Campe, *Väterlicher Rath*, 70.

32 Schindel, *Die deutschen Schriftstellerinnen*.

33 On Goethe and Schiller's marginalization of women writers see Bürger, *Leben Schreiben*, 19–31.

34 June 30, 1797. *Briefwechsel Schiller–Goethe*, 1:412.

35 Schindel, *Die deutschen Schriftstellerinnen*, 3:xx–xxv. Gottschall finds the *Zeitroman* well-suited to the "mehr passiven und reproductiven Talente der Frauen," while declaring them unfit for historical novels about public events (*Die deutsche Nationalliteratur*, 2:275; 2:545).

36 Schmidt, *Geschichte der deutschen Nationalliteratur*, 2:348–49.

37 *Ibid.*, 2:347.

38 For a review of the Clauren–Hauff debate and further references, see Kontje, "Male Fantasies, Female Readers."

39 On the contradiction between genius aesthetics and the commercial demands on the professional artist, see Bosse, *Autorschaft ist Werkherrschaft*, and Woodmansee, *The Author, Art, and the Market*.

40 Huyssen, "Mass Culture as Woman."

41 Both Gottschall (*Die deutsche Nationalliteratur*) and Schmidt (*Geschichte der deutschen Nationalliteratur*) discuss women writers; some even win grudging praise.

42 Both Haym (*Die romantische Schule*) and Dilthey (*Das Erlebnis und die Dichtung*) concentrate almost exclusively on canonical male authors. The same is true of Martini's popular *Deutsche Literaturgeschichte* of the twentieth century, where women receive only the occasional passing reference.

43 Hohendahl, *Building a National Literature*, 153.

44 *Ibid.*, 145.

45 Dilthey, "Die dichterische und philosophische Bewegung," 16.

46 Dilthey, *Leben Schleiermachers*, 317.

47 On the notion that *Bildung* and the *Bildungsroman* were only for men see Kittler, *Discourse Networks*, 125; and Smith, "Sexual Difference." On the subordinate function of women in the genre see Becker–Cantarino, "Priesterin und Lichtbringerin."

48 Kontje, *The German Bildungsroman.*

49 As Schieth suggests, the novel may well have been written by a man ("Elisa"). See also Meise, *Die Unschuld und die Schrift*, for an excellent, Foucault-inspired study of women's novels as agents of social discipline.

50 Wobeser, *Elisa*, 351.

51 On the subversive potential of seemingly conservative women's literature see Weigel's influential essay, "Der schielende Blick." More recent analyses of the critical subtext of novels by German women include Gallas/Heuser, "Einleitung"; Zantop, "Trivial Pursuits?"; and Goodmann/Waldstein, "Introduction."

52 Hunt, *The Family Romance*, xiv.

53 See Cocalis, "'Around 1800,'" for a review of the trend among many contemporary feminist scholars of German literature to adopt the neutral "um 1800" in place of the "Goethezeit."

54 On the establishment of the first university professorships in German literature see Hohendahl, *Building a National Literature*, 201–02.

55 I allude to Mosse's essay on Marlitt, Karl May, and Ludwig Ganghofer, "What the Germans really read."

56 Schieth contends that the genre remains essentially unchanged from LaRoche to Marlitt (*Die Entwicklung des deutschen Frauenromans*, 1, 38, 219). Marlitt, in turn, is often viewed as the originator of today's formulaic pulp fiction (Schenk, *Die Rache der alten Mamsell*, 11, 103). On the historical continuity of English popular fiction from Jane Austen to the Harlequin romance see Modleski, *Loving with a Vengeance*, 35–58.

57 On the concept of "backlash" as an excessive anti-feminist reaction to modest advances in women's rights see Faludi, *Backlash*.

58 Hughes, *Nationalism and Society*, 22. Schulze provides a concise history of *The Course of German Nationalism* from 1763 to 1867.

59 See Mosse, *The Crisis of German Ideology*, for a detailed study of the romantic roots of fascist ideology.

60 See Hobsbawm, "Introduction: Inventing Traditions."

61 On the Restoration backlash against state-sponsored liberal nationalism of the Wars of Liberation, see Johnston, *The Myth of a Nation*. Sheehan stresses the vitality of German liberalism from the early nineteenth century to the "second Reichsgründung" of 1877 (*German Liberalism*).

62 See Huyssen's eloquent call "for the democratic left to reoccupy the discursive terrain of nation" ("Nation, Race, and Immigration," 84).

63 Gallas/Runge, *Romane und Erzählungen*; Eke and Olasz-Eke, *Bibliographie*.

64 A few of the most significant publications, listed in chronological order, include: Touaillon, *Der deutsche Frauenroman* (1919); Möhrmann, *Die andere Frau* (1977); Bovenschen, *Die imaginierte Weiblichkeit* (1979); Blackwell, "Bildungsroman mit Dame" (1982); Meise, *Die Unschuld und die Schrift* (1983); Gnüg/Möhrmann, eds., *Frauen Literatur Geschichte* (1985); Goodman, *Dis/Closures* (1986); Becker-Cantarino, *Der lange Weg zur Mündigkeit* (1987); Schieth, *Die Entwicklung des deutschen Frauenromans* (1987); Brinker-Gabler, ed., *Deutsche Literatur von Frauen* (1988); Bürger, *Leben Schreiben* (1990); Gallas/Heuser, eds., *Untersuchungen zum Roman von Frauen* (1990); Goodman/Waldstein, eds., *In the Shadow of Olympus* (1992).

65 For a recent overview of the achievements and remaining tasks of German feminist scholarship see Clausen/Friedrichsmeyer, "WIG 2000."

66 *Consuming Fiction*, 135–36.

67 Published in the Neuer Kaiser Verlag-Buch und Welt, Hans Kaiser, Klagenfurt.

68 See Tompkins, *Sensational Designs*, 186–201, for an answer to this question in the context of American studies.

69 On "the cultural work of American fiction" see Tompkins, *Sensational Designs*. For a discussion of the novel as an agent of cultural formation in England see Eagleton, *The Rape of Clarissa*; and Armstrong, *Desire and Domestic Fiction*.

2 THE EMERGENCE OF GERMAN DOMESTIC FICTION

1 On Klopstock's nationalist writings see Fischer, *Das Eigene und das Eigentliche*, 131–82.

2 Wellbery, *The Specular Moment*.

3 Wieland, "Der Eifer, unsrer Dichtkunst einen National-Charakter zu geben."

4 Wieland, "Wenn sie fortfahren," 273.

5 Wieland, "Der Eifer," 269.

6 For Wieland's definition of the cosmopolitan see *Die Dialogen des Diogenes*, chapter 32, 72–76.

7 The spelling of LaRoche's last name varies, with the editors of the German Reclam edition choosing "La Roche," and the American edition choosing "LaRoche." I use LaRoche throughout. See Blackwell, "Sophie von La Roche," for an overview of her life and works.

8 Becker-Cantarino, "Nachwort," 386.

9 Touaillon begins her study of *Der deutsche Frauenroman* with an extensive discussion of LaRoche and her imitators (69–229), and Schieth stresses the essential continuity of the tradition LaRoche established (*Die Entwicklung des deutschen Frauenromans*, 219). One of my goals will be to

differentiate historically between novels that Schieth finds monotonously repetitive (161).

10 Michael Maurer, "Das Gute und das Schöne"; Petschauer, "Sophie von LaRoche"; Sudhof, "Sophie Laroche."

11 Bovenschen, *Die imaginierte Weiblichkeit*, 190–200.

12 Assing, *Sophie von La Roche, die Freundin Wielands*; Milch, *Sophie La Roche: Die Großmutter der Brentanos*.

13 Britt, "Introduction," 6.

14 Becker-Cantarino, "Nachwort," 403–05.

15 Cited from LaRoche, *The History of Lady Sophie Sternheim*, 46–47; in German: LaRoche, *Geschichte des Fräuleins von Sternheim*, 10, 12. Subsequent references to the English translation will be included in the text, followed by a page reference to the German edition.

16 Armstrong, *Desire and Domestic Fiction*, 8. Schön argues that the primary readers of eighteenth-century German fiction were women ("Weibliches Lesen").

17 Richardson, *Clarissa*, 53. Hereafter cited in the text.

18 On the social status of Lovelace and the Harlowes see Watt, *The Rise of the Novel*, 220– 21; and Ross, "Introduction," 20–22.

19 Watt, *The Rise of the Novel*, 222.

20 Stone, *The Family, Sex and Marriage*, 4. As Cohen observes, "the novel is more about the *making* of psychological reading and psychological character than it is a psychological text with a heroine driven by her unconscious" (*The Daughter's Dilemma*, 50). On Mr. Harlowe as an authoritarian "figure from the past" see also Haney-Peritz, "Engendering the Exemplary Daughter," 192.

21 Warner pays close attention to the way in which Clarissa works to establish herself as a paragon of virtue and Christian martyr (*Reading Clarissa*). He shares an interest with Castle (*Clarissa's Ciphers*) and Eagleton (*The Rape of Clarissa*) in the hermeneutic aspects of the text. All three argue that events matter less than their interpretation in this novel, and characters are busy trying to understand one another and to influence opinion of themselves. However, Castle and Eagleton direct justified scorn at the implicit misogyny of Warner's deconstructive dogma.

22 Shortly before her death, Belford echoes this position with reference to "the friendly and even *paternal* attendance she had had from Dr. H. and Mr Goddard" (1351).

23 As Haney-Peritz has observed, Clarissa gradually shifts her interest away from reconciliation with her actual father toward a desire for the name of the father ("Engendering the Exemplary Daughter").

24 Much of the novel exhibits the characteristics that Watt identifies as typical of eighteenth-century realism, including truth to individual experience, the representation of recognizable individuals rather than stock types, and a reliance on causality rather than coincidence in the explanation of events (*The Rise of the Novel*, 9–34).

25 On Richardson's use of the set pictorial scene see Doody, *A Natural Passion*, 216–40.
26 *The English Novel*, 49.
27 Warner, *Reading Clarissa*, 75–120. Also Eagleton, *The Rape of Clarissa*.
28 I am indebted to Cohen, *The Daughter's Dilemma*, esp. 54–55.
29 While Christopher Hill argues that Clarissa offers a "damning indictment" of her society ("Clarissa Harlowe and her Times," 332), Van Ghent insists that the "paramount motif is, then, not rebellion and escape, but acquiescence in parental values and return" (*The English Novel*, 60). Eagleton seems to want things both ways, arguing that Clarissa's very submissiveness to the patriarchal order serves as a devastating critique (*The Rape of Clarissa*, 76).
30 Rousseau, *La Nouvelle Héloïse* [English], 144; *La Nouvelle Héloïse* [French], 175–76. All subsequent references to the English translation of the novel are included in the text, followed by page references to the French; passages not translated in the abbreviated English edition are my own. Tanner offers a witty and perceptive Freudian analysis of the relationship between Julie and her father ("Julie and 'La maison paternelle' ").
31 On the coercive nature of the social order in Clarens see Starobinski, *Jean-Jacques Rousseau*, 97–111; and Crocker, "Julie ou la nouvelle duplicité."
32 Several readers have noted the disturbing degree to which Saint-Preux becomes the object of a sadistic experiment in social engineering (Crocker, "Julie ou la nouvelle duplicité," 132–52; Brooks, *The Novel of Worldliness*, 154).
33 On this distinction in Goethe's *Wilhelm Meisters Lehrjahre* see Janz, "Zum sozialen Gehalt der *Lehrjahre*."
34 Touaillon, *Der deutsche Frauenroman*, 104–05; Becker-Cantarino, "Nachwort," 407; Britt, "Introduction," 16–17.
35 Goethe, *Faust*, lines 682–83. *Werke*, 3: 29; English trans. Peter Salm, *Faust*, 45.
36 See the review by "Sr" (Sulzer?) reprinted in LaRoche, *Sternheim*, ed. Becker-Cantarino, 368–70.
37 Even one of the novel's earliest reviewers noted an element of pride in Sophie's altruism: "Sophie thut gute Werke mit Begier, sie freut sich darüber, sie erlangt ihren eigenen Beyfall" (Haller, cited from LaRoche, *Sternheim*, ed. Becker-Cantarino, 367). For more recent critical assessments of Sophie's efforts to right social injustice see Hohendahl, "Empfindsamkeit," 194–98; and Blackwell, "Bildungsroman mit Dame," 125.
38 See Becker-Cantarino on Sophie's move to practical virtue within the limits of the existing patriarchal society ("Nachwort," 407–15).
39 Graf provides a detailed history of eighteenth-century German theatre (*Das Theater im Literaturstaat*, 119–55). Graf works within a German tradition and links changes in theatrical practice to Christian Wolff's

rational philosophy. Mücke details the same changes from a comparative perspective, suggesting that the move from court spectacle to Diderot's *drame sérieux* corresponds to the Foucaultian distinction between a culture of public punishment and one of private discipline (*Virtue and the Veil of Illusion*, 92–96).

40 I am grateful to Wendy K. Arons for calling my attention to Sophie's use of pedagogical theatre in this scene. See her sophisticated discussion of performance, theatricality, and the production of gender in "Sophie Goes to the Theater."

41 LaRoche's novel thus provides a good example of Butler's understanding of gender as a cultural performance. In *Gender Trouble* Butler suggests "that certain cultural configurations of gender take the place of 'the real' and consolidate and augment their hegemony through that felicitous self-naturalization" (32–33).

3 GERMAN WOMEN RESPOND TO THE FRENCH REVOLUTION

1 "The man must go out into hostile life . . . And inside the modest housewife reigns." Schiller, *Sämtliche Werke*, 1:432–33; 440.

2 Campe's treatise was republished in 1790, 1793, 1809, 1819, and 1829.

3 Reported in Caroline Schlegel-Schelling's letter to her daughter Auguste, October 21, 1799. Schlegel-Schelling, *"Lieber Freund,"* 230.

4 Bovenschen points out that the genre's low status facilitated women's entry into publishing, but that as novels such as Goethe's *Wilhelm Meisters Lehrjahre* began to garner respect, women's novels were viewed as *Trivialliteratur* (*Die imaginierte Weiblichkeit*, 200–20).

5 On Wolzogen's biography see Kahn-Wallerstein, *Die Frau im Schatten*; further information in Touaillon, *Der deutsche Frauenroman*, 451–61; Boerner, "Nachwort" to *Agnes von Lilien*; and Fetting, *"Ich fand in mir eine Welt,"* 45–58. These sources also contain information about the composition, publication, and early reception of the novel.

6 The few twentieth-century critics of Wolzogen's work have given her mixed reviews. Touaillon sets the tone by first praising her as one of the most gifted women writers of the eighteenth century, but then asserting that her work lacks vitality, and that her overly idealized characters fail to capture the imagination (*Der deutsche Frauenroman*, 451–54). See similar comments in Boerner, "Nachwort," 402–03; and Fetting, *"Ich fand in mir eine Welt,"* 106–17.

7 Wolzogen, *Agnes von Lilien*, 1:10. Hereafter cited in the text.

8 Frye, *Anatomy of Criticism*, 163–86.

9 For an overview of Unger's life and works, including both primary and secondary bibliography, see Zantop, "Friederike Helene Unger."

10 The exception is Touaillon, who included a discussion of Unger in *Der deutsche Frauenroman*, 244–61. For more recent criticism see Bailet, *Die Frau als Verführte und Verführerin*, 1–50; Grenz, *Mädchenliteratur*, 145–58;

Blackwell, "Bildungsroman mit Dame," 129–58; Meise, *Die Unschuld und die Schrift*, 51–65; Heuser, "'Spuren trauriger Selbstvergessenheit'"; Zantop, "Aus der Not eine Tugend"; "The Beautiful Soul Writes Herself"; and the "Nachwort" to *Julchen Grünthal*.

11 To date *Julchen Grünthal: Eine Pensionsgeschichte* (1798) and *Bekenntnisse einer schönen Seele* (1806) have appeared.

12 Unger, *Julchen Grünthal*, 1:383. Hereafter cited in the text.

13 Meise, *Die Unschuld und die Schrift*, 57–58.

14 "'Der ehrliche Mann that so schmuk und festlich, als wenn sein Hochzeitstag wäre.'" Due to a misprint the page is actually numbered 306.

15 "[D]ie allmähliche Verankerung des Gewissens als innere Instanz." *Die Unschuld und die Schrift*, 55–56.

16 On *Die Franzosen in Berlin* see Zantop, "Aus der Not eine Tugend," 142–47.

17 Zantop examines Unger's ambivalent attitude toward Goethe in later novels, where she alternates between appreciation of his genius and disapproval of his morals. Unger reserves particular scorn for the exaggerated enthusiasm of an idolatrous Goethe cult ("The Beautiful Soul Writes Herself").

18 Heuser, "'Spuren trauriger Selbstvergessenheit,'" 34–35.

19 Blackwell highlights the discrepancy between Julchen's experiences and the reenactment of her virginal innocence, and argues that denial features prominently in forced conclusions to the "female Bildungsroman" ("Bildungsroman mit Dame," 147–53).

20 Heuser, "'Spuren trauriger Selbstvergessenheit,'" 34.

21 For example, Zantop characterizes the novel as a "Trojan Horse" ("Aus der Not eine Tugend," 134–42), and both Grenz and Blackwell underscore the discrepancy between the novel's didactic intent and the psychological realism that encourages identification with the protagonist (*Mädchenliteratur*, 148–50; "Bildungsroman mit Dame," 139).

22 See Schön, "Weibliches Lesen."

23 See Zantop, "Aus der Not eine Tugend," 135–36.

24 Blackwell, "Therese Huber," 189. On Huber's biography see also Touaillon, *Der deutsche Frauenroman*, 324–30; and Heuser, "Nachwort."

25 Richardson's *Pamela* was the most influential eighteenth-century formulation of what his heroine refers to as "the ruin of oppressed innocence" (130). Petriconi traces this theme from its origins in classical antiquity through prominent works by Richardson, Laclos, Sade, and Goethe (*Die verführte Unschuld*).

26 Both Heuser and Peitsch point out Huber's innovative combination of fiction and history in their studies of *Die Familie Seldorf* ("Nachwort," 349–50; "Die Revolution im Familienroman," 263). See also Becker-Cantarino, "Revolution im Patriarchat" and "Poetische Freiheit."

27 Huber, *Die Familie Seldorf*, 2:66. Hereafter cited in the text.

28 Heuser, "Nachwort," 381–82. Earlier Touaillon had contrasted Sara Seldorf's *Sonderentwicklung* with the more directly didactic intention of LaRoche and her followers (*Der deutsche Frauenroman*, 335). Köpke stresses the importance of the theme of *Bildung* as socialization in Huber's *oeuvre* as a whole ("Immer noch im Schatten der Männer?" 122). Peitsch prefers to label the work a *Familienroman*, as the novel's title would seem to indicate ("Revolution im Familienroman," 255). However, Sara Seldorf clearly occupies a central position in the family portrayed in this novel. From this perspective, the distinction between the *Entwicklungs-* or *Bildungsroman* and the *Familienroman* is more a matter of emphasis than an absolute distinction, as individual development always takes place in the context of family and society.

29 On this scene see Meise, *Die Unschuld und die Schrift*, 136–38.

30 As Wild observes, the increased intimacy of the nuclear family leads not to the disappearance of paternal authority, but rather to its internalization (*Die Vernunft der Väter*, 309). We have already seen this process at work in *La Nouvelle Héloïse*.

31 Campe, *Väterliche Rath*, 18.

32 To this extent Huber qualifies his role as "politische[r] Ideenträger des Romans" (Heuser, "Nachwort," 375). The struggle against the aristocracy turns into male fear and resentment of women's seductive charms.

33 Heuser, "Nachwort," 377. Peitsch, "Die Revolution im Familienroman," 263.

34 Kluckhohn, *Die Auffassung der Liebe*, 289; and Touaillon, *Der deutsche Frauenroman*, 336.

35 As both Peitsch and Heuser point out, early reviewers of the novel were disappointed by its ending. Peitsch and Heuser praise Huber's unwillingness to compromise her heroine's desire for sexual fulfillment in marriage with an arrangement based on friendship rather than love ("Revolution im Familienroman," 266; "Nachwort," 379–80).

36 Johann Georg Rist, *Lebenserinnerungen*. Cited from Gersdorff, *"Dich zu lieben,"* 13.

37 Touaillon offers a still-useful introduction to Mereau's life and works (*Der deutsche Frauenroman*, 523–54). See also Gersdorff's biography (*"Dich zu lieben"*). Hammerstein's *Sophie Mereau-Brentano* is the best recent study of Mereau's life and works in socio-historical context.

38 Moens sketches the reception-history of Mereau's work in his "Nachwort" to *Das Blüthenalter der Empfindung*, 23–30.

39 "Frühling" [Spring], "An einem Baum am Spalier" [To a Trellised Tree], and "Die Flucht nach der Hauptstadt" [Flight to the City] in *Bitter Healing*, 369–99.

40 See Weigel, "Sophie Mereau"; Gersdorff, *"Dich zu lieben"*; Kastinger Riley, "Saat und Ernte."

41 Peter Schmidt, "Nachwort" to *Kalathiskos*, 25; 29–30.

42 Moens, "Nachwort" to *Das Blüthenalter der Empfindung*, 2.

43 Bürger, " 'Die mittlere Sphäre,' " 366. Bürger includes a revised version of this essay in *Leben Schreiben*, 33–51.

44 See Bürger's "Einleitung" to *Zur Dichotomisierung von hoher und niederer Literatur.*

45 Bürger, *Leben Schreiben*, 31.

46 *Ibid.*, 30.

47 Bürger, " 'Die mittlere Sphäre,' " 371.

48 Mahoney, *Der Roman der Goethezeit*, 95.

49 Köpke, "Die emanzipierte Frau," 108. Becker-Cantarino demonstrates how Friedrich Schlegel's heroine fulfills just this role for Julius in *Lucinde* (1799) ("Priesterin und Lichtbringerin," 116, 122).

50 Mereau, *Das Blüthenalter der Empfindung*, 84. Hereafter cited in the text.

51 Mereau's first published poem was in celebration of the French Revolution ("Bey Frankreichs Feier des 14. Junius 1790" [1791]). Reprinted in Hammerstein, *Sophie Mereau-Brentano*, 105–07.

52 Mereau, "Flight to the City," 384; "Die Flucht nach der Hauptstadt," 149. Further references to the English translation are included in the text, followed by page references to the original German edition.

53 See Graf, *Das Theater im Literaturstaat*, 130–35.

54 Landes shows how the aristocratic women of the seventeenth-century French salons exercised far greater political power than their bourgeois counterparts around 1800 (*Women and the Public Sphere*, 17–38).

55 Mereau, "Ninon Lenclos," 76. Hereafter cited in the text.

56 See Bremer and Schneider on the composition and publication of the novel ("Wünsche und Verhältnisse," 363–78).

57 Vansant emphasizes Mereau's critique of Schlegel's phallocentric understanding of *Bildung* in her analysis of the novel ("Liebe und Patriarchat," 186; 191–92; 196–200). However, by concentrating on Amanda's resistance to traditional values she oversimplifies her character and therefore overlooks Mereau's implicit critique of Amanda toward the end of the novel. See also Bremer and Schneider, "Wünsche und Verhältnisse."

58 Quoted from Moens, "Nachwort," 23.

59 On Mereau's androgynous narrative perspective as deliberate strategy see Gersdorff, *"Dich zu lieben,"* 48; and Treder, "Sophie Mereau," 175.

60 Both Kastinger Riley and Vansant detail the changes in sequence between the letters published in *Die Horen* and the completed novel ("Saat und Ernte," 71–72; "Liebe und Patriarchat," 190).

61 Gersdorff notes this and other parallels between specific passages of *Amanda und Eduard* and the *Wilhelm Meister* review, which she uses as convincing evidence that the anonymous review is by Mereau and not Clemens Brentano, as earlier readers had assumed (*"Dich zu Lieben,"* 256–61).

62 Bürger, " 'Die mittlere Sphäre,' " 376.

63 On this frequently recurring motif in German thought around 1800 see Abrams, *Natural Supernaturalism*, 197–252.

64 See Bovenschen on the identification of woman with nature in the works of Schiller, Humboldt, and Kant (*Die imaginierte Weiblichkeit*, 220–56).

65 Becker-Cantarino, "Priesterin und Lichtbringerin," 114.

66 Bremer and Schneider cite Mereau's letter to her publisher Wilmans, in which she indicates which passage should serve for the illustration to the second volume. She included the text itself on a separate sheet that has been lost, but the picture itself leaves no doubt as to her choice ("Wünsche und Verhältnisse," 370–71). Reproduced in Weigel, "Der schielende Blick," 94.

67 *Die Horen* 7 (1797), 55–56.

68 Köpke argues that the lack of marital infidelity in the novel reveals a timidity in print that Mereau did not display during her life ("Die emanzipierte Frau," 102). I would agree with Fleischmann that the novel is ambiguous on this point (*Zwischen Aufbruch und Anpassung*, 116–17). The question of whether or not Eduard and Amanda consummate their affair is ultimately less important than the fact that Amanda unabashedly defends her right to experience love outside the bonds of marriage.

69 Mereau had formulated the same idea in her novella *Marie*: "Das meiste von dem, was wir wünschen, geschieht, aber fast nie zu der Zeit, da wir es wünschen" (94). This tale of a woman torn between her feelings for two men represents an earlier version of the theme developed in *Amanda und Eduard*, as does Mereau's translation of *La Princesse de Clèves* in 1799.

70 *Der Mann mit vier Weibern*, 270–71.

71 *Briefwechsel Brentano–Mereau*, 1:62.

72 Wolf, *Kein Ort. Nirgends*, 35–36. On Mereau's preoccupation with death and flirtation with suicide see Hammerstein, *Sophie Mereau-Brentano*, 95–101.

73 Quoted from Fetting, *"Ich fand in mir eine Welt,"* 73.

4 LIBERATION'S AFTERMATH: THE EARLY RESTORATION

1 Schopenhauer paints a vivid picture of the chaotic scene in Weimar in a long letter to her son Arthur written on October 19, 1806. In Schopenhauer, *Im Wechsel der Zeiten*, 316–32.

2 On the development of German nationalism during the Napoleonic Wars see Schulz, *Die deutsche Literatur*; Johnston, *The Myth of a Nation*; Schulze, *The Course of German Nationalism*, 35–63; and Sheehan, *German History*, 371–88.

3 Johnston, *The Myth of a Nation*.

4 Mosse traces the spread of German nationalist sentiments in *The Nationalization of the Masses*.

5 Schulz, *Die deutsche Literatur*, 134–46.

6 Eke and Olasz-Eke, *Bibliographie*, 25.

7 Hauff's *Controvers-Predigt* against Clauren's popular fiction is typical; see Kontje, "Male Fantasies, Female Readers."

8 See Hohendahl, "Literarischer Kommerz," 40.

9 Perthes, *Der deutsche Buchhandel*, 9.

10 Vollmer, *Der deutschsprachige Roman*, 91; Eke and Olasz-Eke arrive at similar figures for the years 1815–1830 (*Bibliographie*, 24).

11 Postwar literary historians continue to portray women writers of the period as a homogenous group of inferior talents. Sengle accuses women writers of the period of lowering literary standards and endangering high culture (*Biedermeierzeit*, 1:102–03), while Schulz writes of the "unübersehbare Menge von Schriftstellerinnen und Schriftstellern" (*Die deutsche Literatur*, 113). Schulz devotes 6 pages of his literary history to the generic category of "female writers," [*Schriftstellerinnen*] and the remaining 800 pages to detailed analyses of works by individual men.

12 See Wilde, *The Romantic Realist*; and Hofacker, "Caroline de la Motte Fouqué," for general overviews of Fouqué's life and works.

13 See Hoffmeister's detailed introduction to the modern reprint of this novel.

14 Fouqué, *Magie der Natur*, 55. Hereafter cited in the text.

15 See Vollmer's discussion of this novel in *Der deutschsprachige Roman* (1993), 63–68.

16 Fouqué, *Edmunds Wege und Irrwege*, 1:103. Hereafter cited in the text.

17 Vollmer, *Der deutschsprachige Roman*, 67.

18 On the history of *Bildungsroman* criticism see Kontje, *The German Bildungsroman*.

19 Fouqué, *Fragmente*, 46. Hereafter cited in the text.

20 Vollmer, "'Die Wahrheit bleibt das Höchste,'" 136–38.

21 Fouqué, *Die beiden Freunde*, 2:157. Hereafter cited in the text.

22 Mosse, *Nationalism and Sexuality*, 101.

23 Fouqué, *Laura*, 207. Hereafter cited in the text.

24 Fouqué, *Das Heldenmädchen*, 2:41. Hereafter cited in the text.

25 Frölich, *Virginia*, 100. Hereafter cited in the text.

26 Steiner, "Nachwort," 231. Steiner provides a good introduction to Frölich's life and situates her work in the context of Restoration Berlin. See also Brandes, "Escape to America"; and Vollmer, *Der deutschsprachige Roman*, 98–102.

27 Hunt, *The Family Romance*.

28 Steiner, "Nachwort," 223.

29 "Vorrede," in Woltmann, *Maria und Walpurgis: Ein Roman* (1817–18). Hereafter cited in the text.

30 Vollmer, *Der deutschsprachige Roman*, 148.

31 See Abbott, *Fictions of Freemasonry*, on the appeal of freemasonry as an alternative to German absolutism. He does not discuss Woltmann's novel, but it too is a significant "fiction of freemasonry."

32 Hobsbawm, *Nations and Nationalism*, 57.
33 See Mosse, *The Crisis of German Ideology*.
34 Peterson, "German Nationalism after Napoleon," 290.
35 "In the midst of the wars of liberation, nationalism and respectability were thus linked, and the restricted, passive role of women legitimized" (Mosse, *Nationalism and Sexuality*, 96).
36 On Schopenhauer's life see Dworetzki, *Johanna Schopenhauer*; and Picket, "Johanna Schopenhauer." Contemporary critics of *Gabriele* include Blackwell, "Bildungsroman mit Dame," 179–93; Bürger, *Leben Schreiben*, 53–79; Fetting, *"Ich fand in mir eine Welt,"* 76–92; 128–42; Goodman, "Johanna Schopenhauer"; and Koranyi, "Nachwort."
37 Schopenhauer, *Gabriele*, 110. Hereafter cited in the text.
38 Menzel (1830); cited from Steinecke, *Romantheorie und Romankritik*, 77.
39 "Ehret die Frauen! sie flechten und weben / Himmlische Rosen ins irdische Leben." Schiller, "Würde der Frauen," in *Sämtliche Werke*, 1:218.
40 Blackwell, "Bildungsroman mit Dame"; Fetting, *"Ich fand in mir eine Welt."*
41 See Frederiksen/Shafi, "Annette von Droste-Hülshoff," 115–16; and Niethammer/Belemann, *Ein Gitter aus Musik und Sprache*, 7–8, on the traditional image of Droste-Hülshoff and its feminist revision. On Droste-Hülshoff's biography see Doris Maurer, *Annette von Droste-Hülshoff*; and Shafi, "Annette von Droste-Hülshoff."
42 See Droste-Hülshoff's poem "Die Stadt und der Dom: Eine Karikatur des Heiligsten." *Sämtliche Werke*, 1:13–16.
43 Niethammer and Belemann observe the increased interest in *Ledwina* in recent years (*Ein Gitter aus Musik und Sprache*, 9–10). Scholarship includes Heselhaus, *Annette von Droste-Hülshoff*, 70–74; Schneider, *Realismus und Restauration*, 100–19; Peucker, "Droste-Hülshoff's Ophelia"; Roebling, "Weibliches Schreiben"; and Frederiksen/Shafi, "Annette von Droste-Hülshoff," 129–33.
44 See *Sämtliche Werke*, 2:835–39, on the composition of *Ledwina*. A fragmentary sketch of the planned continuation is included in the *Historisch-kritische Ausgabe* (1978), vol. 5.1:173–77 ("Zu *Ledwina*").
45 Droste-Hülshoff, *Ledwina*, 509; in German, *Sämtliche Werke*, 2:139. Further references to the English translation of *Ledwina* are included in the text, followed by page references to the German edition.
46 Both Heselhaus (*Annette von Droste-Hülshoff*, 73) and Schneider (*Realismus und Restauration*, 105) stress the socially critical aspect of *Ledwina*.
47 Peucker, "Droste-Hülshoff's Ophelia"; Roebling, "Weibliches Schreiben" and "Heraldik des Unheimlichen."
48 Peucker, "Droste-Hülshoff's Ophelia," 376.
49 Dijkstra, *Idols of Perversity*, 42.
50 Roebling, "Heraldik des Unheimlichen," 57–58.
51 Novalis, "Hymnen an die Nacht." In *Schriften*, 1:139.
52 "Der Hünenstein." In *Sämtliche Werke*, 1:48.

5 FEMINISTS IN THE *VORMÄRZ*

1 Schulze recounts the March events in Berlin in detail in *The Course of German Nationalism*, 5–31.

2 Aston, *Revolution und Contrerevolution*, 2:74. Hereafter cited in the text.

3 See Hamerow, *Restoration*, 1–93; Blasius, "Epoche," 14–31; Sheehan, *German History*, 389–653.

4 Martino, "Publikumsschichten," in *Deutsche Literatur*, vol. 6; Obenaus, "Buchmarkt."

5 Lämmert, *Romantheorie*; Steinecke, *Romantheorie und Romankritik*.

6 Lewald, *Eine Lebensfrage*, 106.

7 See Heintz's critical edition of Gutzkow's *Wally* for extensive documentation of the literary controversies surrounding Young Germany.

8 Möhrmann, *Die andere Frau*, 1.

9 In contrast, Weigel emphasizes the tensions that arise in women's novels of the *Vormärz* between their overt conservatism and latent subversiveness ("Der schielende Blick"). Similar comments in Goetzinger, " 'Allein das Bewußtsein.' "

10 Estimates of the number of German women writers in the nineteenth century range in the thousands. See Herminghouse, "Women and the Literary Enterprise." On women writers in the *Vormärz* see also Boetcher Joeres, "1848 from a Distance."

11 Schmid-Jürgens offers a still-useful overview of Hahn-Hahn's life and works (*Ida Gräfin Hahn-Hahn*). See also Kraft, "Ida Gräfin von Hahn-Hahn."

12 Carl Barthel; cited from Möhrmann, *Die andere Frau*, 172. Möhrmann details Hahn-Hahn's controversial reception in her path-breaking feminist analysis of Hahn-Hahn's work.

13 Lewald, *Diogena*; see further comments on this text below.

14 References to Hahn-Hahn's Catholic admirers in Schmid-Jürgens, *Ida Gräfin Hahn-Hahn*, 9–10; see also Oberembt, *Ida Gräfin Hahn-Hahn*, for a critical account of Hahn-Hahn's "ultramontanism."

15 Most notably Möhrmann, *Die andere Frau*, but see also Geiger, *Die befreite Psyche*.

16 In this vein Herminghouse offers a useful corrective to critics such as Möhrmann and Geiger, arguing that recognition of Hahn-Hahn's early feminism should not obscure her subsequent turn to the right ("Seeing Double").

17 Hahn-Hahn, *Gräfin Faustine*, 21. Hereafter cited in the text.

18 "Als 'Butterbrote' des Mannes"; Möhrmann, *Die andere Frau*, 106.

19 For this reason I disagree with the claim that Hahn-Hahn's primary concern in this novel is to depict Faustine's "Entwicklungsprozess" (Möhrmann, *Die andere Frau*, 105) or her "Drang nach Selbstverwirklichung" (Taeger, "Nachwort," 246).

20 Hahn-Hahn, *Zwei Frauen*, 1:17. Hereafter cited in the text.

21 Oberembt also notes the link between marital infidelity and political revolution in *Zwei Frauen (Ida Gräfin Hahn-Hahn,* 279).

22 Möhrmann attributes the frequent similarities between Hahn-Hahn's early novels to their basis in autobiography (*Die andere Frau,* 99).

23 Hahn-Hahn, *Sibylle,* 1:2. Hereafter cited in the text.

24 Geiger discusses *Sibylle* as "die Geschichte der Genese der weiblichen Kreativität" (*Die befreite Psyche,* 144). While Sibylle eventually does write her memoirs, Hahn-Hahn does not make the act of writing a central thematic concern. Geiger's stress on the positive also sits oddly with the increasingly despairing tone of a narrative that culminates in the writer's death.

25 Lewald, *Diogena,* 122. Hereafter cited in the text.

26 Steinhauer, *Fanny Lewald,* 55–63; Lewis, "The Woman's Novel Parodied."

27 Lewald's autobiography (*Meine Lebensgeschichte* [The Education of Fanny Lewald]) provides the best introduction to her life up to 1845. See also Goodman, *Dis/Closures,* 147–64; and Helmer's "Nachwort" to the German edition. Critical overviews of her life and works include: Steinhauer, *Fanny Lewald*; Möhrmann, *Die andere Frau,* 118–40; Brinker-Gabler, "Fanny Lewald," 72–86; Venske, "Discipline and Daydreaming"; Di Maio, "Fanny Lewald."

28 Lewald, *Clementine,* 16. Hereafter cited in the text.

29 Steinhauer, *Fanny Lewald,* 65; Möhrmann, *Die andere Frau,* 130.

30 Möhrmann, *Die andere Frau,* 131.

31 Venske, "Discipline and Daydreaming," 182.

32 *Ibid.,* 185.

33 *Ibid.,* 188.

34 See Möhrmann, *Die andere Frau,* 134–38; Blackwell, "Bildungsroman mit Dame," 255–74; Helmer, "Nachwort" to *Jenny,* 254–72.

35 In the original 1842 edition of the novel Lewald identified the wave of anti-Semitic violence that swept Germany, Austria, and Denmark "unter dem Feldgeschrei 'Hep-Hep!'" (quoted in Helmer's commentary to *Jenny,* 273). Helmer bases her edition on the slightly revised 1872 edition of the novel.

36 Lewald, *Jenny,* 56–57. Hereafter cited in the text.

37 On the double standard for Jewish men and women regarding conversion see Möhrmann, *Die andere Frau,* 135.

38 Di Maio, "Jewish Emancipation and Integration."

39 Blackwell, "Bildungsroman mit Dame," 271.

40 Gilman, *Jewish Self-Hatred.*

41 Blackwell, "Bildungsroman mit Dame," 272.

42 As Blackwell observes, Lewald blames an intolerant society for her heroine's demise ("Bildungsroman mit Dame," 273). See also Möhrmann, *Die andere Frau,* 138.

43 Lewald, *Eine Lebensfrage,* 76. Hereafter cited in the text.

44 Lewald, *Der dritte Stand,* 6. Hereafter cited in the text.

45 Möhrmann criticizes Lewald's superficial treatment of working conditions in early capitalism (*Die andere Frau*, 143).

46 Lewald wrote *Prinz Louis Ferdinand* between June 1847 and November 1848 (Rogels-Siegel, "Introduction," 57). Rogols-Siegel provides a detailed introduction to the historical background of *Prinz Louis Ferdinand* her translation of the novel.

47 Lewald, *Prinz Louis Ferdinand* (English translation), 120; *Prinz Louis Ferdinand* (in German), 1:22. Further references to the English translation included in the text, followed by page references to the German edition.

48 Di Maio, "Jewish Emancipation and Integration," 284–90.

49 See Mortier, "Une romancière allemande"; Lewis, "Fanny Lewald and the Revolutions of 1848."

50 Lewald, *Erinnerungen aus dem Jahre 1848*, 1:6. Hereafter cited in the text.

51 Lewald, *Auf rother Erde*, 157. Hereafter cited in the text.

52 Boetcher Joeres also notes the conservatism of Lewald's Marie in comparison with other female figures in *Vormärz* fiction ("1848 from a Distance," 607–08).

53 Goetzinger provides the most detailed introduction to Aston's life in a volume that reproduces rare source material by the author and her contemporaries (*Für die Selbstverwirklichung der Frau*). Fingerhut, ed., *Louise Aston: Ein Lesebuch* also contains rare reprints of original material. See also Fingerhut's "Nachwort" in *ibid.*; Geiger, "Louise Aston"; Möhrmann, *Die andere Frau*, 141–50; and Wimmer, *Die Vormärzschriftstellerin Louise Aston*.

54 Carlos von Gagern, "Erinnerung an Louise Aston." Cited from Goetzinger, *Für die Selbstverwirklichung der Frau*, 50.

55 Cited from Goetzinger, *Für die Selbstverwirklichung der Frau*, 31.

56 Rudolf Gottschall, "Aus meiner Jugend." Cited from Goetzinger, *Für die Selbstverwirklichung der Frau*, 45–49.

57 Aston, *Meine Emancipation, Verweisung und Rechtfertigung*; cited from Goetzinger, *Für die Selbstverwirklichung der Frau*, 78.

58 *Meine Emancipation*; Goetzinger, *Für die Selbstverwirklichung der Frau*, 78.

59 Goetzinger, *Für die Selbstverwirklichung der Frau*, 26.

60 *Ibid.*, 123.

61 *Ibid.*, 121.

62 "Free love will liberate the world. You should no longer dedicate tears of resignation to the old bogeyman of shame. The children of this world, not prudish nuns, are our new, holy Madonnas."

63 Goetzinger, *Für die Selbstverwirklichung der Frau*, 43.

64 Cited from Goetzinger, *Für die Selbstverwirklichung der Frau*, 79.

65 Möhrmann, *Die andere Frau*, 142; Geiger, "Louise Aston," 91. Goetzinger wisely cautions against the temptation to read Aston's fiction as unembellished truth (*Für die Selbstverwirklichung der Frau*, 13).

66 Aston, *Aus dem Leben einer Frau*, vi. Hereafter cited in the text.

67 See Weigel's discussion of this preface in "Der schielende Blick," 98–99.

68 As Goodman suggests, Aston's preface may well be directed against Goethe's *Dichtung und Wahrheit* (*Dis/Closures*, 121–29).

69 See McAleer's fascinating study, *Dueling: The Cult of Honor in Fin-de-Siècle Germany.*

70 Aston, *Lydia*, 19. Hereafter cited in the text.

71 Aston wrote the novel in 1849 in Bremen (Wimmer, *Die Vormärzschriftstellerin Louise Aston*, 92). See also Boetcher Joeres, "1848 from a Distance"; Fingerhut, ed., *Louise Aston: Ein Lesebuch*, 75–81; 179–88; Goetzinger, *Für die Selbstverwirklichung der Frau*, 119–22.

72 Aston, *Revolution und Contrerevolution*, 2:6. Hereafter cited in the text.

73 On this enigmatic statement see Fingerhut, ed., *Louise Aston: Ein Lesebuch*, 79; and Wimmer, *Die Vormärzschriftstellerin Louise Aston*, 109–10.

74 Fingerhut, ed., *Louise Aston: Ein Lesebuch*, 183.

75 The stronger Bavarian beer was beginning to displace Berlin's traditional wheat beer in pubs frequented by political radicals, including Louise Aston (Goetzinger, *Für die Selbstverwirklichung der Frau*, 38).

6 EUGENIE MARLITT: THE ART OF LIBERAL COMPROMISE

1 See Belgum, "Domesticating the Reader"; Starcher, "Ernst Keil"; Zahn, "Die Geschichte der 'Gartenlaube'"; Zimmermann, ed., *Die "Gartenlaube."*

2 Reproduced in Klüter, ed., *Facsimile Querschnitt*, 29.

3 Starcher, "Ernst Keil," 212–13.

4 For Marlitt's biography see Peterson, "E. Marlitt"; Potthast, *Eugenie Marlitt*, 3–22; Schenk, *Die Rache der alten Mamsell.*

5 Each of Marlitt's works was first serialized in *Die Gartenlaube*, and then published in book form. I give the date of the first book publication parenthetically, following Peterson's bibliography ("E. Marlitt").

6 Starcher, "Ernst Keil," 213.

7 See Barth, "Zeitschriften"; Bramsted, *Aristocracy and the Middle-Classes*, 200–16; Martino, "Publikumsschichten," in *Deutsche Literatur*, vol. 7.

8 Serialized publication of German novels began in the 1840s (Barth, "Zeitschriften," 83–84).

9 I am particularly indebted to Belgum's study of women and *Die Gartenlaube* ("Domesticating the Reader") for calling attention to Marlitt's role in developing a sense of German national identity through her domestic fictions.

10 The first German women's conference was held in 1865, the same year in which Marlitt published her first story and in which the *Allgemeiner Deutscher Frauenverein* was founded (see Evans, *The Feminist Movement*; Frederiksen, "Einleitung").

11 Potthast's 1926 dissertation, *Eugenie Marlitt*, remains a solid introduction

to Marlitt's life and works. While Potthast draws a sympathetic, if not entirely uncritical portrait of Marlitt, critics of the 1970s were quick to condemn her work as reactionary anti-modernism (Schulte-Sasse/ Werner, E. Marlitts *Im Hause des Kommerzienrates*), or as regressive, narcissistic daydreams (Kienzle, *Erfolgsroman*; "*Reichsgräfin Gisela*"). These scholarly investigations reflect the popular image of Marlitt as an author of "trivial" fiction. More recent studies have attempted a qualified affirmation of the more progressive aspects of Marlitt's admittedly popular fiction. See Arens, *E. Marlitt*; Coupe, "Eugenie Marlitt"; Schenk, *Die Rache der alten Mamsell*; and Wilkie, "Eugenie Marlitt."

12 Marlitt, *Goldelse*, 9. Hereafter cited in the text.
13 Marlitt, *Reichsgräfin Gisela*, 113. Hereafter cited in the text.
14 See Kienzle, "*Reichsgräfin Gisela*," 220.
15 See Potthast for a balanced assessment of Marlitt's moderate feminism (*Eugenie Marlitt*, 45–58).
16 Marlitt, *Das Heideprinzeßchen*, 223. Hereafter cited in the text.
17 Marlitt, *Das Geheimnis der alten Mamsell*, 114. Hereafter cited in the text.
18 Marlitt, *Die zweite Frau*, 219. Hereafter cited in the text.
19 Marlitt, *Im Hause des Kommerzienrates*, 369.
20 Peterson expresses the problem well: "Marlitt's female protagonists . . . without exception . . . renounce their achievements – indeed, their very existence as free human beings – at the precise moment that they have almost succeeded in making independent lives for themselves" ("E. Marlitt," 227). See also Belgum, "Domesticating the Reader," 103.
21 *The Feminist Movement in Germany*, 26.
22 Frederiksen, "Einleitung," 9–10.
23 Lewald, *Für und wider die Frauen*. See Helmer's "Einleitung" to this volume, and Frederiksen's "Einleitung" to the anthology *Die Frauenfrage in Deutschland 1865–1915*.
24 Schenk, *Die Rache der alten Mamsell*, 160.
25 Kienzle, *Der Erfolgsroman*, 74–75.
26 Potthast, *Eugenie Marlitt*, 20.
27 Reproduced in Bernhard, ed., *Herzensangelegenheiten*, 45.
28 Modleski, *Loving with a Vengeance*, 43.
29 Potthast, *Eugenie Marlitt*, 20–21.
30 The various paperback Marlitt editions and Marlitt movies of the 1970s and '80s typify what Jameson terms "nostalgia film (or what the French call *la mode rétro*)" (*Postmodernism*, 19).

Works cited

Abbott, Scott. *Fictions of Freemasonry: Freemasonry and the German Novel.* Detroit: Wayne State University Press, 1991.

Abrams, M. H. *Natural Supernaturalism: Tradition and Revolution in Romantic Literature.* New York: Norton, 1971.

Anderson, Benedict. *Imagined Communities: Reflections on the Origin and Spread of Nationalism.* 2nd rev. edn. London: Verso, 1991.

Arens, Hans. *E. Marlitt: Eine kritische Würdigung.* Trier: Wissenschaftlicher Verlag, 1994.

Ariès, Philippe. *Centuries of Childhood: A Social History of Family Life.* 1960. Trans. Robert Baldick. New York: Vintage, 1962.

Armstrong, Nancy. *Desire and Domestic Fiction: A Political History of the Novel.* New York: Oxford University Press, 1987.

Arons, Wendy K. "Sophie Goes to the Theater: Performance, Theatricality, and the Production of Gender and Identity in Eighteenth-Century German Women's Writing." Diss. University of California, San Diego. 1997.

Assing, L. *Sophie von LaRoche, die Freundin Wielands.* Berlin: Janke, 1859.

Aston, Louise. *Aus dem Leben einer Frau.* 1847. Ed. Karlheinz Fingerhut. Stuttgart: Akademischer Verlag, 1982.

Lydia. Magdeburg: Emil Baensch, 1848.

Revolution und Contrerevolution: Roman. Mannheim: Grohe, 1849.

Bailet, Dietlinde S. *Die Frau als Verführte und als Verführerin in der deutschen und französischen Literatur des 18. Jahrhunderts.* Berne: Lang, 1981.

Barth, Dieter. "Zeitschriften, Buchmarkt und Verlagswesen." *Deutsche Literatur: Eine Sozialgeschichte.* Ed. Horst Albert Glaser. Vol. 7. *Vom Nachmärz zur Gründerzeit: Realismus.* Reinbek: Rowohlt, 1982. 70–88.

Becker-Cantarino, Barbara. *Der lange Weg zur Mündigkeit: Frau und Literatur (1500–1800).* Stuttgart: Metzler, 1987.

"Nachwort." *Geschichte des Fräuleins von Sternheim.* By Sophie von La Roche. Stuttgart: Reclam, 1983. 381–415.

"Poetische Freiheit, Revolution und Patriarchat: Über Therese Hubers Roman 'Die Familie Seldorf.'" *"Der Menschheit Hälfte blieb noch ohne Recht": Frauen und die Französische Revolution.* Ed. Helga Brandes. Wiesbaden: Deutscher Universitätsverlag, 1991. 64–73.

"Priesterin und Lichtbringerin: Zur Ideologie des weiblichen Charakters in der Frühromantik." Ed. Wolfgang Paulsen. *Die Frau als Heldin und Autorin: Neue kritische Ansätze zur deutschen Literatur*. Berne: Francke, 1979. 111–24.

"Revolution im Patriarchat: Therese Forster-Huber (1764–1829)." *Out of Line/Ausgefallen: The Paradox of Marginality in the Writings of Nineteenth-Century German Women*. Ed. Ruth-Ellen Boetcher Joeres and Marianne Burkhard. *Amsterdamer Beiträge zur neueren Germanistik* 28 (1989): 235–53.

Belgum, Kirsten. "Domesticating the Reader: Women and *Die Gartenlaube*." *Women in German Yearbook* 9. Ed. Jeanette Clausen and Sara Friedrichsmeyer. Lincoln: University of Nebraska Press, 1994. 91–111.

Bernhard, Marianne, ed. *Herzensangelegenheiten: Liebe aus der Gartenlaube*. Dortmund: Harenberg, 1978.

Bhabha, Homi K. *The Location of Culture*. London: Routledge, 1994.

Blackwell, Jeannine. "Bildungsroman mit Dame: The Heroine in the German *Bildungsroman*." Diss. Indiana University, 1982.

"Sophie von La Roche (1730–1807)." *German Writers in the Age of Goethe: Sturm und Drang to Classicism*. Ed. James Hardin and Christoph E. Schweitzer. *Dictionary of Literary Biography*. Vol. 94. Detroit: Gale Research, 1990. 154–61.

"Therese Huber (1764–1829)." *German Writers in the Age of Goethe: 1789–1832*. Ed. James Hardin and Christoph E. Schweitzer. *Dictionary of Literary Biography*. Vol. 90. Detroit: Gale Research, 1989. 187–92.

Blackwell, Jeannine and Susanne Zantop, eds. *Bitter Healing: German Women Writers from 1700–1830. An Anthology*. Lincoln: University of Nebraska Press, 1990.

Blasius, Dirk. "Epoche-sozialgeschichtlicher Abriß." *Deutsche Literatur: Eine Sozialgeschichte*. Ed. Horst Albert Glaser. Vol. 6. *Vormärz: Biedermeier, Junges Deutschland, Demokraten 1815–1848*. Ed. Bernd Witte. Reinbek: Rowohlt, 1980. 14–31.

Boerner, Peter. "Nachwort." *Agnes von Lilien*. By Caroline von Wolzogen. Hildesheim: Olms, 1988. 391–410.

Boetcher Joeres, Ruth-Ellen. "1848 from a Distance: German Women Writers on the Revolution." *MLN* 97 (1982): 590–614.

Bosse, Heinrich. *Autorschaft ist Werkherrschaft: Über die Entstehung des Urheberrechts aus dem Geist der Goethezeit*. Paderborn: Schöningh, 1981.

Bovenschen, Silvia. *Die imaginierte Weiblichkeit: Exemplarische Untersuchungen zu kulturgeschichtlichen und literarischen Präsentationsformen des Weiblichen*. Edition Suhrkamp 921. Frankfurt aM: Suhrkamp, 1979.

Bramsted, Ernest K. *Aristocracy and the Middle-Classes in Germany: Social Types in German Literature 1830–1900*. 1937. University of Chicago Press, 1964.

Brandes, Ute. "Escape to America: Social Reality and Utopian Schemes in German Women's Novels Around 1800." *In the Shadow of Olympus: German Women Writers Around 1800*. Ed. Katherine R. Goodman and

Edith Waldstein. Albany: State University of New York Press, 1992. 157–71.

Bremer, Bettina, and Angelika Schneider. "Wünsche und Verhältnisse: Ein Nachwort." Sophie Mereau, *Amanda und Eduard*. Freiburg: Kore, 1993. 317–78.

Brinker-Gabler, Gisela, ed. *Deutsche Literatur von Frauen*. 2 vols. Munich: Beck, 1988.

"Fanny Lewald: 1811–1889." *Frauen: Porträts aus zwei Jahrhunderten*. Ed. Hans Jürgen Schultz. Stuttgart: Kreuz, 1981. 72–86.

Britt, Christa Baguss. "Introduction." *The History of Lady Sophia Sternheim*. By Sophie von LaRoche. Albany: State University of New York Press, 1991. 3–35.

Brooks, Peter. *The Novel of Worldliness: Crébillon Marivaux Laclos Stendhal*. Princeton University Press, 1969.

Bürger, Christa. " 'Die mittlere Sphäre': Sophie Mereau – Schriftstellerin im klassischen Weimar." *Deutsche Literatur von Frauen: Vom Mittelalter bis zum Ende des 18. Jahrhunderts*. Ed. Gisela Brinker-Gabler. Munich: Beck, 1988. 366–88.

"Einleitung." *Zur Dichotomisierung von hoher und niederer Literatur*. Ed. Christa Bürger, et al. Frankfurt aM: Suhrkamp, 1982. 9–39.

Leben Schreiben: Die Klassik, die Romantik und der Ort der Frauen. Stuttgart: Metzler, 1990.

Butler, Judith. *Gender Trouble: Feminism and the Subversion of Identity*. New York: Routledge, 1990.

Campe, Joachim Heinrich. *Väterlicher Rath für meine Tochter: Ein Gegenstück zum Theophron*. 1796. Paderborn: Hüttemann, 1988.

Castle, Terry. *Clarissa's Ciphers: Meaning & Disruption in Richardson's "Clarissa."* Ithaca: Cornell University Press, 1982.

Clausen, Jeanette, and Sara Friedrichsmeyer. "WIG 2000: Feminism and the Future of *Germanistik*." *Women in German Yearbook* 10 (1995): 267–72.

Cocalis, Susan L. " 'Around 1800': Reassessing the Role of German Women Writers in Literary Production of the Late Eighteenth and Early Nineteenth Centuries. Review Essay." *Women in German Yearbook* 8 (1993): 159–77.

Cohen, Paula Marantz. *The Daughter's Dilemma: Family Process and the Nineteenth-Century Domestic Novel*. Ann Arbor: University of Michigan Press, 1991.

Coupe, W. A. "Eugenie Marlitt: In Defence of a Writer of Kitsch." *German Life and Letters* 49 (1996): 42–58.

Crocker, Lester G. "*Julie* ou la nouvelle duplicité." *Annales de la Société Jean-Jacques Rousseau* 36 (1963–65): 105–52.

Dijkstra, Bram. *Idols of Perversity: Fantasies of Feminine Evil in Fin-de-Siècle Culture*. New York: Oxford University Press, 1986.

Dilthey, Wilhelm. *Das Erlebnis und die Dichtung: Lessing, Goethe, Novalis, Hölderlin. Vier Aufsätze*. 1906. Berlin: Teubner, 1916.

"Die dichterische und philosophische Bewegung in Deutschland 1770–1800. Antrittsvorlesung in Basel 1867." *Gesammelte Schriften.* Vol. 5.1. Stuttgart: Teubner, 1957. 12–27.

Leben Schleiermachers. 1870; Berlin: de Gruyter, 1922.

Di Maio, Irene Stocksieker. "Fanny Lewald (1811–1889)." *Nineteenth-Century German Writers, 1841–1900.* Ed. James Hardin and Siegfried Mews. *Dictionary of Literary Biography.* Vol. 129. Detroit: Gale Research, 1993. 202–13.

"Jewish Emancipation and Integration: Fanny Lewald's Narrative Strategies." *Autoren Damals und Heute: Literaturgeschichtliche Beispiele veränderter Wirkungshorizonte. Amsterdamer Beiträge zur neueren Germanistik* 31–33 (1990–91): 273–301.

Doody, Margaret Anne. *A Natural Passion: A Study of the Novels of Samuel Richardson.* Oxford: Clarendon Press, 1974.

Droste-Hülshoff, Annette von. *Ledwina.* Trans. David Ward. *Bitter Healing: German Women Writers from 1700–1830.* Ed. Jeannine Blackwell and Susanne Zantop. Lincoln: University of Nebraska Press, 1990. 480–526.

Sämtliche Werke. Ed. Bodo Plachta and Winfried Woesler. 2 vols. Frankfurt aM: Deutscher Klassiker Verlag, 1994.

"Zu *Ledwina*: Entwurf einer Fortsetzung." *Historisch-kritische Ausgabe.* Ed. Walter Huge. Vol. 5.1. Tübingen: Niemeyer, 1978. 171–77.

Dworetzki, Gertrud. *Johanna Schopenhauer: Ein Charakterbild aus Goethes Zeiten.* Düsseldorf: Droste, 1987.

Eagleton, Terry. *The Rape of Clarissa: Writing, Sexuality and Class Struggle in Samuel Richardson.* Oxford: Basil Blackwell, 1982.

Eke, Norbert Otto, and Dagmar Olasz-Eke. *Bibliographie: Der deutsche Roman 1815–1830. Standortnachweise, Rezensionen, Forschungsüberblick.* Munich: Fink, 1994.

Engelsing, Rolf. *Der Bürger als Leser: Lesergeschichte in Deutschland 1500–1800.* Stuttgart: Metzler, 1974.

Evans, Richard J. *The Feminist Movement in Germany 1894–1933.* SAGE Studies in 20th Century History 6. London: SAGE, 1976.

Faludi, Susan. *Backlash: The Undeclared War Against American Women.* New York: Doubleday, 1991.

Fetting, Friederike. *"Ich fand in mir eine Welt": Eine sozial- und literaturgeschichtliche Untersuchung zur deutschen Romanschriftstellerin um 1800.* Munich: Fink, 1992.

Fingerhut, Karlheinz, ed. *Louise Aston: Ein Lesebuch: Gedichte, Romane, Schriften in Auswahl* (1846–49). Stuttgart: Akademischer Verlag, 1983.

Fischer, Bernd. *Das Eigene und das Eigentliche: Klopstock, Herder, Fichte, Kleist: Episoden aus der Konstruktionsgeschichte nationaler Intentionalitäten.* Berlin: Erich Schmidt, 1995.

Fleischmann, Uta. *Zwischen Aufbruch und Anpassung: Untersuchungen zum Werk und Leben der Sophie Mereau.* Frankfurt aM: Lang, 1989.

Fouqué, Caroline de la Motte. *Das Heldenmädchen aus der Vendée: Ein Roman.* Leipzig: Fleischer, 1816.
Die beiden Freunde: Ein Roman. Berlin: Schlesinger, 1824.
Edmunds Wege und Irrwege: Ein Roman aus der nächsten Vergangenheit. 3 vols. Leipzig: Fleischer, 1815.
Fragmente aus dem Leben der heutigen Welt. Berlin: Schlesinger, 1820.
Laura: Eine Begebenheit aus der französischen Revolution. Erzählungen. Vol. 2. Jena: Schmid, 1821. 169–235.
Magie der Natur: Eine Revolutions-Geschichte. 1812. Ed. Gerhart Hoffmeister. Berne: Lang, 1989.
Frederiksen, Elke. "Einleitung: Zum Problem der Frauenfrage um die Jahrhundertwende." *Die Frauenfrage in Deutschland 1865–1915.* Stuttgart: Reclam, 1981. 5–43.
Frederiksen, Elke and Monika Shafi. "Annette von Droste-Hülshoff (1797–1848): Konfliktstrukturen im Frühwerk." *Out of Line/Ausgefallen: The Paradox of Marginality in the Writings of Nineteenth-Century German Women.* Ed. Ruth-Ellen Boetcher Joeres and Marianne Burkhard. *Amsterdamer Beiträge zur neueren Germanistik* 28 (1989): 115–36.
Frölich, Henriette [Jerta]. *Virginia oder Die Kolonie von Kentucky: Mehr Wahrheit als Dichtung.* 1820. Berlin: Aufbau, 1963.
Frye, Northrop. *Anatomy of Criticism: Four Essays.* Princeton: Princeton University Press, 1957.
Gallas, Helga and Magdalene Heuser. "Einleitung." *Untersuchungen zum Roman von Frauen um 1800.* Ed. Gallas and Heuser. Tübingen: Niemeyer, 1990. 1–9.
Gallas, Helga and Magdalene Heuser, eds. *Untersuchungen zum Roman von Frauen um 1800.* Tübingen: Niemeyer, 1990.
Gallas, Helga, and Anita Runge. *Romane und Erzählungen deutscher Schriftstellerinnen um 1800: Eine Bibliographie mit Standortnachweisen.* Stuttgart: Metzler, 1993.
Geiger, Gerlinde Maria. *Die befreite Psyche: Emanzipationsansätze im Frühwerk Ida Hahn-Hahns (1838–48).* Frankfurt aM: Lang, 1986.
Geiger, Ruth-Esther. "Louise Aston 1818–1871: Das Recht der freien Persönlichkeit ist in mir beleidigt!" *Frauen: Porträts aus zwei Jahrhunderten.* Ed. Hans Jürgen Schultz. Stuttgart: Kreuz, 1981. 88–100.
Gersdorff, Dagmar von. *"Dich zu lieben kann ich nicht verlernen": Das Leben der Sophie Brentano-Mereau.* Frankfurt aM: Insel, 1984.
Gilman, Sander. *Jewish Self-Hatred: Anti-Semitism and the Hidden Language of the Jews.* Baltimore: Johns Hopkins University Press, 1986.
Gnüg, Hiltrud, and Renate Möhrmann, eds. *Frauen Literatur Geschichte: Schreibende Frauen vom Mittelalter bis zur Gegenwart.* Stuttgart: Metzler, 1985.
Goethe, Johann Wolfgang. *Faust. Goethes Werke.* Ed. Erich Trunz. Vol. 3. Hamburg: Wegner, 1949.
Faust: Part I. Trans. Peter Salm. Toronto: Bantam, 1962.
Goethe, Johann Wolfgang and Friedrich Schiller. *Der Briefwechsel zwischen*

Schiller und Goethe. Ed. Emil Staiger. 2 vols. Frankfurt aM: Suhrkamp, 1977.

Goetzinger, Germaine. " 'Allein das Bewußtsein dieses Befreienkönnens ist schon erhebend.' " Emanzipation und Politik in Publizistik und Roman des Vormärz." *Deutsche Literatur von Frauen.* Ed. Gisela Brinker-Gabler. Vol. 2. Munich: Beck, 1988. 86–104.

Für die Selbstverwirklichung der Frau: Louise Aston in Selbstzeugnissen und Dokumenten. Frankfurt aM: Fischer, 1983.

Goodman, Katherine. *Dis/Closures: Women's Autobiography in Germany between 1790 and 1914.* New York: Lang, 1986.

"Johanna Schopenhauer (1766–1838), or Pride and Resignation." *Out of Line/Ausgefallen: The Paradox of Marginality in the Writings of Nineteenth-Century German Women.* Ed. Ruth-Ellen Boetcher Joeres and Marianne Burkhard. *Amsterdamer Beiträge zur neueren Germanistik* 28 (1989): 187–209.

Goodman, Katherine R. and Edith Waldstein. "Introduction." *In the Shadow of Olympus: German Women Writers around 1800.* Ed. Goodman and Waldstein. Albany: State University of New York Press, 1992. 1–27.

Goodman, Katherine R., and Edith Waldstein, eds. *In the Shadow of Olympus: German Women Writers around 1800.* Albany: State University of New York Press, 1992.

Gottschall, Rudolph. *Die deutsche Nationalliteratur der ersten Hälfte des neunzehnten Jahrhunderts.* 2 vols. Breslau: Trewendt & Granier, 1855.

Graf, Ruedi. *Das Theater im Literaturstaat: Literarisches Theater auf dem Weg zur Bildungsmacht.* Tübingen: Niemeyer, 1992.

Grenz, Dagmar. *Mädchenliteratur: Von den moralisch-belehrenden Schriften im 18. Jahrhundert bis zur Herausbildung der Backfischliteratur im 19. Jahrhundert.* Stuttgart: Metzler, 1981.

Gutzkow, Karl. *Wally, die Zweiflerin.* 1835. Ed. Günter Heintz. Stuttgart: Reclam, 1983.

Habermas, Jürgen. *The Structural Transformation of the Public Sphere: An Inquiry into a Category of Bourgeois Society.* 1962. Trans. Thomas Burger. Cambridge: MIT, 1991.

Hahn-Hahn, Ida Gräfin. *Gräfin Faustine.* 1841. Ed. Norbert Altenhofer. Bouviers Bibliothek 2. Bonn: Bouvier, 1986.

Sibylle: Eine Selbstbiographie. Berlin: Duncker, 1846.

Zwei Frauen. Berlin: Duncker, 1845.

Hamerow, Theodore S. *Restoration, Revolution, Reaction: Economics and Politics in Germany, 1815–1871.* Princeton University Press, 1958.

Hammerstein, Katharina von. *Sophie Mereau-Brentano: Freiheit – Liebe – Weiblichkeit. Trikolore sozialer und individueller Selbstbestimmung um 1800.* Heidelberg: Winter, 1994.

Haney-Peritz, Janice. "Engendering the Exemplary Daughter: The Deployment of Sexuality in Richardson's *Clarissa.*" *Daughters and Fathers.*

Ed. Lynda E. Boose and Betty S. Flowers. Baltimore: Johns Hopkins University Press, 1989. 181–207.

Hausen, Karin. "Family and Role-Division: The Polarisation of Sexual Stereotypes in the Nineteenth Century: An Aspect of the Dissociation of Work and Family Life." *The German Family: Essays on the Social History of the Family in Nineteenth- and Twentieth-Century Germany.* Ed. Richard J. Evans and W. R. Lee. London: Croom Helm, 1981. 51–83.

Haym, Rudolf. *Die romantische Schule: Ein Beitrag zur Geschichte des deutschen Geistes.* 1870. Hildesheim: Olms, 1961.

Helmer, Ulrike. "Einleitung." *Politische Schriften Für und wider die Frauen.* By Fanny Lewald. Ed. Ulrike Helmer. Frankfurt aM: Helmer, 1989. 5–13.

"Nachwort." *Jenny.* By Fanny Lewald. Frankfurt aM: Helmer, 1988. 254–72.

"Nachwort." *Meine Lebensgeschichte.* By Fanny Lewald. Vol. 1. Frankfurt aM: Helmer, 1988. 271–88.

Herminghouse, Patricia A. "Seeing Double: Ida Hahn-Hahn (1805–1880) and her Challenge to Feminist Criticism." *Out of Line/Ausgefallen: The Paradox of Marginality in the Writings of Nineteenth-Century German Women.* Ed. Ruth-Ellen Boetcher Joeres and Marianne Burkhard. *Amsterdamer Beiträge zur neueren Germanistik* 28 (1989): 255–78.

"Women and the Literary Enterprise in Nineteenth-Century Germany." *German Women in the Eighteenth and Nineteenth Centuries: A Social and Literary History.* Ed. Ruth-Ellen B. Joeres and Mary Jo Maynes. Bloomington: Indiana University Press, 1986. 78–93.

Heselhaus, Clemens. *Annette von Droste-Hülshoff: Werk und Leben.* Düsseldorf: Bagel, 1971.

Heuser, Magdalene. "Nachwort." *Die Familie Seldorf.* By Therese Huber. *Romane und Erzählungen.* Ed. Magdalene Heuser. Vol. 1. Hildesheim: Olms, 1989. 347–89.

"'Spuren trauriger Selbstvergessenheit': Möglichkeiten eines weiblichen Bildungsromans um 1800: Friederike Helene Unger." *Frauensprache-Frauenliteratur/Für und Wider einer Psychoanalyse literarischer Texte.* Vol. 6 of *Kontroversen, alte und neue.* Akten des VI. Internationalen Germanisten-Kongresses. Göttingen, 1985. 30–42.

Hill, Christopher. "Clarissa Harlowe and her Times." *Essays in Criticism* 5 (1955): 315–40.

Hobsbawm, E. J. "Introduction: Inventing Traditions." *The Invention of Tradition.* Ed. E. J. Hobsbawm and Terence Ranger. Cambridge University Press, 1983. 1–14.

Nations and Nationalism since 1780: Programme, Myth, Reality. 2nd rev. edn. Cambridge University Press, 1992.

Hofacker, Erich P. Jr. "Caroline de la Motte Fouqué (1774–1843)." *German Writers in the Age of Goethe: 1789–1832.* Ed. James Hardin and Christoph

E. Schweitzer. *Dictionary of Literary Biography.* Vol. 90. Detroit: Gale Research, 1989. 78–83.

Hoffmeister, Gerhart. "Einführung." *Magie der Natur: Eine Revolutionsgeschichte.* By Caroline de la Motte Fouqué. Ed. Gerhart Hoffmeister. Berne: Lang, 1989. 5–46.

Hohendahl, Peter Uwe. *Building a National Literature: The Case of Germany 1830–1870.* Trans. Renate Baron Franciscono. Ithaca: Cornell University Press, 1989.

"Empfindsamkeit und gesellschaftliches Bewusstsein: Zur Soziologie des empfindsamen Romans am Beispiel von *La Vie de Marianne, Clarissa, Fräulein von Sternheim* und *Werther. Jahrbuch der deutschen Schillergesellschaft* 6 (1972): 176–207.

"Literarischer Kommerz: Zum Verhältnis von Trivialliteratur und Kulturindustrie." *Die Fürstliche Bibliothek Corvey: Ihrer Bedeutung für eine neue Sicht der Literatur des frühen 19. Jahrhunderts.* Ed. Rainer Schöwerling and Harmut Steinecke. Munich: Fink, 1992. 35–49.

The Institution of Criticism. Ithaca: Cornell University Press, 1982.

Huber, Therese. *Die Familie Seldorf.* 1795–96. *Romane und Erzählungen.* Ed. Magdalene Heuser. Frühe Frauenliteratur in Deutschland 10. Vol. 1. Hildesheim: Olms, 1989.

Hughes, Michael. *Nationalism and Society: Germany 1800–1945.* London: Arnold, 1988.

Hunt, Lynn. *The Family Romance of the French Revolution.* Berkeley: University of California Press, 1992.

Huyssen, Andreas. "Mass Culture as Woman: Modernism's Other." *After the Great Divide: Modernism, Mass Culture, Postmodernism.* Bloomington: Indiana University Press, 1986. 44–62.

"Nation, Race, and Immigration: German Identities after Unification." *Twilight Memories: Marking Time in a Culture of Amnesia.* New York: Routledge, 1995. 67–84.

Jameson, Fredric. *Postmodernism, or, The Cultural Logic of Late Capitalism.* Durham: Duke University Press, 1991.

Janz, Rolf-Peter. "Zum sozialen Gehalt der *Lehrjahre.*" *Literaturwissenschaft und Geschichtsphilosophie: Festschrift für Wilhelm Emrich.* Berlin: de Gruyter, 1975. 320–40.

Johnston, Otto W. *The Myth of a Nation: Literature and Politics in Prussia under Napoleon.* Studies in German Literature, Linguistics, and Culture 32. Columbia, SC: Camden House, 1989.

Kahn-Wallerstein, Carmen. *Die Frau im Schatten: Schillers Schwägerin Karoline von Wolzogen.* Berne: Francke, 1970.

Kastinger Riley, Helene M. "Saat und Ernte: Sophie Mereaus Forderung geschlechtlicher Gleichberechtigung." *Die weibliche Muse: Sechs Essays über künstlerisch schaffende Frauen der Goethezeit.* Columbia, SC: Camden House, 1986. 54–88.

Kienzle, Michael. *Der Erfolgsroman: Zur Kritik seiner poetischen Ökonomie bei Gustav Freytag und Eugenie Marlitt.* Stuttgart: Metzler, 1975.

"Eugenie Marlitt: *Reichsgräfin Giesela* (1869): Zum Verhältnis zwischen Politik und Tagtraum." *Romane und Erzählungen des bürgerlichen Realismus: Neue Interpretationen.* Ed. Horst Denkler. Stuttgart: Reclam, 1980. 217–30.

Kittler, Friedrich A. *Discourse Networks 1800/1900.* 1985. Trans. Chris Cullens and Michael Metteer. Stanford: Stanford University Press, 1990.

Kluckhohn, Paul. *Die Auffassung der Liebe in der Literatur des 18. Jahrhunderts und in der deutschen Romantik.* 1921. Halle: Niemeyer, 1931.

Klüger, Ruth. "Zum Außenseitertum der deutschen Dichterinnen." *Untersuchungen zum Roman von Frauen um 1800.* Ed. Helga Gallas and Magdalene Heuser. Tübingen: Niemeyer, 1990. 13–19.

Klüter, Heinz, ed. *Facsimile Querschnitt durch die Gartenlaube.* Stuttgart: Scherz, 1963.

Köpke, Wulf. "Die emanzipierte Frau in der Goethezeit." *Die Frau als Heldin und Autorin: Neue kritische Ansätze zur deutschen Literatur.* Ed. Wolfgang Pausen. Berne: Francke, 1979. 96–110.

"Immer noch im Schatten der Männer? Therese Huber als Schriftstellerin." *Der Weltumsegler und seine Freunde: Georg Forster als gesellschaftlicher Schriftsteller der Goethezeit.* Ed. Detlef Rasmussen. Tübingen: Narr, 1988. 116–32.

Körner, Theodor. *Leier und Schwert.* 1814. *Körners Werke.* Ed. Hans Zimmer. Vol. 1. Leipzig: Bibliographisches Institut, 1893. 65–121.

Kontje, Todd. *The German Bildungsroman: History of a National Genre.* Columbia, SC: Camden House, 1993.

"Male Fantasies, Female Readers: Fictions of the Nation in the Early Restoration." *The German Quarterly* 68 (1995): 131–46.

"Socialization and Alienation in the Female Bildungsroman." *Impure Reason: Dialectic of Enlightenment in Germany.* Ed. W. Daniel Wilson and Robert Holub. Detroit: Wayne State University Press, 1993. 221–41.

Koonz, Claudia. *Mothers in the Fatherland: Women, the Family, and Nazi Politics.* New York: St. Martin's Press, 1987.

Koranyi, Stephan. "Nachwort." *Gabriele.* By Johanna Schopenhauer. Munich: Deutscher Taschenbuch Verlag, 1985. 403–16.

Kraft, Helga W. "Ida Gräfin von Hahn-Hahn." *Nineteenth-Century German Writers to 1840.* Ed. James Hardin and Siegfried Mews. *Dictionary of Literary Biography.* Vol. 133. Detroit: Gale Research, 1993. 150–55.

Kunze, Michael. *Highroad to the Stake: A Tale of Witchcraft.* 1982. Trans. William E. Yuill. Chicago University Press, 1987.

Kuzniar, Alice A., ed. *Outing Goethe and His Age.* Stanford: Stanford University Press, 1996.

Lämmert, Eberhard, ed. *Romantheorie: Dokumentation ihrer Geschichte in Deutschland 1620–1880.* Berlin: Kiepenheuer & Witsch, 1971.

Landes, Joan B. *Women and the Public Sphere in the Age of the French Revolution.* Ithaca: Cornell University Press, 1988.

Laqueur, Thomas. *Making Sex: Body and Gender from the Greeks to Freud.* Cambridge: Harvard University Press, 1990.

LaRoche, Sophie von. *Geschichte des Fräuleins von Sternheim.* 1771. Ed. Barbara Becker-Cantarino. Stuttgart: Reclam, 1983.

The History of Lady Sophia Sternheim. Ed. and trans. Christa Baguss Britt. Albany: State University of New York Press, 1991.

Lewald, Fanny. *Auf rother Erde: Eine Novelle.* Leipzig: Weber, 1850.

Clementine. Berlin: Janke, 1842.

Der dritte Stand: Novellistisches Zeitbild. 1846. Berlin: Gerschel, 1862.

Diogena: Roman von Iduna Gräfin H. . . H. . . Leipzig: Brockhaus, 1847.

Eine Lebensfrage: Roman. 1845. 2 vols. Berlin: Janke, 1872.

Erinnerungen aus dem Jahre 1848. 2 vols. Braunschweig: Vieweg, 1850.

Für und wider die Frauen. 1870. *Politische Schriften für und wider die Frauen.* Ed. Ulrike Helmer. Frankfurt aM: Helmer, 1989. 97–204.

Jenny. 1843. Ed. Ulrike Helmer. Frankfurt aM: Helmer, 1988.

Meine Lebensgeschichte. 1861–62. Ed. Ulrike Helmer. 3 vols. Frankfurt aM: Helmer, 1988– 89.

Prinz Louis Ferdinand: Ein Zeitbild. 1849. 3 vols. Berlin: Hofmann, 1859.

Prinz Louis Ferdinand. Trans. Linda Rogols-Siegel. Studies in German Thought and History 6. Lewiston/Queenston: Mellen, 1988.

The Education of Fanny Lewald: An Autobiography. Trans. and ed. Hanna Ballin Lewis. Albany: State University of New York Press, 1992.

Lewis, Hanna B. "Fanny Lewald and the Revolutions of 1848." *Horizonte: Festschrift für Herbert Lehnert zum 65. Geburtstag.* Ed. Hannelore Mundt, Egon Schwarz, William J. Lillyman. Tübingen: Niemeyer, 1990. 80–91.

"The Woman's Novel Parodied: Fanny Lewald's *Diogena.*" *Continental, Latin-American and Francophone Women Writers: Selected Papers from the Wichita State University Conference on Foreign Literature, 1984–1985.* Ed. Eunice Myers and Ginette Adamson. Lanham: University Press of America, 1987. 107–117.

Lorenz, Dagmar. "Vom Kloster zur Küche: Die Frau vor und nach der Reformation Dr. Martin Luthers." *Die Frau von der Reformation zur Romantik: Die Situation der Frau vor dem Hintergrund der Literatur- und Sozialgeschichte.* Ed. Barbara Becker-Cantarino. Bonn: Bouvier, 1980. 7–35.

Lovell, Terry. *Consuming Fiction.* London: Verso, 1987.

Mahoney, Dennis. *Der Roman der Goethezeit (1774–1829).* Stuttgart: Metzler, 1988.

Marlitt, E. [Eugenie John]. *Das Geheimnis der alten Mamsell.* 1868. *E. Marlitts gesammelte Romane und Novellen.* Vol. 1. 2nd edn. Leipzig: Ernst Keils Nachfolger, 1891.

Das Heideprinzeßchen. 1872. Vol. 2.

Die zweite Frau. 1874. Vol. 7.

Goldelse: Roman. 1867. Vol. 8.

Im Hause des Kommerzienrates. 1877. Vol. 6.

Reichsgräfin Gisela. 1870. Vol. 3.

Martens, Wolfgang. *Die Botschaft der Tugend*. Stuttgart: Metzler, 1971.

Martini, Fritz. *Deutsche Literaturgeschichte von den Anfängen bis zur Gegenwart*. 1949. 16th edn. Stuttgart: Kröner, 1972.

Martino, Alberto. "Publikumsschichten und Leihbibliotheken." *Deutsche Literatur: Eine Sozialgeschichte*. Ed. Horst Albert Glaser. Vol. 6: *Vormärz: Biedermeier, Junges Deutschland, Demokraten 1815–1848*. Ed. Bernd Witte. Reinbek: Rowohlt, 1980. 32–43.

"Publikumsschichten und Leihbibliotheken." *Deutsche Literatur: Eine Sozialgeschichte*. Ed. Horst Albert Glaser. Vol. 7: *Vom Nachmärz zur Gründerzeit: Realismus*. Reinbek: Rowohlt, 1982. 59–69.

Maurer, Doris. *Annette von Droste-Hülshoff: Ein Leben zwischen Auflehnung und Gehorsam*. Bonn: Keil, 1982.

Maurer, Michael. "Das Gute und das Schöne: Sophie von La Roche (1730–1807) wiederentdecken?" *Euphorion* 79 (1985): 111–38.

Mauzi, Robert. "La Conversion de Julie dans *La Nouvelle Héloïse*." *Annales de la Société Jean-Jacques Rousseau* 35 (1959–62): 29–47.

May, Kurt. " 'Wilhelm Meisters Lehrjahre': Ein Bildungsroman?" *Deutsche Vierteljahresschrift* 31 (1957): 1–37.

McAleer, Kevin. *Dueling: The Cult of Honor in Fin-de-Siècle Germany*. Princeton University Press, 1994.

Meise, Helga. "Der Frauenroman: Erprobungen der 'Weiblichkeit.' " *Deutsche Literatur von Frauen*. Ed. Gisela Brinker-Gabler. Vol. 1. Munich: Beck, 1988. 434–52.

Die Unschuld und die Schrift: Deutsche Frauenromane im 18. Jahrhundert. Marburg: Guttandin and Hoppe, 1983.

Mereau, Sophie. *Amanda und Eduard: Ein Roman in Briefen*. 1803. Ed. Bettina Bremer and Angelika Schneider. Freiburg: Kore, 1993.

"Briefe von Amanda und Eduard." *Die Horen: Eine Monatsschrift* 6 (1797): 49–68; 7 (1797): 38–55.

Briefwechsel zwischen Clemens Brentano und Sophie Mereau. Ed. Heinz Amelung. 2 vols. Leipzig: Insel, 1908.

Das Blüthenalter der Empfindung. 1794. Ed. Herman Moens. Stuttgart: Akademischer Verlag, 1982.

Der Mann mit vier Weibern. Bunte Reihe kleiner Schriften. Frankfurt aM: Wilmans, 1805. 111–281.

"Die Flucht nach der Hauptstadt." *Taschenbuch für das Jahr 1806*. Frankfurt aM: Wilmans, 1806. 139–84.

"Flight to the City." Trans. Jacqueline Vansant. *Bitter Healing: German Women Writers 1700–1830*. Ed. Jeannine Blackwell and Susanne Zantop. Lincoln: Nebraska University Press, 1990. 369–99.

Kalathiskos. 1801–02. Ed. Peter Schmidt. Heidelberg: Lambert Schneider, 1968.

Marie. Flora: Teutschlands Töchtern geweiht. Tübingen: Cotta, 1798. 41–103.

"Ninon de Lenclos." 1801–02. *Kalathiskos.* 1801–02. Ed. Peter Schmidt. Heidelberg: Lambert Schneider, 1968. 52–126.

Milch, Werner. *Sophie La Roche: Die Großmutter der Brentanos.* Frankfurt aM: Societätsverlag, 1935.

Modleski, Tania. *Loving with a Vengeance: Mass-Produced Fantasies for Women.* 1982. New York: Routledge, 1990.

Möhrmann, Renate. *Die andere Frau: Emanzipationsansätze deutscher Schriftstellerinnen im Vorfeld der Achtundvierziger-Revolution.* Stuttgart: Metzler: 1977.

Möhrmann, Renate, ed. *Frauenemanzipation im deutschen Vormärz: Texte und Dokumente.* Stuttgart: Reclam, 1978.

Moens, Herman. "Nachwort." *Das Blüthenalter der Empfindung.* By Sophie Mereau. Stuttgart: Heinz, 1982. 1–30.

Mortier, Roland. "Une romancière allemande spectatrice de la Révolution française de 1848." *Littérature et Culture Allemandes.* Brussels: Université de Bruxelles, 1985. 147–63.

Mosse, George L. *Nationalism and Sexuality: Respectability and Abnormal Sexuality in Modern Europe.* New York: Fertig, 1985.

The Crisis of German Ideology: Intellectual Origins of the Third Reich. 1964. New York: Schocken, 1981.

The Nationalization of the Masses: Political Symbolism and Mass Movements in Germany from the Napoleonic Wars through the Third Reich. Ithaca: Cornell University Press, 1975.

"What the Germans really read." *Masses and Man: Nationalist and Fascist Perceptions of Reality.* New York: Fertig, 1980. 52–68.

Mücke, Dorothea E. von. *Virtue and the Veil of Illusion: Generic Innovation and the Pedagogical Project in Eighteenth-Century Literature.* Stanford University Press, 1991.

Niethammer, Ortrun, and Claudia Belemann. *Ein Gitter aus Musik und Sprache: Feministische Analysen zu Annette von Droste-Hülshoff.* Paderborn: Schöningh, 1993.

Novalis [Friedrich von Hardenberg]. "Hymnen an die Nacht." *Schriften.* Ed. Paul Kluckhohn and Richard Samuel. Vol. 1. Stuttgart: Kohlhammer, 1960. 130–57.

Obenaus, Sibylle. "Buchmarkt, Verlagswesen und Zeitschriften." *Deutsche Literatur: Eine Sozialgeschichte.* Ed. Horst Albert Glaser. Vol. 6. *Vormärz: Biedermeier, Junges Deutschland, Demokraten 1815–1848.* Ed. Bernd Witte. Reinbek: Rowohlt, 1980. 44–62.

Oberembt, Gert. *Ida Gräfin Hahn-Hahn: Weltschmerz und Ultramontanismus. Studien zum Unterhaltungsroman im 19. Jahrhundert.* Bonn: Bouvier, 1980.

Parker, Andrew, Mary Russo, Doris Sommer, and Patricia Yaeger. "Introduction." *Nationalism and Sexualities.* Ed. Andrew Parker, et al. New York: Routledge, 1992. 1–18.

Peitsch, Helmut. "Die Revolution im Familienroman: Aktuelles politisches Thema und konventionelle Romanstruktur in Therese Hubers *Die*

Familie Seldorf." *Jahrbuch der deutschen Schiller Gesellschaft* 28 (1984): 248–69.

Perthes, Friedrich. *Der deutsche Buchhandel als Bedingung des Daseyns einer deutschen Literatur.* Hamburg: Hanseatische Verlagsanstalt, 1816.

Peterson, Brent O. "E. Marlitt (Eugenie John) (1825–87)." *Nineteenth-Century German Writers, 1841–1900.* Ed. James Hardin and Siegfried Mews. *Dictionary of Literary Biography.* Vol. 129. Detroit: Gale Research, 1993. 223–28.

"German Nationalism after Napoleon: Caste and Regional Identities in Historical Fiction, 1815–1830." *The German Quarterly* 68 (1995): 287–303.

Petriconi, H. *Die verführte Unschuld: Bemerkungen über ein literarisches Thema.* Hamburg: Cram, de Gruyter & Co., 1953.

Petschauer, Peter. "Sophie von LaRoche: Novelist between Reason and Emotion." *Germanic Review* 57 (1982): 70–77.

Peucker, Brigitte. "Droste-Hülshoff's Ophelia and the Recovery of Voice." *Journal of English and Germanic Philology* 82 (1983): 374–91.

Pickett, T. H. "Johanna Schopenhauer (1766–1838)." *German Writers in the Age of Goethe: 1789–1832.* Ed. James Hardin and Christoph E. Schweitzer. *Dictionary of Literary Biography.* Vol. 90. Detroit: Gale Research, 1989. 299–302.

Potthast, Bertha. *Eugenie Marlitt: Ein Beitrag zur Geschichte des deutschen Frauenromans.* Bielefeld: Rennebohm, 1926.

Richardson, Samuel. *Clarissa or the History of a Young Lady.* 1749. Ed. Angus Ross. London: Penguin, 1985.

Pamela or Virtue Rewarded. 1740–41. Ed. Peter Sabor. London: Penguin, 1980.

Ridderhoff, Kuno. *Sophie von La Roche, die Schülerin Richardsons und Rousseaus.* Einbeck: Schroedter, 1895.

Roebling, Irmgard. "Heraldik des Unheimlichen: Annette von Droste-Hülshoff (1797–1848). Auch ein Portrait." *Deutsche Literatur von Frauen.* Ed. Gisela Brinker-Gabler. Vol. 2. Munich: Beck, 1988. 41–68.

"Weibliches Schreiben im 19. Jahrhundert: Untersuchungen zur Natur-metaphorik der Droste." *Der Deutschunterricht* 18 (1986): 36–56.

Rogols-Siegel, Linda. "Introduction." *Prinz Louis Ferdinand.* By Fanny Lewald. Lewiston/Queenston: Mellen, 1988. 1–92.

Ross, Angus. "Introduction." *Clarissa or the History of a Young Lady.* By Samuel Richardson. London: Penguin, 1985. 15–29.

Rousseau, Jean-Jacques. *Emile.* 1762. Trans. Barbara Foxley. London: Everyman, 1911.

Julie, ou La Nouvelle Héloïse. 1761. Ed. Bernard Gagnebin and Marcel Raymond. *Œuvres complètes.* Vol. 2. Paris: Pléiade, 1961.

La Nouvelle Héloïse. Trans. and abridged by Judith H. McDowell. University Park: Penn State Press, 1968.

Sammons, Jeffrey L. "The Mystery of the Missing *Bildungsroman,* or: What happened to Wilhelm Meister's Legacy?" *Genre* 14 (1981): 229–46.

Schenk, Herrad. *Die Rache der alten Mamsell: Eugenie Marlitts Lebensroman.* Düsseldorf: Claassen, 1986.

Schieth, Lydia. *Die Entwicklung des deutschen Frauenromans im ausgehenden 18. Jahrhundert: Ein Beitrag zur Gattungsgeschichte.* Frankfurt aM: Lang, 1987.

" 'Elisa oder das Weib wie es seyn sollte': Zur Analyse eines Frauen-Romanbestsellers." *Untersuchungen zum Roman von Frauen um 1800.* Ed. Helga Gallas and Magdalene Heuser. Tübingen: Niemeyer, 1990. 114–31.

Schiller, Friedrich. *Sämtliche Werke.* Ed. Gerhard Fricke and Herbert G. Göpfert. 5 vols. Munich: Hanser, 1980.

Schindel, Carl Wilhelm Otto August von. *Die deutschen Schriftstellerinnen des neunzehnten Jahrhunderts.* 3 vols. Leipzig: Brockhaus, 1823–25.

Schlegel-Schelling, Caroline. *"Lieber Freund, ich komme weit her schon an diesem frühen Morgen": Briefe.* Ed. Sigrid Damm. Darmstadt: Luchterhand, 1980.

Schmid-Juergens, Erna Ines. *Ida Gräfin Hahn-Hahn.* Berlin: Emil Ebering, 1933.

Schmidt, Julian. *Geschichte der deutschen Nationalliteratur im neunzehnten Jahrhundert.* 2 vols. Leipzig: Herbig, 1853.

Schmidt, Peter. "Nachwort." *Kalathiskos.* By Sophie Mereau. Ed. Peter Schmidt. Heidelberg: Lambert Schneider, 1968. 3–43.

Schmidt, Siegfried J. *Die Selbstorganisation des Sozialsystems Literatur im 18. Jahrhundert.* Frankfurt aM: Suhrkamp, 1989.

Schneider, Ronald. *Realismus und Restauration: Untersuchungen zu Poetik und epischem Werk der Annette von Droste-Hülshoff.* Kronberg: Scriptor, 1976.

Schön, Erich. "Weibliches Lesen: Romanleserinnen im späten 18. Jahrhundert." *Untersuchungen zum Roman von Frauen um 1800.* Ed. Helga Gallas and Magdalene Heuser. Tübingen: Niemeyer, 1990. 20–40.

Schopenhauer, Johanna. *Gabriele: Ein Roman.* 1819. Ed. Stephan Koranyi. Munich: Deutscher Taschenbuch Verlag, 1985.

Im Wechsel der Zeiten, im Gedränge der Welt: Jugenderinnerungen, Tagebücher, Briefe. Ed. Rolf Weber. Munich: Winkler, 1986.

Schulte-Sasse, Jochen, and Renate Werner. "E. Marlitts 'Im Hause des Kommerzienrates': Analyse eines Trivialromans in paradigmatischer Absicht." Eugenie Marlitt. *Im Hause des Kommerzienrates.* Munich: Fink, 1977. 389–434.

Schulz, Gerhard. *Die deutsche Literatur zwischen französischer Revolution und Restauration: Das Zeitalter der napoleonischen Kriege und der Restauration 1806–1830.* Vol. 7, part 2, of *Geschichte der deutschen Literatur von den Anfängen bis zur Gegenwart.* Munich: Beck, 1989.

Schulze, Hagen. *The Course of German Nationalism: From Frederick the Great to Bismarck 1763–1867.* 1985. Trans. Sarah Hanbury-Tenison. Cambridge University Press, 1991.

Schwab, Dieter. "Familie." *Geschichtliche Grundbegriffe: Historisches Lexikon zur politisch-sozialen Sprache in Deutschland.* Ed. Otto Brunner et al. Vol. 2. Stuttgart: Klett, 1975. 253–301.

Sedgwick, Eve Kosofsky. *Between Men: English Literature and Male Homosocial Desire.* New York: Columbia University Press, 1985.

Sengle, Friedrich. *Biedermeierzeit: deutsche Literatur im Spannungsfeld zwischen Restauration und Revolution 1815–1848.* 2 vols. Stuttgart: Metzler, 1971.

Shafi, Monika. "Annette von Droste-Hülshoff." *Nineteenth-Century German Writers to 1840.* Ed. James Hardin and Siegfried Mews. *Dictionary of Literary Biography.* Vol. 133. Detroit: Gale Research, 1993. 49–60.

Sheehan, James J. *German History 1770–1866.* Oxford: Clarendon, 1989.

German Liberalism in the Nineteenth Century. University of Chicago Press, 1978.

Smith, John H. "Sexual Difference, *Bildung,* and the *Bildungsroman.*" *Michigan Germanic Studies* 13 (1987): 206–25.

Sommer, Doris. *Foundational Fictions: The National Romances of Latin America.* Berkeley: University of California Press, 1991.

Starcher, B. K. "Ernst Keil und die Anfänge der *Gartenlaube.*" *Seminar* 17 (1981): 205–13.

Starobinski, Jean. *Jean-Jacques Rousseau: Transparency and Obstruction.* 1957. Trans. Arthur Goldhammer. University of Chicago Press, 1988.

Steinecke, Hartmut. *Romantheorie und Romankritik in Deutschland.* 2 vols. Stuttgart: Metzler, 1975–76.

Steiner, Gerhard. "Nachwort." *Virginia oder die Kolonie von Kentucky: Mehr Wahrheit als Dichtung.* By Henriette Frölich. Berlin: Aufbau, 1963. 205–33.

Steinhauer, Marieluise. *Fanny Lewald, die deutsche George Sand. Ein Kapitel aus der Geschichte des Frauenromans im 19. Jahrhundert.* Berlin: Hoffmann, 1937.

Stone, Lawrence. *The Family, Sex and Marriage in England 1500–1800.* New York: Harper & Row, 1977.

Sudhof, Siegfried. "Sophie Laroche." *Deutsche Dichter des 18. Jahrhunderts: Ihr Leben und Werk.* Ed. Benno von Wiese. Berlin: Erich Schmidt, 1977. 300–19.

Taeger, Annemarie. "Nachwort." *Gräfin Faustine.* By Ida Gräfin Hahn-Hahn. Bonn: Bouvier, 1986. 245–68.

Tanner, Tony. "Julie and 'La Maison paternelle': Another Look at Rousseau's *La Nouvelle Héloïse.*" *Jean-Jacques Rousseau: Modern Critical Views.* Ed. Harold Bloom. New York: Chelsea House, 1988. 119–47.

Theweleit, Klaus. *Male Fantasies.* 1977–78. Trans. Erica Carter, Stephen Conway, and Chris Turner. 2 vols. Minneapolis: University of Minnesota Press, 1987–89.

Tompkins, Jane. *Sensational Designs: The Cultural Work of American Fiction 1790–1860.* New York: Oxford University Press, 1985.

Touaillon, Christine. *Der deutsche Frauenroman des 18. Jahrhunderts.* Vienna: Braumüller, 1919.

Treder, Uta. "Sophie Mereau: Montage und Demontage einer Liebe." *Untersuchungen zum Roman von Frauen um 1800.* Ed. Helga Gallas and Magdalene Heuser. Tübingen: Niemeyer, 1990. 172–83.

Unger, Friederike Helene. *Julchen Grünthal*. 1784–98. 2 vols. Frühe Frauenliteratur in Deutschland 11. Ed. Anita Runge. Hildesheim: Olms, 1991.

Van Ghent, Dorothy. *The English Novel: Form and Function*. New York: Rinehart & Co., 1953.

Vansant, Jacqueline. "Liebe und Patriarchat in der Romantik: Sophie Mereaus *Amanda und Eduard*." *Der Widerspenstigen Zähmung: Studien zur bezwungenen Weiblichkeit in der Literatur vom Mittelalter bis zur Gegenwart*. Ed. Sylvia Wallinger and Monika Jones. Innsbruck: Institut für Germanistik, 1986. 185–200.

Venske, Regula. "Discipline and Daydreaming in the Works of a Nineteenth-Century Woman Author: Fanny Lewald." *German Women in the Eighteenth and Nineteenth Centuries: A Social and Literary History*. Ed. Ruth-Ellen Boetcher Joeres and Mary Jo Maynes. Bloomington: Indiana University Press, 1986. 175–92.

Vollmer, Hartmut. *Der deutschsprachige Roman 1815–1820: Bestand, Entwicklung, Gattungen, Rolle und Bedeutung in der Literatur und in der Zeit*. Munich: Fink, 1993.

" 'Die Wahrheit bleibt das Höchste': Die historischen Romane Caroline de la Motte Fouqués." *Geschichten aus (der) Geschichte: Zum Stand des historischen Erzählens im Deutschland der frühen Restaurationszeit*. Ed. Norbert Otto Eke and Hartmut Steinecke. Munich: Fink, 1994. 109–41.

Ward, Albert. *Book Production, Fiction, and the German Reading Public: 1740–1800*. Oxford: Clarendon Press, 1974.

Ward, Margaret E. "*Ehe* and *Entsagung*: Fanny Lewald's Early Novels and Goethe's Literary Paternity." *Women in German Yearbook* 2 (1986): 57–77.

Warner, William Beatty. *Reading Clarissa: The Struggles of Interpretation*. New Haven: Yale University Press, 1979.

Watt, Ian. *The Rise of the Novel: Studies in Defoe, Richardson and Fielding*. Berkeley: University of California Press, 1957.

Weber-Kellermann, Ingeborg. *Die deutsche Familie: Versuch einer Sozialgeschichte*. Frankfurt aM: Suhrkamp, 1974.

Weigel, Sigrid. "Der schielende Blick: Thesen zur Geschichte weiblicher Schreibpraxis." *Die verborgene Frau: Sechs Beiträge zu einer feministischen Literaturwissenschaft*. Berlin: Argument, 1983. 83–137.

"Sophie Mereau." *Frauen: Porträts aus zwei Jahrhunderten*. Ed. Hans Jürgen Schultz. Stuttgart: Kreuz, 1981. 20–32.

Wellbery, David E. *The Specular Moment: Goethe's Early Lyric and the Beginnings of Romanticism*. Stanford University Press, 1996.

Wieland, Christoph Martin. "Der Eifer, unsrer Dichtkunst einen National-Charakter zu geben." *Werke*. Ed. Fritz Martini and Hans Werner Seiffert. Vol. 3. Munich: Hanser, 1967. 267–72.

Sokrates Mainomenos oder die Dialogen des Diogenes von Sinope. Werke. Ed. Fritz Martini and Hans Werner Seiffert. Vol. 2. Munich: Hanser, 1966. 7–120.

"Wenn sie fortfahren die Teutschen des achtzehnten Jahrhunderts für Enkel Tuiskons anzusehen." *Werke.* Ed. Fritz Martini and Hans Werner Seiffert. Vol. 3. Munich: Hanser, 1967. 273–74.

Wild, Reiner. *Die Vernunft der Väter: Zur Psychographie von Bürgerlichkeit und Aufklärung in Deutschland am Beispiel ihrer Literatur für Kinder.* Stuttgart: Metzler, 1987.

Wilde, Jean T. *The Romantic Realist: Caroline de la Motte Fouqué.* New York: Bookman, 1955.

Wilkie, Claudia. "Eugenie Marlitt vor 100 Jahren gestorben." *Neue Deutsche Hefte* 34 (1987): 331–47.

Wimmer, Barbara. *Die Vormärzschriftstellerin Louise Aston: Selbst- und Zeiterfahrung.* Frankfurt aM: Lang, 1993.

Wobeser, Wilhelmine Karoline von. *Elisa oder das Weib wie es seyn sollte.* 1795. Frühe Frauenliteratur in Deutschland 8. Ed. Anita Runge. Hildesheim: Olms, 1990.

Wolf, Christa. *Kein Ort. Nirgends.* Berlin: Aufbau, 1979.

Woltmann, Karoline von. *Maria und Walpurgis: Ein Roman.* 2 vols. Leipzig: Deutsches Museum, 1817–18.

Wolzogen, Caroline von. *Agnes von Lilien.* 1798. *Gesammelte Schriften.* Vol. 1. Ed. Peter Boerner. Hildesheim: Olms, 1988.

Woodmansee, Martha. *The Author, Art, and the Market: Rereading the History of Aesthetics.* New York: Columbia University Press, 1994.

Zahn, Eva. "Die Geschichte der 'Gartenlaube.'" *Facsimile Querschnitt durch die Gartenlaube.* Ed. Heinz Klüter. Stuttgart: Scherz, 1963. 5–14.

Zantop, Susanne. "Aus der Not eine Tugend: Tugendgebot und Öffentlichkeit bei Friederike Helene Unger." *Untersuchungen zum Roman von Frauen um 1800.* Ed. Helga Gallas and Magdalene Heuser. Tübingen: Niemeyer, 1990. 132–47.

"Friederike Helene Unger (1741?–21 September 1813)." *German Writers in the Age of Goethe: Sturm und Drang to Classicism.* Ed. James Hardin and Christoph E. Schweitzer. *Dictionary of Literary Biography.* Vol. 94. Detroit: Gale Research, 1990. 288–93.

"Nachwort." *Julchen Grünthal.* By Friederike Helene Unger. Hildesheim: Olms, 1991. 361–92.

"The Beautiful Soul Writes Herself: Friederike Helene Unger and the 'Große Göthe.'" *In the Shadow of Olympus: German Women Writers Around 1800.* Ed. Katherine R. Goodman and Edith Waldstein. Albany: State University of New York Press, 1992. 29–51.

"Trivial Pursuits? An Introduction to German Women's Writing from the Middle Ages to 1830." *Bitter Healing: German Women Writers from 1700–1830. An Anthology.* Ed. Jeannine Blackwell and Susanne Zantop. Lincoln: University of Nebraska Press, 1990. 9–50.

Zimmermann, Magdalene, ed. *Die "Gartenlaube" als Dokument ihrer Zeit.* Munich: Heimeran, 1963.

Index

Adorno, Theodor W., 8
"Age of Goethe," xi, 11, 43, 205 n.53
America, 77–79, 81, 108, 112–14, 121–22, 190, 195
American Revolution, 65
Anderson, Benedict, xii
androgyny, 84
anti-Semitism, 14, 117, 156–59, 167, 217 n.35; see also Jews, Jewish emancipation
Arons, Wendy K., 209 n.40
Aston, Louise (Hoche), 11, 12, 13, 14, 138, 139, 170–72, 185, 191, 197
  Aus dem Leben einer Frau, 172–76, 179
  Freischärler, Der, 172
  Lydia, 172, 176–79, 182
  Meine Emancipation, Verweisung und Rechtfertigung, 172, 175
  Revolution und Contrerevolution, 136, 172, 179–82
  Wilde Rosen, 171–72
Aston, Samuel, 173
Aquinas, Thomas, 2
aristocracy (nobility), 10, 30, 78, 94, 100, 113, 118, 129, 143, 159
  and capitalism, 145, 150–51, 163–64, 175, 185, 189
  and decadence (libertinage, vice), 20, 33, 38, 42, 49, 52–54, 61, 64–70, 81, 111–12, 123, 138, 144–48, 153, 163–64, 167, 174–78, 181–82, 185–91, 195
  family, attitude toward, 22, 25–26, 124–25, 130–31
  and feminism, 2, 13, 81–82, 104–07, 122, 140–46, 153, 176, 180–82, 212 n.54
  marriage, understanding of, 4, 25, 28, 67, 77, 119–20, 123–25, 154–55
  progressive-conservative (benevolent, enlightened), 11, 13, 30–31, 33, 45, 48–51, 55–56, 99–104, 107–10, 116–18, 140, 151, 154, 160–62, 174, 181–82
  see also bourgeoisie, nationalism

Armstrong, Nancy, xiii
autobiography, religious, 2, 33–34, 40; see also Pietism

Balzac, Honoré de, 137
Becker-Cantarino, Barbara, 15
Beethoven, Ludwig van, 151
Belgum, Kirsten, 219 n.9
Berlin, xi, 15, 44, 51–56, 58, 74, 79, 108, 136, 137, 139, 155, 160, 163–65, 168, 169, 170–71, 179–82
Beulwitz, Friedrich Wilhelm Ludwig von, 43
Bible, 1–3, 52, 56–57, 81
Biedermeier, 12, 97, 104, 132–33, 162
Bildung, 9–10, 44, 50, 77, 83–85, 116, 128
Bildungsroman, Entwicklungsroman, xi–xiii, 62, 76–78, 91–92, 100, 144, 147, 211 n.28
  German nationalism, ties to, 9–10
  "female *Bildungsroman*," xiii, 83, 127–28, 202 n.7
  women's role in, 9, 77–78, 84–85, 128, 205 n.47
Bismarck, Otto von, 201
Blackwell, Jeannine, 75
Börne, Ludwig, 96, 138
bourgeoisie (middle class), 203 n.9
  alliance with nobility, 116, 164
  children, attitude toward, 4
  education, 31–32, 164, 193
  gender roles for women (domestic virtue), 1–5, 7–8, 12–13, 19, 38–40, 41–42, 52–54, 57–60, 62–69, 71–73, 74, 78–83, 87–93, 97–98, 104–07, 110–13, 122, 138–42, 148–49, 154–59, 173, 176–78, 185–95, 199
  liberalism, 11, 13, 154, 156
  marriage and family, understanding of, 1, 4, 21–22, 25–34, 38, 40, 41, 52–55, 62, 65–69, 77–81, 87, 120, 124, 154–55, 158–59, 160–61, 166–70, 183, 185–99
  paternal authority in, 21–29, 32, 41, 58–60, 62–69, 86–87, 109–12, 114, 118–20,

124–25, 128, 134, 151, 154–56, 158,
161–64, 173, 175, 211 n.30
see also aristocracy, nationalism
Bremer, Bettina, 75
Brentano, Bettina, 19
Brentano, Clemens, 19, 74
Bürger, Christa, 75–76, 84
Burschenschaft movement, 12, 137, 156–57, 174

Campe, Joachim Heinrich, 7, 17
Väterliche Rath für meine Tochter, 42
capitalism, 21, 145, 151, 163–64, 175, 189
Catholic Church, Catholicism, 2, 129, 135,
140, 147, 152, 161–62
Chodowiecki, Daniel Nikolaus, 53
Clauren, H. (Carl Heun), 8
Congress of Vienna, 93, 95–96
Cooper, James Fenimore, 153
cosmopolitanism, 14, 19–20, 98, 112, 117, 122,
123, 206 n.6
cross-dressing, 105–07, 170, 176, 182

Declaration of the Rights of Man, 41
Dickens, Charles, 137
Dijkstra, Bram, 133
Dilthey, Wilhelm, 9
Di Maio, Irene Stocksieker, 157
divorce, 160–63, 165, 170, 175
domestic fiction, xiii–xiv, 1, 3, 10–11, 20–21,
40, 43, 61, 86, 108, 118, 125, 130, 139–40,
173–74, 191, 195, 199, 200
Droste-Hülshoff, Annette von, 13, 129–30
"Heidebilder," 129
Judenbuche, Die, 129, 131
Ledwina, 129–35
Durova, Nadezhda, *The Calvalry Maiden*, 105

Eichendorff, Joseph von, 181
Ahnung und Gegenwart, 100
Elisa oder das Weib wie es seyn sollte (Wobeser),
xi, 10
England, 20, 21, 30–31, 33–35, 40, 49, 55, 97,
101, 109, 123, 137, 147, 150–51, 167, 170,
195
Enlightenment, 13–14, 19–20, 75, 98, 115, 117
Epicurus, 81
Evans, Richard, 195

feminist movements, 12, 75, 138, 185, 195, 200
Fichte, Johann Gottlieb, 44, 74
Reden an die deutsche Nation, 95, 116
Fingerhut, Karlheinz, 181
Forster, Georg, 60, 91
Fouqué, Caroline de la Motte, 13, 97–98, 114,
121, 130–31, 144–45, 185

beiden Freunde, Die, 101–04, 105
Edmunds Wege und Irrwege, 99–100, 102, 103,
105, 122
Fragmente aus dem Leben der heutigen Welt,
100–01
Heldenmädchen aus der Vendée, Das, 105–07, 110
Laura, 105–06
Magie der Natur, 98–99, 104–05
Fouqué, Friedrich de la Motte, 98
France, 101, 104, 122, 147
cultural hegemony of, 18, 31
decadence of, 40, 48, 52, 81–82, 188, 191
democratic (revolutionary), 42, 54–55, 59,
60–73, 107–12
Old Regime, 4, 12, 20–21, 65, 73, 81–82,
146
war with Germany, 93–95, 116–17, 126–27,
165–68
see also French Revolution, Paris
Frauenroman, xiii, 12, 202 n.7
French Revolution,
gender roles in, 4–5, 10–11
German response to, 10–11, 12, 14, 41–93,
95–95, 97–102, 105–06, 108–13, 123, 130,
137, 145, 188
Friedrich Wilhelm II ("the Great"), king of
Prussia, 165
Friedrich Wilhelm III, king of Prussia, 165
Friedrich Wilhelm IV, king of Prussia, 183
Freud, Sigmund, xiii
Frölich, Henriette [Jerta], 14, 97, 130
Virginia, oder die Kolonie von Kentucky, 107–14,
121–22, 123
Frye, Northrop, 46

Gartenlaube, Die, 12, 183–85, 190, 191, 197, 199
German Classicism, see Weimar Classicism
Gervinus, Georg Gottfried, 9
Gilman, Sander, 158
Goethe, Johann Wolfgang, xi, xiv, 7, 8, 9, 11,
12, 19, 44, 75–76, 101, 112, 116, 118, 123,
137
Faust, 34, 141
Götz von Berlichingen, 18
Hermann und Dorothea, 41–42
Leiden des jungen Werther, Die, 18, 19, 77, 125
"Literary Sansculottism," 97
"Sesenheimer Lieder," 18
Stella, 56
Wahlverwandtschaften, Die, xiii–xiv, 125
Wilhelm Meisters Lehrjahre, 9, 51, 77, 79, 84,
100, 116, 125
Wilhelm Meisters Wanderjahre, 125
Gouges, Olympia de, xiv
Gottschall, Rudolf, 171

Gründerzeit, xiii, 185
Gryphius, Andreas, 152
Günderrode, Karoline von, 93, 104
Gutzkow, Karl, *Wally, die Zweiflerin*, 138

Habermas, Jürgen, 4
Hahn-Hahn, Ida Gräfin, 8, 11, 12, 13, 138,
    139, 140
    Gräfin Faustine, 122, 140–42, 152
    Sibylle, 140, 147–52
    Zwei Frauen, 140, 142–47, 150, 153
Hardenberg, Karl August von, 96
Hauff, Wilhelm, 8
Heine, Heinrich, 138
    Deutschland: Ein Wintermärchen, 14
Herder, Johann Gottfried, 11, 95
    *Ideen zur Philosophie der Geschichte der
        Menschheit*, 116–17
    Journal meiner Reise im Jahr 1769, 18
Heyse, Paul, 129
Hippel, Theodor Gottlieb von, *Über die
    bürgerliche Verbesserung der Weiber*, xiv, 42
Hobsbawm, E. J., xii, 117
Hoffmann, Ernst Theodor Amadeus, xi
Hofmannswaldau, Christian, 152
Hogarth, William, 23
Hohendahl, Peter Uwe, xii, 9
Hölderlin, Friedrich, 9
Homer, 44
Horen, Die, 44, 82, 84, 86, 116
Horkheimer, Max, 8
Huber, Ludwig Ferdinand, 60–61
Huber, Therese, xi, 11, 13, 42, 60–61, 93, 109
    Familie Seldorf, Die, 61–73, 80, 110
    Luise, 197
    Morgenblatt für gebildete Stände, 61
Hughes, Michael, 13
Humboldt, Alexander von, 44
Humboldt, Wilhelm von, 42, 44
Hunt, Lynn, 10–11, 110
Huyssen, Andreas, 202 n.4, 205 n.62

industrial revolution, 21, 137

Jacobi, Friedrich Heinrich, 44
Jacobi, Johann Georg, 44
Jean Paul (Johann Paul Friedrich Richter), 9
Jews, xii, 57, 139, 144, 152–54, 171, 192
    Jewish emancipation, 156–59, 165, 167
    see also anti-Semitism
Junges Deutschland, see Young Germany

Keil, Ernst, 183–85
Kipp, Johann Heinrich, 74
Kleist, Heinrich von, *Hermannsschlacht, Die*, 95

Klopstock, Friedrich Gottlob, 95
Körner, Theodor, *Leier und Schwert*, 5–6, 95,
    104
Kosciusko, Thadeus, 146
Kotzebue, August von, 121
Kurz, Hermann, 129

Landes, Joan, 4–5, 10
Laqueur, Thomas, 203 n.12
LaRoche, Sophie von, xiv, 12, 13, 19–21, 42,
    49, 50, 95, 109, 151, 200, 206 n.7
    Pomona für Teutschlands Töchter, 20
    Geschichte des Fräuleins von Sternheim, xi, 11,
        15, 19–21, 30–40, 45, 49–50, 52–55, 57,
        59, 60, 80, 81, 111, 118, 140, 147, 174–75,
        178, 186, 187, 195
Laube, Heinrich, 138
Lengefeld, Charlotte von, 43–44
Lenz, Jakob Michael Reinhold, 19
Lessing, Gotthold Ephraim, 11, 95
    17th *Literaturbrief*, 18
    Hamburgische Dramaturgie, 18
Lewald, Fanny, xiv, 11, 13, 14, 138, 139, 140,
    152–54, 181, 192, 197
    Auf rother Erde, 168–70
    Clementine, 154–56
    Diogena, 152–53
    dritte Stand, Der, 163–64
    Erinnerungen aus dem Jahre 1848, 168, 179
    Für und wider die Frauen, 195
    Jenny, 156–59, 167, 170
    Lebensfrage, Eine, 137, 160–63, 167, 175
    Prinz Louis Ferdinand, 165–68
London, 20, 94, 97, 127
Louis Philippe, king of France, 136, 168
Lovell, Terry, 15
Luther, Martin, 2–3

Mainz Republic, 12, 60
Mann, Thomas, 132–33
Marat, Jean Paul, 54, 59
Marie Antoinette, queen of France, 146
Marlitt, Eugenie (John), xiv, 11–12, 13, 14, 15,
    183–85
    Geheimnis der alten Mamsell, Das, 189–94,
        196, 198
    Goldelse, 184, 185–87, 191, 192, 196, 201
    Heideprinzeßchen, Das, 191, 192, 193
    Im Hause des Kommerzienrates, 190–94, 201
    Reichsgräfin Gisela, 187–89, 196–97, 198
    zweite Frau, Die, 192–94, 196, 198–99
    zwölf Apostel, Die, 184
Marx, Karl, 164
Meise, Helga, 54
Menzel, Wolfgang, 125

Mereau, Karl, 74
Mereau, Sophie (Schubart, Brentano), xi, 7,
    11, 12, 13, 42, 74–76, 94, 98, 109
    Amanda und Eduard, 75, 76, 82–93, 142
    Blüthenalter der Empfindung, Das, 75, 76–79,
        81, 82, 83–84, 92, 93
    Flucht nach der Hauptstadt, Die, 76, 79–81, 88
    Kalathiskos, 75
    Mann mit vier Weibern, Der, 89, 92
    "Ninon de Lenclos," 76, 81–82, 87, 92,
        122, 146, 176, 182
Metternich, Klemens von, 121, 136, 139
Modleski, Tania, 198
Moens, Herman, 75
Möhrmann, Renate, 138–39, 141
Montaigne, Michel de, 81
Mosse, George, 4
Müchler, Karl, 114
Mühlbach, Luise, 129, 138, 139
Mundt, Theodor, *Madonna: Unterhaltungen mit
    einer Heiligen*, 138

Nachmärz, 12
Napoleon I, emperor of France, 5, 12, 14,
    99–103, 108, 111, 146
Napoleonic Wars, 42, 54, 94–96, 104–05, 127,
    130, 137, 147, 165–67, 184, 213 n.2
nationalism, German, xi–xiii, 4, 11, 13–14,
    54–56, 59, 94–98, 100, 107–08, 116–18,
    121–22, 126–28, 136–40, 171, 179–82, 213
    n.2
    and aristocracy, 55, 98–107, 122, 129, 151
    and bourgeoisie, 1, 3–4, 41, 166–70, 185,
        191
    and liberalism, 13–14, 96, 122, 151, 157, 159,
        162, 165–70, 174, 183–85, 205 n.61
    and gender roles, 5–7, 10–11, 104–07,
        110–11, 118–22, 138–40, 160, 186, 204
        n.27, 215 n.35
    and national literature (canon-formation),
        xii–xiii, 1, 3, 9–12, 14, 16, 18–20, 55–56,
        96–97, 137–40, 200, 214 n.11
    and reunification (1989), ix, 201
    romantic, 13–14, 98
    and unification (1871), 9, 137–38, 165–68,
        183, 185, 200–01
    see also aristocracy, bourgeoisie,
        cosmopolitanism
Nibelungenlied, Das, 12
nobility, see aristocracy
Novalis (Friedrich von Hardenberg), xi, 9,
    135

Old Regime, see France
Otto-Peters, Louise, 129, 138, 139

Peterson, Brent O., 220 n.20
Peucker, Brigitte, 133
Pietism, 33, 186; see also autobiography,
    religious
proletariat, 180–82

Robespierre, Maximilien, 54, 59, 94, 108
Restoration, xiii, 11, 12, 14, 94–135, 136–39,
    164–65
Revolution of 1830 (July Revolution), 137,
    145, 146, 162
Revolution of 1848 (March Revolution), 12,
    14, 136–37, 165, 168–70, 171, 179–82,
    201
Richardson, Samuel, xi, xiii, xiv, 11, 20, 29,
    31
    Clarissa, 20, 21–25, 30, 33, 34, 36–37, 40,
        50, 54, 59, 124–25, 178, 195
Rochow, Friedrich von, 98
Roebling, Irmgard, 133
Romanticism, 11, 13, 18, 42–43, 51, 74–75, 98,
    131–32
Rousseau, xi, xiii, xiv, 7, 11, 17, 20, 44, 56, 77,
    81, 83, 113
    Emile, 3–4, 20
    Julie, ou La Nouvelle Héloïse, 20–21, 25–30,
        31, 40, 52, 87, 117, 124

Sade, Marquis de, 197
St. Paul, 2
Sand, George, *Lelia*, 143
Schiller, Friedrich, 7–9, 42, 43–44, 74–76, 82,
    84, 116, 126–27
    Aesthetic Education, 85, 118
    Jungfrau von Orleans, Die, 107
    Kabale und Liebe, 175
    "Lied von der Glocke, Das" 41–42
Schindel, Carl Wilhelm von, 7
Schlegel, Dorothea, 98
Schlegel, Friedrich, 44, 83–84
    Lucinde, 77–78, 85
Schlegel-Schelling, Caroline, 42, 98
Schleiermacher, Friedrich, 9
Schmidt, Georg Philipp, 74
Schmidt, Julian, 8
Schmidt, Peter, 75
Schneider, Angelika, 75
Schopenhauer, Arthur, 122–23
Schopenhauer, Johanna, 94, 97, 145, 197
    Gabriele, 16, 122–29, 140, 173, 195
Schcking, Levin, 129
Sealsfield, Charles, 153
Shakespeare, 18, 31, 132
Sommer, Doris, xii
Stein, Karl von, 96

Steiner, Gerhard, 108, 113
Stone, Lawrence, 22
Stutz, Johann Jakob, 51

theatre, 2, 18, 37, 79–80, 81, 134, 161, 182, 208
    n.39
Theweleit, Klaus, 6
Tieck, Ludwig, xi, 9

Unger, Friederike Helene, xi, 11, 42, 93
    Franzosen in Berlin, Die, 54
    Julchen Grünthal 42, 51–60, 79, 80, 158
Unger, Johann Friedrich, 44, 51

Van Ghent, Dorothy, 23
Varnhagen, Rahel von, 167–68
Venske, Regula, 156
Vormärz, xiii, 11, 12, 116, 129, 136–82, 183,
    185, 191, 197, 199
Voss, 173
Vulpius, Christiane, 123

Wars of Liberation, 5, 95, 162

Weimar, 43–44, 49, 74, 89, 94, 123, 183
Weimar Classicism (German Classicism), 11,
    43, 44, 74–76, 85, 94, 116–17, 172
Wieland, Christoph Martin, 19–20, 36
Wienbarg, Ludolf, 138
Wolf, Christa, *Kein Ort. Nirgends*, 93
Wolfe, Thomas, 60
Wollstonecraft, Mary, xiv
Woltmann, Karl Ludwig, 115–16
Woltmann, Karoline von, 97, 130
    Bildhauer, Die, 114
    Euphrosyne, 114
    Maria und Walpurgis, 114–22, 123
Wolzogen, Caroline von (Lengefeld), xi, 11,
    13, 42, 43–44, 55, 109
    Agnes von Lilien, 44–51, 52, 60, 111, 118, 173,
    186
    Cordelia, 44
Wolzogen, Wilhelm von, 43

Young Germany, 138, 146, 161–62, 183

Zantop, Susanne, 75